Praise for *It's*

"A refreshing and engaging exploration of astrology that transcends traditional interpretations. . . . Wells expertly unpacks the intricate meanings behind Mercury, Venus, and Mars, offering insights that resonate with both astrology enthusiasts and newcomers alike. . . . The book not only educates but also entertains."
—**MICHAEL HERKES**, author of *Glamstrology*

"If you're looking for a no-nonsense, fun guide to astrology, *It's All About Astrology* is it. Wells delivers astrology with a side of sass and a down-to-earth style that's refreshing and approachable. Perfect for beginners and anyone who's curious about the cosmic mechanics behind their personality quirks, the book offers digestible insights into each sign, along with just the right amount of practical advice. This isn't some lofty astrology textbook; instead, Wells brings the zodiac down to Earth, helping you see how it plays out in everyday life. Whether you're a novice or someone in need of a little astro-entertainment, this book offers something for everyone."
—**STORM CESTAVANI**, creator of Astro Magic candles and sprays and the cohost of the *Curse Breakers* podcast

"An absolute joy to read, blending astrology with practical advice and plenty of humor that had me laughing out loud. . . . Nicole has a way of making the cosmic feel personal, relatable, and downright hilarious. What I adore is how the humor never detracts from the depth of the information—it only enhances it. Whether you're diving into ways to pamper yourself based on your Moon sign or cracking the code on your partner's Venus sign quirks, Nicole's wisdom feels like your best friend letting you in on all the secrets of the universe. This book is perfect for anyone wanting to bring astrology into their daily routine. . . . A brilliant blend of practical advice and celestial wit, it's a must-have for anyone curious about the stars."

—DR. STORMIE GRACE, astrologer

"An easy-to-read, yet highly informative introduction to all things relational when it comes to astrology. Written in modern, accessible language, Nicole's voice is fun, knowledgeable, and feels like you're chatting with your best friend. This book is fantastic for getting to know the signs beyond just the quintessential Sun sign, and through the lens of not only yourself, but the important, close connections in your life. The advice in this book is practical and thought provoking, and aids readers in understanding how the signs show up in real people. The value provided in this book, paired with its flippable layout, makes it a fantastic reference people will turn to time and again."

—AUBREY HOUDESHELL, author of *The Cosmic Symposium*

"Witty, no-nonsense, and frankly essential, this sparkling guide to the heavens takes you beyond the sun sign for a clearer view of who you, and those in your life, really are—and have the potential to be. Keep it handy: you'll find yourself returning to these pages again and again."

—ZOË HOWE, author of *Witchful Thinking* and coauthor of *Scorpio Witch*

"*It's All About Astrology* is the book I wish I had when I was starting out on my astrology journey. This book has it all, from a unique perspective on your Big Three (Sun, Moon, and Rising), how to understand your emotional and creative needs, as well as insightful journal prompts that really illuminate the archetypes of each sign. I also appreciate Nicole's refreshing guidance on how to have success with your Mars sign and what to avoid doing. Having an Aquarius Mars myself, I find it to be a complicated placement to understand. Nicole's perspective felt very accurate. This is a must-have astrology book to add to your collection that is easy to connect with and a joy to read!"

—**MAJORIE GATSON**, the Punk Priestess

"Whether you're new to astrology or have been dabbling for some time and want to go deeper, this book is a comprehensive resource for anyone looking to familiarize themself with the signs and planets. It's approachable, beautifully organized, and full of practical insights on how to use astrology to learn more about yourself and relate well with others."

—**SARA MELLAS**, author and food stylist

"A true gem for anyone curious about astrology. . . . Her relatable, conversational style makes it feel like you're chatting with a wise, funny bestie who just gets it. She takes what can be an intimidating subject and breaks it down into bite-sized, easy-to-understand insights. . . . What truly sets this book apart, though, is Nicole's unique approach. It's not the usual 'What does a Libra man love?' kind of guide—it's a deep dive into the personality planets that feels both accessible and refreshingly insightful. . . . It's a perfect resource for beginners to truly grasp the personal planets and seasoned astrologers to gain new, nuanced understandings. . . . Nicole's wisdom and wit shine through on every page!"

—**LEAH R. PATTERSON**, CEO of MOVE Makeup, professional salsa instructor, natural beauty and wellness mentor, confidence coach

IT'S ALL ABOUT
ASTROLOGY

ABOUT THE AUTHOR

Nicole Wells (she / her) is a Virgo Sun, Pisces Moon, Taurus rising. In her free time, Nicole can be found reading, watching horror movies, or playing *The Sims*. She lives in the Twin Cities with her cats. Connect with her on Instagram and TikTok: @nicolewellwell.

IT'S ALL ABOUT
ASTROLOGY

ADVICE YOU
DIDN'T KNOW
YOU NEEDED

NICOLE WELLS

LLEWELLYN
WOODBURY, MINNESOTA

First Edition
First Printing, 2025

Cover design by Shira Atakpu
Book design by Lauryn Heineman

Llewellyn Publications is a registered trademark of Llewellyn Worldwide Ltd.

Library of Congress Cataloging-in-Publication Data (Pending)
ISBN: 978-0-7387-7894-5

Llewellyn Worldwide Ltd. does not participate in, endorse, or have any authority or responsibility concerning private business transactions between our authors and the public.

All mail addressed to the author is forwarded but the publisher cannot, unless specifically instructed by the author, give out an address or phone number.

Any internet references contained in this work are current at publication time, but the publisher cannot guarantee that a specific location will continue to be maintained. Please refer to the publisher's website for links to authors' websites and other sources.

Llewellyn Publications
A Division of Llewellyn Worldwide Ltd.
2143 Wooddale Drive
Woodbury, MN 55125-2989
www.llewellyn.com

Printed in the United States of America

To Bella. I miss you. I love you. Always.

CONTENTS

INTRODUCTION

The more I've gotten into astrology, the more I find myself having to explain it to people I've just met. It almost always comes up on my first dates, mostly because I like making astrology a conversation topic so I can vibe-check the person I'm sitting across from. If I'm trying to gauge how compatible I am with a potential new friend, I'll ask their sign and see how they respond. I've also gotten into the habit of guessing the Sun sign of my servers when I go to a restaurant, which sparks a fun conversation whether or not I've guessed correctly. (Though, more often than not, I have!) As I've became more comfortable bringing up astrology, I've learned that even skeptics are willing to have a conversation; there's a lot of curiosity surrounding the topic. Every time I have the chance to get on my "Astrology is so much more than a vague horoscope in a newspaper" soapbox, I take it.

This is how I explain astrology to skeptics: Most people associate the word *astrology* with their Sun sign, also known colloquially as the zodiac sign. However, the Sun sign barely scratches the surface of astrology. The only reason so many people know their Sun sign is because the Sun changes signs at a pace that is compatible with the Gregorian calendar. A birth chart shows the signs all the planets were in at the moment of birth, not just the Sun. Each planet impacts us in different ways, but they all move at different speeds.

Sun signs are the only aspect of astrology that has made it to the mainstream because Sun sign dates are set in stone, more or less—they shift a bit year-to-year because the planet rotates 360 degrees and there are 365 days in a year. However, the Moon, for example, switches signs every two and a half days, and rising signs change about every two *hours*. So it's understandable that the complexities of a birth chart have led to astrology being reduced to nothing more than a Sun sign and a general horoscope in a newspaper. (By this point in the conversation, the person I'm talking to has usually stopped listening.)

All of that is to say, when it comes to astrology, you really have to look at a person's entire birth chart. Not only does a birth chart reading factor in the sign of each planet, but it also looks at the house each planet is in, the sign each house is in, and the aspect patterns (angles) being created by the planets. And, as if that isn't complicated enough, birth charts also include things that aren't planets but that still create aspect patterns and can be interpreted, like the north and south nodes, Chiron, and something called the Midheaven.

I won't be covering nodes or Chiron or any of that in this book. Astrology is a vast, complicated subject, but I want this work to be beginner-friendly. You could spend your whole life studying astrology and still have more to learn! (If you are interested in diving into the more complex facets of a birth chart, I've listed some fantastic resources at the back of the book.)

In this book, I'll be focusing on the rising sign and the five planets that have the strongest influence on personality, often called the *inner planets* or the *personal planets* (the Sun, the Moon, Mercury, Venus, and Mars). Now, you may be thinking, *Wait, the moon isn't a planet.* Technically, the moon isn't a planet, and neither is the sun. However, in astrology, they are referred to as planets, so that is the terminology I'll be using. When I am speaking of these celestial bodies as astrological planets, I capitalize *Sun* and *Moon*.

Nowadays, you may hear people talking about their "big three": This means their Sun, Moon, and rising signs. It makes sense that these three placements are grouped together, as they significantly influence how we engage with the world. Many people who are interested in astrology start out by learning about their big three, myself included. This is a great starting point if the information in this book overwhelms you. Once you have a solid grasp of your big three and how these energies work together, it will be much easier for you to absorb information about the other planets in your chart.

I want to stress that astrology is a study and a practice, just like anything else. To become comfortable with the signs, houses, aspects, and other facets of a birth chart, you must keep seeking information. Find ways to consume astrological content that are fun for you. For some, that will mean continuing to read books on astrology or following astrological content creators. In my case, I engage with astrology every day by following dozens of astrological meme accounts.[1] While this may sound ludicrous, seeing lighthearted astro memes on my social media feed every day has been integral to my continued interest in astrology.

Finally, please remember that a birth chart is as unique as a fingerprint. If you are not connecting with one of your placements, do not fret. The signs and the planets are the foundation of astrological interpretation, but there are other factors to consider. Perhaps the house the planet is in or its aspect patterns have influenced the way it impacts your life. Not only that, but your lived experiences play a part in how your life has panned out as well. So take the content in this book with a grain of salt, but keep an open mind, and know that this book only scratches the surface of astrology.

A NOTE ON THE ORIGINS OF ASTROLOGY

I want to take a moment to acknowledge that when I talk about astrology, I am referring to the Western tropical zodiac. Astrology is an ancient practice

....

1   The recommended reading list in the back of this book includes the Instagram handles of my favorite astrological meme accounts and content creators.

that originated in the East, and like many Eastern concepts, it has been appropriated and transformed. I express my gratitude to all of those who came before me who spent time studying astrology and sharing their knowledge.

CREATING A BIRTH CHART

To create a birth chart for yourself or someone else, this is the information you'll need to know:

1. Birthdate

2. Place of birth (city)

3. Exact time of birth

Most people can tell you numbers one and two off the top of their head, but they only have a vague guess for their time of birth. Each bit of information here is needed—exact time of birth matters. If the time of birth isn't exact, the birth chart will be able to convey some accurate information (like the sign Saturn is in, for example, because Saturn changes signs every two and a half years), but other information will be off. Remember, rising signs change every two hours, so if your rising sign is miscalculated, all your house placements will be inaccurate. This is why it's so crucial to include the exact time of birth. Most people can find this information on their birth certificate or by talking to a family member.

There are tons of websites that will create a birth chart for free. My personal favorite is astro-charts.com, but visit a few different websites to see what you're drawn to. Each website will give you the same information, but it'll be displayed in different ways. Once a birth chart is in front of you, pay attention to where the Sun, the Moon, Mercury, Venus, and Mars are. Also check what sign begins the first house, often denoted with the letters *Asc* or *AC*. Write down this information so you can find the appropriate sections in this book.

A GENERAL OVERVIEW OF THE INNER PLANETS

If you're totally new to astrology, or if you just need a refresher, here is a brief overview of the inner planets and what each of them indicate in a birth chart:

Sun: Overall personality and character traits; general essence of who you are

Moon: Emotion; how you naturally feel your feelings and what makes you feel nurtured

Mercury: Communication; how you interact with others and prefer to be interacted with

Venus: Love; how you love others and how you want to be shown love in return

Mars: Passion and drive; sex; how you behave when you feel strongly about something; chaos and self-destruction

I call these the *inner planets* throughout the book, though they are also known as the *personal planets* because of their strong influence on personality. There are five other planets denoted in a birth chart: In order, they are Jupiter, Saturn, Uranus, Neptune, and Pluto. Sometimes, people lump Jupiter and Saturn in with the inner planets, but I consider them to be more transpersonal planets than personal planets, and as such, I group them with the outer planets. Outer planets change signs more slowly and, in general, they have a less-intense impact on a birth chart, so we'll be sticking to the inner planets and the rising sign in this book.

One more thing worth mentioning is that every zodiac sign has a planetary ruler. For the inner planets, the Sun rules Leo, the Moon rules Cancer, Mercury rules Gemini and Virgo, Venus rules Taurus and Libra, and Mars rules Aries. (The outer planets are associated with the remaining zodiac signs: Jupiter/Sagittarius, Saturn/Capricorn, Uranus/Aquarius, Neptune/Pisces, and Pluto/Scorpio.) Planetary rulers are important to note because when a planet is in a sign it rules, it is comfortable. Planetary energy flows easily and the volume is turned up—everything is amplified.

Planets for Sex and Love

Venus is associated with love, whereas Mars is associated with sex. This perplexes some people: Why are these two topics separate? Astrologically, Venus can tell us what sorts of relationships and people we are drawn to, as well as what our intimate relationships need to thrive in the long run, whereas Mars highlights our sexual desires. Most people who have dated around can tell you that while you may be romantically compatible with someone, you are not necessarily sexually compatible, and vice versa.

It is impossible to discuss relationship needs without considering Venus *and* Mars placements. For this reason, if you are especially interested in your compatibility with another person, I recommend reading about that individual's Venus and Mars placements. To learn even more about this topic, see the recommended reading list in the back of this book.

The Rising Sign

While the rising sign is not a planet, it is crucial to astrological interpretation because it has a powerful influence on how others perceive you. The rising sign is how you come across to people you've just met. If your rising sign and Sun sign are the same, then what you see is what you get. But, for most people, these signs are different. People usually seem one way when you're first getting to know them and then, as time goes on, you see another side to them. This is because you were drawn in by their rising sign, but once they shed this mask, so to speak, you are able to see their Sun sign and their true personality. This may explain why you are instantly drawn to some people, only to discover, over time, that you are not compatible. Astrology can help you make sense of this, and in the long run, it can save you from investing a lot of time and energy on the wrong people.

THE SECTIONS IN THIS BOOK

Each chapter covers one zodiac sign and its Sun, Moon, rising, Mercury, Venus, and Mars expressions. Some of these sections will apply directly to you, and others are great ways to learn more about your friends, family members, coworkers, supervisors, or partners. Remember that you'll need to know an exact time of birth if you want a birth chart analysis to be accurate!

In the Sun section of each chapter, you'll find:

★ Pure *Sun Sign* Energy

★ Gifts for a *Sun Sign*

★ So Your Boss Is a *Sun Sign* . . .

★ So Your Coworker Is a *Sun Sign* . . .

★ So Your Partner Is a *Sun Sign* . . .

In the Moon section:

★ Restorative Activities for a *Moon Sign*

★ Journal Prompts for a *Moon Sign*

★ So Your Partner Is a *Moon Sign* . . .

In the rising section:

★ Ways to Spot a *Rising Sign*

★ Downsides of Being a *Rising Sign*

★ Using Your *Rising Sign* to Your Advantage

In the Mercury section:

★ Communicating with a *Mercury Sign*

★ Questions to Ask a *Mercury Sign*

In the Venus section:

★ Self-Love for a *Venus Sign*

★ Seducing a *Venus Sign*

★ So Your Partner Has a *Venus Sign* . . .

In the Mars section:

★ *Mars Sign* Behind Closed Doors

★ Things *Not* to Do to a *Mars Sign*

★ Things a *Mars Sign* Probably Needs to Hear (But Definitely Doesn't Want To)

As you can see, each section has something of value for the individual and for the people in their life who have that placement.

THE PURPOSES OF ASTROLOGY

I don't know who needs to hear this, but astrology does not predict the future. Astrology can indicate likely trajectories, but it cannot predict, as nothing in life is set in stone; all of us have the power of free will.

Personally, I see astrology as a tool for self-development and self-reflection. Astrology has been an incredibly healing subject for me because it's helped me understand why I behave the way I do and what I need to feel my best. I have a better understanding of the people in my life and the ways we interact. Astrology has even helped me make sense of why I am drawn to certain people and the kind of energy I need in my life. For example, I only have one fire sign placement in my entire birth chart, and it's not an inner planet placement. I naturally lack the spontaneity, courage, and resilience that fire signs have, so I unconsciously seek out that energy to bring balance to my life. Imagine my surprise when I realized that every person I've seriously dated had a fire Sun sign, and my best friends are all fire Sun signs as well!

Understanding astrology has changed my life. I have happier, healthier relationships and complete confidence in the Universe's grand design. My hope for you is that this book leads to new discoveries about yourself and others and that these discoveries enrich your life. A birth chart is a powerful tool once you know how to use it.

★ 1 ★
ARIES

An Aries's personality is large and in charge. They leave a lasting impression on everyone they meet. Those who are lucky enough to befriend an Aries are guaranteed to have a partner in crime. Aries love to laugh and have a good time. I have to say, I love being around people with Aries placements. They are the most lively, loving, *fun* friends I've ever had.

At their best, Aries are exuberant, confident, hilarious, and brave. There are few things in life that best them; this is because at their core, Aries believe they can do anything they set their mind to. They are natural leaders who inspire everyone around them.

Of course, there are downsides to every sign. Aries are reckless and impulsive, and they lack foresight. They tend to be super happy or incredibly cranky. And, while we're on the subject, they are outright *loud*, which can be tough for earth and water signs to handle.

Before we dive into Aries placements, there are a few logistics that are good to know. Aries rules the first house, the house of self (personality, self-expression, individuality, etc.). And Aries is the first sign of the zodiac, making them the "youngest" sign in astrology, so they're often likened to a child. I think of Aries like a toddler: On a good day, they are a delight to be around. They're goofy and down for anything; they laugh loudly and often; their smile lights up a room. But on a bad day? Watch out. Adult Aries never really outgrew the terrible twos. Grown Aries have been known to throw a temper tantrum.

Aries's symbol is the ram. This accurately sums up their stubbornness. If there's an obstacle in their way, they'll just use their horns to shove it aside so they can get where they're going. The ram is certain of its path and has no problem telling others what they believe their path to be too. If you've never been on the receiving end of advice from an Aries, I'll just tell you now, your feelings are probably going to get hurt. An Aries doesn't beat around the bush. They give fantastic advice—*if* you can get past the way they deliver it.

Aries is a fire sign. All fire signs (Aries, Leo, and Sagittarius) share similar traits: They are passionate, loud, and confident. They don't shy away from the spotlight, and they rarely back down from a fight. Even when the flame of a fire sign is sputtering, it stays lit; others may balk at their never-ending charisma, even at their lowest moments. And when the flame of a fire sign roars to life, well, let's just say there's no doubting their presence.

Aries is a cardinal sign. All cardinal signs (Aries, Cancer, Libra, and Capricorn) go *fast*. Anytime an Aries is involved, chaos will ensue. Aries is the best person to go barhopping with, but you might need to have an energy drink beforehand to keep up. They're sort of like the Energizer Bunny. They go, go, go—until they crash. A tired Aries, an Aries who has fully expended their cardinal energy, must be left alone. Much like a hibernating bear, they'll return when the time is right. In the meantime, leave them be. Their rebound time is faster than most, so they'll be taking tequila shots with you again in no time.

☉

ARIES SUN

The Sun is typically in the sign of Aries from March 21 to April 19. When individuals have an Aries Sun, they are pretty genial people, though you don't want to cross them, because they will rain hellfire down on you. This is one of the most spiteful signs, so Aries never forgets the ways they've been wronged. The good news is that Aries loses interest in things pretty fast, so if you've pissed one off, you just have to hold out until they find someone new to hate.

For those with an Aries Sun, every section in this chapter will apply to some degree. The Sun is the most powerful planetary force, so it has a huge impact on personality. While an Aries Sun may not have an Aries Mars, for example, they will undoubtedly find something in that section that they relate to.

Pure Aries Energy

If you've ever been in a room with a person who radiates confidence, they're probably an Aries. Even when they're totally quiet (which doesn't happen very often, to be fair), they give off a badass energy that's hard to describe.

Aries Suns do not care what other people think of them. If someone cuts in line, Aries will speak up. If a performer asks for a volunteer, Aries raises their hand. If their order gets messed up at a restaurant, Aries will send it back—and with their charm, they might even finagle a free dessert out of the situation. An Aries's straightforwardness is refreshing, if a bit abrasive at times.

★ **Aries Suns are incredibly spontaneous.** For example, Aries is the sort of person who walks into a tattoo shop in the middle of the day and picks a random flash design to put on their body, just because. Then, when someone points to their new ink and asks what the tattoo means, Aries will shrug and say, "I don't know. I just liked it." They never second-guess an inspired action.

★ **Most Aries Suns have at least one area of life that they are constantly switching up,** whether it's the car they drive, their hairstyle, or the business idea they're developing. They don't like it when things become too predictable or familiar. They believe life is too short to continue with the same old, same old. Earth signs will struggle to understand Aries's impermanence.

★ **Aries Suns are convinced that they are a better driver than everyone else on the road.** If you've ever driven with an Aries Sun, you already know their road rage is through the roof. Aries Suns regularly cuss out other drivers. If they have a more subdued Mercury or Mars, however, they'll be more likely to keep their nasty thoughts to themselves. Whenever an Aries is not in control of the car, they're sure to be a backseat driver.

★ **There is nothing an Aries hates more than being bored.** It may seem like every time you talk to an Aries, they have a new hobby. These flavor-of-the-month obsessions will ebb and flow. Just when you think you've gotten the hang of their latest obsession, they're on to the next.

★ **Aries Suns are polarizing—you either love them or hate them.** Oftentimes, Aries rub people the wrong way. They are not very careful with their delivery, and more sensitive signs such as Cancer take this bluntness personally. Those who are compatible with Aries Suns appreciate their honesty, whereas those who aren't will think they are mean.

Gifts for an Aries Sun

Aries aren't sentimental people, so don't bother getting them one of those "Someone in [Location] loves you"–type of things. They'd rather receive an experience than a tangible item. Memories are forever, but that glass souvenir isn't—it'll break when Aries moves and decides not to bother with bubble wrap.

★ **Aries loves versatility,** so take them to a brewery where they can create their own flight, or visit a winery to do a taste testing.

* **Buy Aries a gift card to a tattoo shop** so they can get a spur-of-the-moment tattoo or, if they're a little more reserved, a piercing that they can take out when they get tired of it in a few months.

* **Visit an amusement park, play laser tag, or see a horror movie in theaters.** Basically, take them somewhere they can shout without freaking someone out.

* **Pay attention to what an Aries's latest hobby is and purchase a gift accordingly.** Don't spend too much money on it, though—Aries is guaranteed to have a new passion project within a few months.

So Your Boss Is an Aries Sun . . .

This is not the easiest Sun sign to have as a boss. It's basically impossible to suck up to them, and their moods can flip like a switch. If you get on their bad side, you might as well put in your two weeks' notice. But if you can manage to win them over, you've secured a ride-or-die colleague.

* **Don't make them ask you for something twice.** If your boss asks you to do something, do it immediately. Nothing irritates an Aries more than repeating themselves.

* **Aries believes they can do things better than most, so make sure you're putting your best foot forward.** If you're unsure how to improve a project, your Aries boss is *not* the person to ask. They'll have good ideas, sure, but then they'll question your ability and decide to just do it themselves. Instead, go find a quiet and capable coworker and request their feedback. Then take the revised work to your boss.

* **Fake it 'til you make it!** Never show weakness in front of your Aries boss, especially not at the beginning of your relationship. If you're unsure about your work, plaster on a big smile and sell it. If you notice your Aries boss still isn't convinced, be quick to admit fault and defer to their wisdom. Essentially, if your Aries boss isn't buying it, your best bet is to tuck tail and admit they could do it better, then ask them for guidance. They'll appreciate the ego boost.

★ **Dealing with personal issues? Your Aries boss should never know about it.** Do not—I repeat, *do not*—come into work crying. Do not tell your Aries boss that you need time off because your boyfriend just broke up with you; make up an excuse. Always leave your emotional distress at home, because Aries is not sensitive to your issues. They come into work and get shit done, and they expect you to do the same. So that runny nose you have from crying all night? As far as your boss is concerned, that's actually a seasonal allergy.

So Your Coworker Is an Aries Sun . . .

You definitely want your Aries coworkers in your corner. An Aries will fight tooth and nail for you. When you're in an Aries's good graces, they'll say nice things about you behind your back. Bonus points if you hate the same people—that's great bonding material with an Aries.

★ **Thank them for the work they do.** Aries works hard, and they appreciate recognition. Unlike some signs who will work and work without ever needing to hear a thank you (*cough, cough,* Pisces), words of appreciation go a long way with an Aries.

★ **Ask them out to lunch every once in a while.** Aries likes feeling important, and they like being around people they can talk to. Asking them out to lunch makes them feel valued and also shakes up their otherwise-boring workday routine. And it probably goes without saying that you should let them pick the restaurant.

★ **If you sense they're in a bad mood, leave them alone.** Don't ask them what is wrong. If they want to talk about it, they will. You're better off just staying out of their way until they've self-regulated.

So Your Partner Is an Aries Sun . . .

I take it you're not a boring person. It's impossible to be boring when you love an Aries Sun. More than likely, you're the quieter one. You follow your partner's lead, and they love that about you!

★ **Take no shit.** An angry Aries can be petty or brutish; they may even fall into the role of bully. They don't do this intentionally, but when they're in a bad mood, they just want to watch the world burn. Stand up for yourself. Don't argue, because you won't win. Hold your ground and let them know what's up. Aries respects people who have a backbone.

★ **Spend time with them.** Aries may not be the most touchy-feely sign, but they do value quality time. Having a spontaneous adventure, creating a little chaos, and laughing the whole time is Aries's recipe for a perfect day.

★ **Remember why you love them.** Sometimes their blunt advice or targeted quips can be too much, and it's easy to wonder what you liked about them in the first place. In those moments, think back to all the fun times you've had together. Remember that they are a good person with a bit of a temper, and do everything you can not to engage with them when they're angry—you'd only add more fuel to the fire.

★ **Work alongside them.** If you want your relationship to grow—and if both of you want to grow as people—you need to do it together. On their own, Aries rarely pursues self-development. Working through their triggers and choosing healthier responses to stress is something they'll need a little help with. At the end of the day, they need you to be the bucket of water that (gently) reduces their inferno to a smolder.

☽

ARIES MOON

This is a tough placement. The Moon rules emotion, and Aries is either glad or mad, with little variation. That means an Aries Moon may be a bit volatile. Aries Moons are hard to get close to and even harder to maintain a long-term relationship with. The good news is, once you're aware of an Aries Moon placement, you'll be better prepared to handle the accompanying emotional outbursts.

Ideally, an Aries Moon's partner would have their Moon in an air sign (Gemini, Libra, and Aquarius) because an air Moon won't want to argue but can hold their own if need be, and they're able to do so without bursting into tears. Both an Aries Moon and an air Moon move on quickly.

Aries Moons are least compatible with water Moons (Cancer, Scorpio, and Pisces). They find water Moons to be overly sensitive, melancholic, and dramatic. Relationships with other fire Moons (Aries, Leo, and Sagittarius) will be explosive at best.

An Aries Moon may be compatible with an earth Moon (Taurus, Virgo, and Capricorn), depending on other placements. Compatibility will be better determined by the individuals' Venus and Mars signs.

Restorative Activities for an Aries Moon

Aries Moons are a bit like a pot that is about to boil over. If you don't blow off some steam, disaster will ensue.

- ★ **Vent often.** The healthiest thing you can do for yourself is purge all your emotions in a safe space. Perhaps you don't even need to vent to another person—just talking out loud to yourself can soothe frustration. If you have a loved one or therapist who will listen as you get things off your chest, all the better.

- ★ **Move your body.** I recommend going for a walk, if possible. Decide whether you want to exercise alone, bring a pet, or invite a friend. Then, get moving. Try to move at a pace fast enough that holding a conversation would be challenging. The goal here is to push your body so that when you are finished, you feel pleasantly fatigued.

- ★ **Bake or cook.** The more time-intensive or laborious the recipe, the better. When you are in the kitchen, you are out of your head and in your body. Your focus is on chopping, kneading, or measuring, not on how you have been slighted. By the time your masterpiece is finished, the irritations of the day will have melted away and you'll have created something tasty with your own two hands. Alternatively, order food from a restaurant you have never tried before and savor each flavor.

★ **Go for a drive alone.** If listening to music or a podcast soothes you, by all means, turn up the volume. Otherwise, embrace the ambiance of road noise. Drive with no destination in mind. Turn down roads in your neighborhood that you haven't explored before. If at any point you notice yourself becoming irritated by other drivers, it's time to head home. Alternatively, sit outside and immerse yourself in the noises of nature.

Journal Prompts for an Aries Moon

If you have an Aries Moon, it's unlikely that journaling comes naturally to you. Writing about your emotions might seem counterintuitive because you prefer acting on them, but I promise there is value to be found in journaling. Journaling can help you get to the root cause of some of your habitual responses, and it might help you determine healthier ways to respond in certain situations. Bear with me, Aries Moons, and give it a try.

★ Think about the last time you were angry. What triggered that emotion? Is it a regular trigger for you? How did you handle the situation? Were you happy with the outcome? What could you do to handle that situation differently next time?

★ What contributes to your mood swings? For example, are you sleeping enough? What are some things you do to feel rejuvenated? Is there a correlation between how happy you are and how regularly you're practicing self-care?

★ What is an emotional topic you hate talking about? Why don't you like talking about it? Is it benefiting you to keep it inside, or is there someone in your life whom you should be talking about this with?

So Your Partner Is an Aries Moon . . .

First of all, you must really love this person to enter a relationship with them, and they must really love you back. This placement makes love complicated, but you've deemed each other worth the effort, and that's beautiful. Hopefully, with a little TLC and a lot of patience, you can help your partner learn to better regulate their emotions.

★ **Find ways to laugh together.** Remember, emotions are powerful for an Aries Moon, and they're usually very happy or very upset. Making laughter a foundation of your relationship will help them naturally recalibrate to happier territory.

★ **When they're angry, leave them alone so they can let it out.** Aries Moons need a tried-and-true way to release their anger, and that will look different for everyone. But what all Aries Moons need is to be left alone so they can work through their strong emotions. Talking to an angry Aries Moon will never lead to a positive outcome. If you're having a conversation and it's becoming heated, put a pin in it and wait to revisit the topic until you're both in a better mood.

★ **Telling an Aries Moon that you love them is great, but they'll really feel loved when you show them.** This might look like making a dinner reservation at the new restaurant they've been dying to try, offering them a massage after a long day, or signing up for a fun couples class and securing a babysitter.

↑
ARIES RISING

The rising sign is how we appear to people when we first meet them. More than likely, Aries risings are extroverts—or at least they appear to be. It's easy for them to chat with strangers; they're not shy. Aries risings are great wingmen because they can strike up a conversation with anyone, even on their friends' behalf.

Aries risings are naturally drawn to people who have Libra placements. They likely get along well with Libras; they may have close friends with Libra placements or a partner who has plenty of Libra in their chart. Libra's calm, even-keeled demeanor balances them out, and Aries rising's feisty attitude adds some much-needed fun to Libra's day-to-day life. If an Aries rising is single, they should pay special attention to the Libras they encounter. (And if an Aries rising and a Libra end up marrying after reading this, I expect an invitation to the wedding.)

Ways to Spot an Aries Rising

Aries risings like to hang out in areas where they can talk, laugh, and shoot the shit. They're not likely to frequent quieter areas like the library or a coffee shop. For this reason, studying or getting work done may be a bit of a struggle for them; quiet environments may seem stifling.

★ **Aries risings have loud voices or loud laughs.** They don't even try to be loud—it just happens. Their charisma and confidence naturally draw people in, and you can usually find them at the center of a crowd.

★ **Aries risings are social butterflies.** They have a long list of people they can call if they have a favor to ask, and they likely have more acquaintances than the average Joe. With their innate friendliness and warmth, an acquaintance quickly feels like a friend.

★ **When the spotlight shines on them, Aries risings don't shy away.** It won't take much convincing to get an Aries rising to jump onstage at a karaoke bar.

Downsides of Being an Aries Rising

It's all fun and games when you're the life of the party, but the party doesn't last forever. Once the Aries rising mask falls off, people may be startled by what's actually underneath.

★ **It might be hard for Aries risings to form long-lasting relationships.** Because you naturally come off as a bundle of fun, you may form friendships that lack depth. Fair-weather friends turn tail when the Aries rising mask slips off and there is a real, flawed human underneath.

★ **Your larger-than-life demeanor might scare away people** you would otherwise connect with. An Aries rising could inadvertently repel people with more reserved Sun and rising signs who mistakenly believe they can't keep up. In reality, you may have other placements that make you a lot more laidback than you appear.

★ **Aries risings may suffer from "always the bridesmaid, never the bride" syndrome.** You're a lot of fun to have around, so you make connections easily. But others may not perceive you as a serious person, and you might be passed over when it comes to dating or other commitments.

Using Your Aries Rising to Your Advantage

Aries rising is an attention-grabbing placement. Others will certainly be aware of your presence. You never have to worry about blending in with the crowd!

★ **You are a natural leader.** Your strong voice and capable demeanor command attention. Whether you are surrounded by friends or colleagues, others look to you to make decisions for the group. This puts you in a position of power, and with great power comes great responsibility.

★ **Others see you as very confident.** When you feel nervous or insecure, nobody will pick up on it. You seem to have everything under control, even if you know it is a façade. This is a fantastic trait to have when it comes to your profession because customers and coworkers will naturally rely on you, and it benefits your love life too, since most people find confidence incredibly attractive.

★ **You are fun to be around.** Strangers see you as high-energy and excitable. New people, places, and experiences bring out your curious side. You roll with the punches and make every situation an adventure. Of course, once people get to know you, they will learn that no one—not even an Aries rising—can uphold this level of energy at all times.

☿
ARIES MERCURY

The planet Mercury rules communication. Aries is a spontaneous, fun-loving sign. Thus, chatting with an Aries Mercury is an adventure—you never know where the conversation will lead! Someone with an Aries Mercury quickly becomes the life of the party. Even the dullest anecdotes are entertaining when Aries Mercury is the storyteller.

Communicating with an Aries Mercury

If you're shy, communicating with an Aries Mercury is a blessing because you won't be expected to contribute much to the conversation anyway. An Aries Mercury could talk to a brick wall. If you like to contribute to a conversation, though, you may struggle to get a word in edgewise.

★ **Try not to raise your voice**—positively or negatively—because that will just lead to them raising theirs. An Aries Mercury always ends up being the loudest person in the room, whether that's accidental or on purpose. Keep your voice low and hope they follow suit.

★ **Make eye contact.** An Aries Mercury likes knowing they have your attention. If your focus drifts while talking to an Aries Mercury, correct it quickly, before they notice and become offended.

★ **Avoid controversial subjects.** Aries Mercury has an opinion on pretty much everything, and you never know what is going to come out of their mouth next. Especially if you're talking in a public area, it's safest to stick to small talk.

Questions to Ask an Aries Mercury

An Aries Mercury is super easy to strike up a conversation with. Ask broad questions and see where that takes you. Once Aries Mercury finds a subject they like talking about, they can go on for a while, so get comfortable!

★ Who is on your last nerve right now?

★ What are you passionate about? What couldn't you care less about?

★ If you were in charge, how would things be different?

♀
ARIES VENUS

Venus is the planet of love, beauty, and pleasure, and it becomes all gas, no brakes in the sign of Aries. This is because Aries likes the chase. They approach dating as a bit of a game. If it's too easy to win someone's affection, they lose interest. But they're probably going to lose interest anyway, if we're being honest.

Self-Love for an Aries Venus

An Aries Venus speeds through life. You're not terribly concerned if potential partners can't keep up.

★ **Try something new.** Variety is the spice of life for an Aries Venus. Is there a restaurant, activity, or small business that's been on your mind? Once you know what you want to explore, have an adventure. Aries is an independent sign—its cosmic opposite is Libra, the sign of partnership—so you thrive on your own. For that reason, explore solo if possible.

★ **Delete and block to your heart's content.** You appreciate the finality of blocking someone, and it gives you the illusion of having control over the situation. Fill your block list with ex-friends, former lovers, and inconsiderate strangers. But remember that this is an incomplete solution, as you may still encounter those you have blocked in everyday life.

★ **Make a list of everyone who has wronged you.** If it feels right, get into the nitty-gritty details of what happened. Write down all the resentments you are harboring. Essentially, create your own version of the *Mean Girls* Burn Book. When you've gotten out all your frustrations, rip up the paper(s) and burn the pieces, or if you wrote your list on a device, delete the document. Try to leave these wounds behind; don't let them make you bitter.

Seducing an Aries Venus

Aries rules the head, and seducing an Aries Venus definitely requires a cerebral approach. Keep them intrigued as long as you can. They're drawn to the physical, and they dislike the emotional. An Aries Venus is easily aroused and easily put off; proceed with caution.

★ **Aries Venus will want to play the dating game.** Think through your strategy. If you're too restrained, Aries will deem you boring and cut you off. If you decide to come on strong, it should be a sexual kind of strong. For example, right off the bat, you could send them a risqué photo (with consent, of course), rather than asking them how many children they want.

★ **Practice saying yes to whatever an Aries Venus suggests.** Obviously, if it goes against your moral compass or makes you feel uncomfortable or unsafe in any way, you should say no. But, within reason, say yes! *Yes* is one of Aries's favorite words. It makes them feel so loved. "You want to grab a beer at 11:00 a.m. on Friday?" Yes! "Can we go for a drive and listen to music?" Yes! "Will you help me dye my hair?" Yes!

★ **Propose unusual date ideas.** Nothing sounds more boring to an Aries than meeting for coffee. Ask Aries to visit a petting zoo, go thrift shopping, or join you for any other activity. Emphasis on *activity*—this is not the sign to Netflix and chill with. Also, Aries is one of the only signs that truly embraces spontaneity, so don't be afraid to ask them on a date the day of.

So Your Partner Has an Aries Venus ...

There is nothing boring about this placement! Embrace your partner's fun-loving spirit. At home and in public, Aries Venus just wants to have a good time.

★ **Keep things fun and flirty.** Aries Venus is happiest when they're laughing, and they find long, heartfelt conversations laborious and uncomfortable. For example, instead of reading your Aries Venus partner a long, cheesy love letter, sit for a caricature artist and hang the portrait in your home.

★ **It's unlikely that your Aries Venus partner knows how to help when you're going through an emotional situation.** You can and should ask for what you need, but nobody is capable of being everything to everyone, not even your partner—adjust your expectations accordingly. Aries Venus is capable of depth and intimacy, certainly, but not in the prolonged, patient way that some people require; they simply don't have the attention span to sit in heavy emotions for long. If you're going through a rough patch, accept the support your Aries Venus partner offers *and* seek the support of trusted friends, family members, or a therapist.

★ **Do your best to stay calm, cool, and collected in difficult situations.** An Aries Venus may not verbalize it, but they appreciate having a level-headed presence nearby, especially if their own temper is rising. A peaceful approach is a good way to neutralize a hotheaded temperament.

♂
ARIES MARS

Mars—the planet of passion, aggression, sex, and chaos—heightens the energy of whatever sign it is in. Mars rules the sign of Aries, making this a very comfortable (and powerful) position for Mars. This is an intense placement, and wrangling an Aries Mars is not for the faint of heart.

Aries Mars Behind Closed Doors

Aries Mars expresses themselves through sex and aggression. If you are the more reserved one in the relationship (and, let's face it, unless you also have a fiery Mars, you probably are), this placement will challenge you.

★ **Be open to interesting sex.** Aries like to keep things fun and exciting. They're likely to experiment. If you've never taken the BDSM quiz, this might be a good time to. If you have traits like "pillow princess," an Aries Mars will probably be way too much for you. But if you're into bondage, voyeurism, or anything not-quite-vanilla, full steam ahead!

★ **Anything that challenges social norms piques the interest of an Aries Mars.** Roleplay, nonmonogamy, and experimenting with dominant/submissive dynamics are all things your partner might be curious about. They may bring up taboo topics just to see how you react.

★ **Aries Mars is prone to temper tantrums.** They become easily frustrated, and when things are consistently not going their way, anger is their natural response. Since anger is a familiar emotion for them, large reactions often accompany minor irritation. Old habits die hard, so they may raise their voice or appear much angrier than they actually are.

Things *Not* to Do to an Aries Mars

There's no way to sugarcoat this: You don't want to be on an Aries Mars's bad side. Do everything in your power to stay in their good graces. Hell hath no fury like an Aries Mars.

★ **If you can help it, don't yell.** Easier said than done, certainly, but an Aries Mars is going to intensify whatever energy you bring to the table, and fighting fire with fire isn't going to do either of you any good.

★ **Don't provoke them.** It's easy to piss off an Aries Mars, but it's almost impossible to calm them back down. They don't forgive and it'll take a while for them to forget, so bite your tongue. You'll save yourself a lot of trouble.

★ **Don't put them in incongruous situations.** Aries Mars is always in pursuit of a good time, and that often includes hooting and hollering. If you want to bring a friend to the orchestra, find someone with more soft-spoken tendencies. An Aries Mars is much better suited for rock concerts and rodeos.

Things an Aries Mars Probably Needs to Hear (But Definitely Doesn't Want To)

Critiquing an Aries Mars is asking for trouble, but everyone has room to grow.

★ **For the love of god, buy a punching bag.** Lift some weights. Pound the pavement. See a therapist! You have so much energy inside you, and you have to let it out. If you're holding it in, not only are you making yourself miserable, but you are making the people around you miserable too!

★ **You aren't a toddler; you can't just stomp around and pout.** You have to learn how to channel your energy in a healthier way, and that starts with communication. Humans evolved for a reason. Make your ancestors proud. Read a book; reflect; journal.

★ **Stop! Yelling!** I know it comes naturally, but raising your voice when you're upset never leads to anything good. You have to find a calmer way to communicate when you're feeling strong emotions.

★ **You are not the easiest person to be around.** Take a moment to think about the people in your life who consistently show up for you, then find a way to thank them. It doesn't have to be a verbal thank-you if that feels out of character; you could buy them a drink next time you're out. Ride-or-die friends are rare, so let yours know how much you appreciate them every once in a while.

★ **Let someone else win.** Not everything in life is a competition.

QUICK GUIDE TO

ARIES

PLACEMENTS

If someone in your life has Aries placements . . .

DO

★ Share the spotlight—or better yet, let them take center stage.

★ Laugh with them, not at them.

★ Follow their lead and embrace spontaneity.

DON'T

★ Try to force them into having emotional conversations.

★ Expect them to handle every situation perfectly.

★ Suppress or shame their childlike nature.

★ 2 ★
TAURUS

I'm going to be totally honest right up front: Taurus is my favorite sign—and no, I'm not a Taurus. I love the reliability of Taurus placements, the silent strength. Every Taurus I have ever met is peaceable and reliable, and most of them have a wicked sense of humor as well. Taurus is one of the funniest signs, though their humor is usually dry or sarcastic.

At their best, Tauruses are resilient, unflappable, calm, determined, hardworking, committed, and patient. They enjoy the finer things in life. The life of a Taurus is full of soft fabrics, rich foods, and cozy nights at home. All of this makes sense: Taurus is ruled by the planet Venus, which is notoriously loving and luxe.

Of course, Tauruses have flaws. They are incredibly stubborn. Tauruses are also cheap—sometimes embarrassingly so. They don't like change, and they have a difficult time accepting viewpoints that differ from their own. The phrase "My way or the highway" was probably coined by a Taurus; it's energy they all embody.

Taurus rules the second house, the house of finances and material affairs, and this explains their money-conscious tendencies. As the second sign of the zodiac, Taurus has been around the block a time or two. However, Taurus is still pretty "young" astrologically, so they have a lot to learn. If Aries is the child, Taurus is the preteen starting to save up their money, perhaps working their first job as a babysitter or lawn mower. The shackles of adulthood are starting to take hold, but there is still childlike mirth to be found underneath the grown-up exterior; Tauruses are more lighthearted than they appear.

The symbol for Taurus is the bull. The bull is steadfast, sturdy, and determined. From afar, bulls look pretty approachable; they keep to themselves, quietly munching on grass or dozing. But when crossed, bulls become aggressive. Anyone who's pissed off a bull immediately regrets it. Taurus is the same—their good nature only lasts so long. Once they reach the end of their rope, Taurus snaps, revealing a totally different side to their personality. The good news is that Taurus is one of the most patient signs, mostly because they don't enjoy being upset—it's too much effort for their limited energy supply.

Taurus is an earth sign. Earth signs (Taurus, Virgo, and Capricorn) are even-tempered, hardworking, and responsible. These are the perfect signs to have in your corner because earth signs will drop everything for the people they love. Their affection may be hard-won, but it's for a lifetime. Earth signs take things slow, including building trust. But, like most things that build up slowly, eventually there is a breaking point. Earth signs are notorious for suffering in silence; your earth sign loved ones are unlikely to ask for help.

Taurus is a fixed sign, along with Leo, Scorpio, and Aquarius. This means exactly what it sounds like: They latch on to something and stay put. Persistence has benefits, especially in situations where perseverance leads to career advances or monetary gain, but it also can be incredibly off-putting. Sometimes you have to let go of things that aren't working in order to make room for better things to fall into place; this is a lesson fixed signs have a hard time learning. Releasing—whether it's a relationship, a financial opportunity, or a career—does not come easily to Taurus. On the other hand, if you're in a relationship with a Taurus, their fixed modality means they're unlikely to stray. If Taurus chooses you, you are blessed indeed, because you've found a partner for life.

⊙

TAURUS SUN

The Sun is in Taurus between April 20 and May 20, give or take a few days depending on the year. Individuals born under the Taurus Sun are loyal friends and devoted family members. They can be trusted to remain calm in chaotic situations, and their mere presence deescalates tension.

For those with a Taurus Sun, every section in this chapter will apply to some degree. The Sun is the most powerful planetary force, so it has a huge impact on personality. While a Taurus Sun may not have a Taurus Venus, for example, they will undoubtedly find something in that section that they relate to.

Pure Taurus Energy

Don't be surprised if you rarely cross paths with a Taurus. They aren't out and about often—they'd much rather be at home.

★ **Taurus Suns are incredibly money conscious.** When they go out with friends and the waiter brings one bill, Taurus will calculate exactly what they owe down to the penny. When paying someone back, Tauruses rarely round up or down—every cent counts.

★ **A Taurus's social battery depletes quickly.** Their favorite way to preserve their energy is by sleeping. Tauruses *love* taking naps. In fact, naps are an integral part of their self-care routine. If you haven't heard from your Taurus loved one for a while, don't be alarmed—they're probably asleep.

★ **Comfort is paramount for a Taurus Sun.** After a long day at work, they immediately change into sweatpants, slippers, and their favorite robe. They prefer to spend the weekend lounging in clothes without zippers and buttons, and they don't forsake comfort easily. If you text a Taurus at 7:00 p.m. and ask them if they want to go out later, they'll say, "Sorry, can't. Already in my pajamas." Once the sun sets, Taurus is in for the night.

★ **Because Taurus is ruled by the planet Venus, they have expensive taste.** For example, at a wine tasting, Taurus is the person who performs every step of the process perfectly. They don't just sip; they sniff and swirl so they can taste every flavor. And at home, their bathroom counters are covered with moisturizers, lotions, and potions. Ask a Taurus for skincare recommendations and be ready to take notes.

★ **Typically, Taurus is an introverted sign.** At a party, Tauruses are the people in the background. They won't be tearing up the dance floor—they're more likely to be bobbing to the beat from the corner of the room. Loud noises and small spaces test their patience, and the moment they arrive somewhere, they're already daydreaming about going home and crawling into bed.

★ **The characteristic Taurus stubbornness often shows up in their personal relationships.** Taurus Suns don't dislike many people, but once someone pushes them to their limit, they will hold a lifelong grudge. Taurus will never be outright cruel; instead, they give a cold shoulder so intense even passersby can feel the chill.

Gifts for a Taurus Sun

When it comes to gifts for a Taurus Sun, you can't go wrong with luxury. Taurus appreciates the finer things in life, but they hate dipping into their bank account. Give them the gift of indulgence.

★ **A Taurus Sun always appreciates a new blanket.** They may be something of a connoisseur. In fact, in their living room or bedroom, you'll likely find a basket full of blankets: light, heavy, soft, and more. Give them a blanket that stands out in some way; perhaps it's weighted or handwoven, or it's the very same shade of taupe as the bedroom curtains.

★ **Splurge on something expensive.** Whether it's a designer watch or a Michelin-star dinner, Taurus loves feeling wealthy, especially on someone else's dime.

★ **If you can't afford luxury, you're better off buying Taurus an experience than a cheap gift.** Stay away from active experiences—Taurus would rather float in a lazy river than go rock climbing. Give them a gift certificate to a winery or nice restaurant, or pay for them to attend a cooking class. You could also give them a gift certificate to a local spa for a day of pampering.

★ **As an earth sign, Taurus enjoys being in nature, but they don't like overexerting themselves.** Find a way for them to enjoy the great outdoors without having to work too hard. Go for a picnic, hang a hammock in a patch of shade, or take a boat tour.

★ **Honor their aversion to change.** If the Taurus in your life has an established favorite—whether it's a favorite author, a favorite candy, or a favorite brand of pen—you can't go wrong contributing to their supply. Tauruses don't like to try new things, so once they've found a tried-and-true favorite, they love to stock up.

★ **When all else fails, give a Taurus a candle.** Go for a clean, simple scent—nothing too floral or sweet, which could be overpowering. Candles scented with essential oils are a great option.

So Your Boss Is a Taurus Sun . . .

This is a fantastic placement to have in a leadership role. Taurus bosses are reliable, consistent, and calm under pressure. They may be hard to please at first, but once you've won them over, they'll trust you unconditionally. Count your lucky stars!

★ **Master the art of sucking up in small ways.** Nobody likes a kiss-ass, but a little appreciation goes a long way with a Taurus. Offer to grab them a cup of coffee when you're already on your way to the break room, leave a card on their desk on their birthday, or ask them to lunch.

★ **Laugh at their jokes.** Remember, Tauruses have an understated sense of humor, and they like to keep things light. Laughing at their jokes is a surefire way to stay in their good graces.

★ **Ask for help when you need it.** It's unlikely that a Taurus will admit when they're struggling, but they respect and appreciate when other people are able to do so. Taurus doesn't find it cumbersome to lend a hand; instead, they're happy the situation will be handled correctly.

★ **Try to keep your personal life and your professional life separate.** Taurus is a pro at this, so crossing the invisible line at work may make them bristle. They're happy to hear what's going on in your life, but only to a certain degree. This is not the person you should be venting to, especially not on company property.

★ **Remain as organized as possible.** Your Taurus boss appears to have it all together, and whether or not that's actually the case, they appreciate employees who follow suit. Keep your workspace clean, stay on top of your projects, and compose thoughtful emails—Taurus bosses appreciate emails that have a salutation, a clear message, and a formal signature.

★ **If you are facing a problem, think of a few possible solutions.** Then present your ideas to your boss and ask for their feedback. Taurus will see this as a learning opportunity, and even if they don't think your solutions are the best approach, they'll appreciate that you came prepared.

So Your Coworker Is a Taurus Sun . . .

This is a coworker you want to make nice with. More than likely, your Taurus coworker is easy to get along with and pretty laidback, so that shouldn't be too hard. Make an effort to befriend your Taurus coworker, because they might be your boss someday.

★ **Casually find out what their interests are, and make a point to remember the answers.** Everyone finds it touching when someone remembers the little things about them, but especially Taurus. A little kindness goes a long way.

★ **Collaborate with them when you can.** Remember, Taurus tends to suffer in silence, so if they solicit your help, find a way to make it happen. This is an opportunity to prove your trustworthiness. Likewise, ask Taurus for help when you're faced with a sticky situation; they like feeling useful. But don't fall into a routine of asking for help too often—only ask for help when it's really necessary.

★ **The way to a Taurus's heart is through their stomach, so find a way to treat them once in a while.** This can be super simple: Tell them you're grabbing a coffee and ask if they want anything, or offer to bring them back something if you go out for lunch. If sharing food is acceptable in your office, find out what kinds of snacks your Taurus coworker likes and keep them in mind. And if you bring in Taurus's favorite snack on their birthday, well, you've just made a friend for life.

So Your Partner Is a Taurus Sun . . .

Life with a Taurus partner is steady, loving, and easy—until you change the brand of cereal you buy and they freak out. Taurus doesn't like change, and they also have a tough time admitting when they're wrong, which is probably the source of a lot of your arguments. But isn't it worth it, really, to be loved by a Taurus?

★ **Let them make the decisions once in a while.** Tauruses are notorious for letting their partner choose, but once in a blue moon, shake things up by letting them pick where you go on date night or what you're having for dinner. They don't need to make these choices every time—nor do they want to—but letting them decide every so often is a nice gesture.

★ **Find a way to appeal to their sensual side.** This could be through massage, cuddling, or just a romantic dinner at home. When it comes to a Taurus, you can't go wrong with good food, good wine, and some candlelight.

★ **More than likely, your Taurus Sun partner loves physical touch.** In fact, it might be their love language! Incorporate more consensual physical touch into your relationship. Rub their shoulders after a long day, run your fingers through their hair, hold their hand when you're walking around the grocery store, or wind your arm around them while waiting in line. And always remember to kiss them good night!

★ **Gently challenge their stubbornness once in a while.** As hard as it might be for Taurus to believe, change is good from time to time. Life begins outside of your comfort zone, after all. When attempting to broaden your Taurus partner's horizons, do so delicately. In a perfect world, they won't even realize they've stepped outside of their comfort zone until after the fact. I'm not suggesting you pull a fast one on them—quite the opposite, actually. Work in change slowly. Add a new vegetable to your stir-fry; go see a movie in theaters without watching the trailer first; rearrange some of the furniture in your home.

☽
TAURUS MOON

Because Taurus is ruled by the planet Venus, it's a very sensual and luxurious sign. Taurus is calm, cool, and collected. When combined with the Moon, which rules emotion, Taurus is even calmer and even cooler, believe it or not! Unlikely to raise their voice, they're also unlikely to change their mind about anything—ever. Nobody's perfect.

Taurus Moons are most compatible with earth Moons (Taurus, Virgo, and Capricorn) or water Moons (Cancer, Scorpio, and Pisces). Other earth Moons can match Taurus's levelheadedness, and water Moons can appeal to their sensitive side.

Taurus Moons are least compatible with air Moons (Gemini, Libra, and Aquarius). Air Moons process emotions by talking through them, but Taurus Moons don't want to talk about how they're feeling; they prefer to keep it all inside. They're masters of internalization.

An exception to the rule is Libra Moon. Because both Taurus and Libra are ruled by Venus, they will understand each other on an intrinsic level. Beyond that, neither Taurus nor Libra are interested in debates or dramatics, meaning their relationship would be a peaceful and harmonious one.

Taurus Moons may be compatible with fire Moons (Aries, Leo, and Sagittarius), depending on other placements. Because Taurus and Leo are both fixed signs, couples with this combination are slightly more compatible, though neither of them will want to admit defeat during an argument.

Restorative Activities for a Taurus Moon

What do you think of when you hear the word *cozy*? More than likely, whatever comes to mind is one of many ways a Taurus Moon can practice self-care.

★ **Embrace the concept of hygge.** *Hygge* is a Scandinavian word that roughly translates to "comfort" and "coziness." The goal is to foster "a sense of coziness, contentment, and well-being."[2] When I think of representations of hygge, I think of rooms lit only by candlelight, reading during a rainstorm, snuggling up under a blanket, and other scenarios that elicit that warm and fuzzy feeling. Prioritize moments of coziness in everyday life.

★ **Volunteer at an animal shelter.** You enjoy spending time with animals: They don't talk back, they don't pressure you to share how you're feeling before you're ready, and they are innately gentle and pure. If your local animal shelter is not in need of volunteers at this time, make a donation instead. Alternatively, you could spend time with

---

2 *Merriam-Webster*, s.v. "hygge (*adj.*)," accessed December 21, 2023, https://www.merriam-webster.com/dictionary/hygge.

animals by offering to walk your neighbor's dog, taking pet-sitting gigs, adopting a pet yourself, or visiting the zoo.

★ **Invite family and friends over for a campfire,** or see if one of your loved ones would be willing to host. The ambiance of a fire can be so soothing: the smell of the wood burning, the crackling sounds, the heat combating the chill evening air. As you sit around the fire with the people you love most, feel your spirit lightening.

Journal Prompts for a Taurus Moon

Because Taurus Moons are internal processors, journaling is a fantastic way to work through things. If you have a Taurus Moon, you are naturally reflective, but you may have a hard time putting words to what you're feeling. There is nothing wrong with this—it's just how you're wired—but you may find it easier to put the words together on paper. Oftentimes, journaling allows connections to be made that you might've missed while turning things over in your mind.

★ If you could have anything in the world right now, what would you wish for? Is your goal attainable? What small actions can you take to turn your dream into a reality? If your goal doesn't feel attainable, how can you modify it?

★ What's something that's weighing heavily on your mind right now? Is there anything you can do to improve the situation? If not, what can you do to decompress and redirect your focus?

★ What is something you strongly believe? What comforts you about this belief? How do you react when that belief is threatened? In what ways is your belief flexible?

So Your Partner Is a Taurus Moon . . .

Getting a strong reaction out of your partner may be difficult. This sounds like a good thing until you're asking them why they love you and they only string a few words together. At the end of the day, you know your Taurus

Moon partner will always be there for you, even if they're not the best at verbalizing it.

★ **Your partner needs alone time**; this is a crucial aspect of their well-being. Taurus Moons don't like talking through their emotions, nor do they like acting on them. They need time to process and reflect, and that's best done in solitude.

★ **Don't force them to talk about something if they're not ready.** The more you poke and prod, the less responsive they'll become. This is their stubbornness in action.

★ **Spoil them in small ways.** You don't need to do anything grand to impress a Taurus Moon. Leave sticky notes around the house with sweet messages, pick up their favorite snack the next time you go to the store, or randomly text them a heart emoji. Just knowing they're on your mind is enough to warm a Taurus Moon's heart.

★ **It's hard for Taurus Moons to express their needs, so ask questions to find out how you can best support them.** When they're upset, do they like to be held, or do they prefer not to be touched? If they're dealing with something heavy, do they want to talk about it, or would they prefer to work through it on their own? When faced with a problem, do they want you to propose solutions, or do they just need you to listen?

↑
TAURUS RISING

Taurus risings typically come off as shy, perhaps even a little dull. Their stoic expression can easily be interpreted as a lack of interest. This might frustrate them, especially if their placid demeanor leads to people assuming they don't have much going on underneath the surface.

Taurus risings are naturally drawn to people with Scorpio placements. There is something about dark, broody Scorpio that sucks Taurus right in. Both signs are deeply loyal and incredibly stubborn. Taurus risings and people with Scorpio placements become great friends and dedicated romantic partners. Single Taurus risings should not be surprised if they fall for a Scorpio—this would be a true power couple.

Ways to Spot a Taurus Rising

I once heard this first impression of a Taurus rising: "When I met you, I thought you were a stoner." Because Taurus risings come off so calm and laidback, it is assumed they must be under the influence of *something*. Nope! That's just a Taurus rising.

★ Remember the symbol for Taurus, the bull? **Like a bull, many Taurus risings have nose piercings.** Unlike some astrologers, I do not believe the rising sign affects physical appearance, but this is one physical correlation that I have seen time and time again.

★ **A Taurus rising prefers to hang around the outskirts of a situation.** They're not going to be the person at an event making the rounds. They'd rather wait for someone to come to them, at which point they are perfectly capable of making polite small talk.

★ **Taurus risings might appear quiet or introverted.** They are more likely to listen to a conversation than to contribute to it. Once in a while, they'll slip a sarcastic joke in, but they prefer to let other people do the talking.

★ **They seem to be very easygoing.** If someone asks what they want—whether it's something to drink or eat, or which game they want to play, or where they'd like to go—they always say, "I don't care!" And most of the time, they really don't; they're just along for the ride.

Downsides of Being a Taurus Rising

Taurus risings tend to blend in. This can be a great quality to have in certain situations, but it also means that people often make broad assumptions that might not match what's underneath the mask; it's automatically assumed

Taurus risings are always quiet, nice, easygoing, and unemotional. However, Taurus risings are as complex and multifaceted as everyone else.

★ **Your laidback demeanor means you tend to attract people who like to walk all over others.** Because of this, you may slowly become surrounded by manipulators, narcissists, energy vampires, and other toxic people.

★ Because **it takes a while for you to warm up to people,** others may have a hard time picking up on your likes and dislikes or your emotions in certain situations. As a result, you may feel misunderstood, overlooked, or unimportant.

★ **Most Taurus risings have severe RBF** (resting bitch face). This is just the way your face looks! But an uninviting expression isn't the social norm, so RBF may make it hard for you to meet new people or partners. It may also lead to being perceived as mean, unfriendly, or uninterested.

★ **You don't show your emotions right away,** so once you lower your mask and start to express how you're feeling, others might perceive you as hysterical. The emotions were always there—they were just hidden. This can be tough to navigate, especially if it's a recurring problem in your relationships. You should share your emotions earlier in relationships so that the shift doesn't seem so abrupt to others.

Using Your Taurus Rising to Your Advantage

While some see Taurus risings as quiet, even unfriendly, others perceive you as intentional and calm. You will know you have found your people when you encounter the latter.

★ **Taurus risings seem unflappable.** Your ability to appear level-headed in challenging circumstances is admirable. When you remain calm, you are also able to calm down others. This will benefit you greatly at work, especially if you work in customer service.

★ **Because you tend to keep your thoughts to yourself, others see you as trustworthy and confide in you.** You may become the go-to person for stressed coworkers or disgruntled customers. This can be a heavy burden to bear at times, so practice setting boundaries and protecting your energy. Overall, though, it is a wonderful thing that others consider you a safe space.

★ **Others have realistic expectations for you.** You don't seem flaky (like Gemini risings) or overly ambitious (like Capricorn risings). Instead, you simply seem, well, average. This means that with a little effort, you will be seen as going above and beyond. Be wary about making this a habit, though, because once people see you as a high achiever, any attempts to slow down will be cause for concern.

$$☿$$

TAURUS MERCURY

Mercury is the planet of communication, and we've already established that Taurus is selective with their words. When Taurus Mercury decides to share an opinion, they aren't interested in hearing opposing viewpoints; they are set in their ways and unwilling to change their mind. This can be a great thing, because they have a strong conviction, but it can also narrow their perspectives.

Communicating with a Taurus Mercury

Talking to a Taurus Mercury feels like talking to a brick wall from time to time, especially when they've made up their mind about something. However, once you get to know a Taurus Mercury, they have more to say than you might think.

★ **Be patient.** Taurus Mercury may shut down when faced with conflict, a behavior known as stonewalling. This usually isn't intentional; it's part of Taurus's natural urge to retreat and reflect.

★ **Don't rush to fill occasional pauses in conversation.** Taurus Mercury doesn't need constant chatter to have a fulfilling conversation. Plus, sometimes they like having a moment of silence to collect their thoughts.

★ **Don't bother trying to change their mind.** Taurus Mercury is stubborn with a capital *S*. If they say something you don't agree with, you're better off casually changing the subject than engaging.

Questions to Ask a Taurus Mercury

Getting a Taurus Mercury to open up takes a little bit of work. Your best bet is to ask open-ended questions. If you know what they're interested in, that's another great way to get conversation flowing.

★ If money was no object, what is the first big purchase you would make?

★ How do you treat yourself?

★ What's the best gift you've ever received? What about the worst?

★ When do you feel the most relaxed?

♀
TAURUS VENUS

Ooh la la! What a phenomenal placement. Venus is comfortable in Taurus, as it rules this sign. The planet Venus represents love, beauty, pleasure, and sensuality. This means people with a Taurus Venus are incredibly romantic, though this energy depletes quickly. The good news is that there is a lifetime to collect romantic moments, because Taurus Venus loves forever.

Self-Love for a Taurus Venus

If you have a Taurus Venus, you are pretty good at showing yourself love, but it is never a bad idea to commit to a dedicated self-care routine.

★ **Pamper yourself.** The act of applying lotion or washing your hair can be deeply sensual. Rub your own shoulders, hands, and feet. Trim your nails and apply cuticle oil. Change your bedsheets and put on a silk pillowcase. These simple actions will make you feel like a million bucks. Alternatively, schedule an appointment with a skilled body worker.

★ **Meditate or do a gentle movement practice.** There are plenty of YouTube creators who upload relaxed yoga practices; choose one that is meant to be done right before bed or can be done in a chair. Stretching and slow movement are remarkably beneficial even though they get a bad rap for not being "intensive enough."

★ **Receiving gifts makes you feel cared for,** so get yourself a little treat. Perhaps this means ordering a coffee even though you could brew a pot at home or freshening up your space with a new set of curtains. Don't go overboard—the goal here is to offer yourself a small token of appreciation, not to splurge.

★ **Set aside time to read.** If you don't think you have enough time to read, check out an audiobook from your local library or browse Spotify's collection. It's relaxing to get lost in a story, and when you are able to fully unplug from the world around you for a while, you will return to everyday tasks with a renewed sense of energy.

Seducing a Taurus Venus

Taurus Venus is one of the easiest placements to seduce. What comes to mind when you hear the word *romance*? That's really all you need to do to win over a Taurus Venus. Keep in mind that public displays of affection and throes of passion don't mean much to a Taurus Venus. They're simple: They love nothing more than cuddling up to the person they love after a long day.

★ **When you have plans, show up on time.** Better yet, show up a few minutes early! Nothing is sexier to a Taurus Venus than someone who keeps their promises.

★ **Never run out of candles.** Want to set the mood? Light a candle. Preparing to have a difficult conversation? Light a candle. Helping Taurus Venus de-stress after a long day? Light a candle. When all else fails, light a candle.

★ **Incorporate texture** in a way that feels right for your relationship. If you're just getting to know each other, cuddle up under a chunky blanket (or a weighted blanket, if you really want to blow a Taurus Venus's mind). If you want to make texture sexy, try fuzzy handcuffs, silk sheets, undergarments made of lace or chiffon, or a satin eye mask.

★ **Lean into romance.** Plan an elaborate date night complete with delicious food, a chilled beverage, rose petals, and candlelight (naturally). Chocolate-covered strawberries are always a good idea. Intimate moments are more important to Taurus Venus than sexual ones; they always appreciate extra effort.

So Your Partner Has a Taurus Venus . . .

Your partner is a very loving person, but they probably have a hard time showing it. You may be underwhelmed by the amount of effort Taurus Venus puts into seducing you. If you want grand gestures, look elsewhere.

★ **Take comfort in the fact that Taurus Venus is unlikely to stray.** Of course, stranger things have happened, but most Taurus Venuses are loyal and faithful. This is for several reasons: They love love. They prefer to stay in their comfort zone and abhor change, so once they've established a relationship with someone, they don't want to have to start over. And their energy reserves aren't as robust as other signs, which means chasing after someone else is simply too much work.

★ **Don't bog down your relationship with intense emotions.** Tauruses are peaceable and patient, but they also have a limited energy supply. When you're feeling incredibly angry or downright depressed, there's only so much emotional heavy lifting a Taurus Venus is capable of. Have a support system in place, and turn to them after your Taurus Venus partner gets tired.

★ **Embody the word *cozy* in your relationship** as much as possible. Taurus Venus loves all things warm and fuzzy, whether that's watching a rom-com, going glamping, or spending the entire weekend in pajamas. These kinds of moments are deeply rejuvenating for a Taurus Venus.

★ **Don't try to change them.** Instead, make an effort to accept them exactly as they are. This is for your benefit and theirs, because they are unlikely to change anyway. Yes, your Taurus Venus partner is stubborn, but they are also incredibly sweet at their core. Protect this at all costs.

♂

TAURUS MARS

Mars is the planet of passion, drive, chaos, aggression, and sex. Taurus's number one priority is stability. Nothing brings a Taurus Mars more joy than concrete plans, a comfortable routine, and a sizable bank account balance.

Taurus Mars Behind Closed Doors

Mars is a planet of movement, yet in slow, steady Taurus, it pumps the brakes.

★ **When it comes to sex, what you see is what you get.** Unless a Taurus Mars has strong Scorpio placements or a fiery Sun or Moon, they're probably pretty vanilla in the bedroom. They are unlikely to have strong kinks; they'd rather make love. If you crave spice in your love life, you're unlikely to find it here.

★ **Taurus Mars struggles to find motivation.** They would rather rest in the familiar than venture into the unknown. Others may accuse them of being lazy, but the truth is their energy depletes quickly, and new experiences deplete them faster than anything else. In a world that prizes unending drive and determination, Taurus Mars's commitment to comfort is admirable.

★ **Taurus Mars is incredibly stubborn.** They are easygoing to a degree, but once their patience has worn thin, they do not budge. They may have strict rules around mealtime or bedtime. Alternatively, they may not let anyone eat in their car or wear shoes indoors. Taurus Mars's attempts to control their environment bring them peace, but if they are not careful, this can become dictatorial.

★ **Taurus Mars is prone to stonewalling.** Family members, close friends, and partners know that when Taurus Mars is pushed too far, they shut down and then shut others out. Their cold shoulder takes days, if not weeks, to thaw. This is a self-protective measure, but it is an unhealthy response. Taurus Mars should work to resolve this tendency lest their intimate relationships suffer the consequences.

Things *Not* to Do to a Taurus Mars

Taurus Mars isn't prone to emotional outbursts. They show their irritability in other ways: the cold shoulder, the silent treatment, or pointed quips. An angry Taurus Mars will dig their heels in and refuse to cooperate. You'll know you've upset a Taurus Mars when they stop responding to you.

★ **Don't change plans at the last minute.** This is super frustrating for Taurus Mars because they thrive in reliable, predictable situations. Not only will it disturb their routine, but it also means they have to rearrange their schedule, which cuts into their valuable relaxation time.

★ **Don't expect them to be on board with an activity that costs money.** You can extend an invitation, certainly, but they'll probably decline. Taurus Mars is stingy; in their mind, the money in their bank account was hard-won, and they would like it to stay where it is. Once in a while, they are willing to spend their money, but it's usually on something solitary and luxurious, like a mani-pedi or a facial.

★ **Don't overexert them.** Taurus Mars has a limited energy supply, and once it runs out, they're ready to go home and take a bubble bath. They tend to shut down when overexerted, both emotionally and verbally. Taurus Mars thinks they have more stamina than they really do, so they might agree to something only to realize halfway through that their battery is totally drained. Keep this in mind before asking your Taurus Mars friend to run a 5K with you.

★ **Don't expect them to throw caution to the wind.** Taurus Mars likes to have a plan, and they are relatively reserved. Taurus Mars is not spontaneous and doesn't take kindly to people who are rash, boisterous, or overwhelming. This is how they are, and they're not likely to change that.

Things a Taurus Mars Probably Needs to Hear (But Definitely Doesn't Want To)

Taurus is a fixed sign, so if you have a Taurus Mars, thinking about how you could better yourself is not high on your priority list. You like everything exactly as it is, thank you very much. But self-improvement is just as important as self-care—maybe even more so.

★ **It's healthy to loosen your grip on control once in a while.** Relax your shoulders, unclench your jaw, and try to have fun in a way you normally wouldn't. Fun is relative, sure, and I know you enjoy just hanging out at home, but are those the stories you want to tell your grandchildren someday? It might be a good idea to try axe throwing or meet up with a new friend. You never know what surprises are waiting on the other side of the experience.

★ **Change can be a good thing.** Do you really want to stay the same for the rest of your life? To grow and evolve, you have to open the door to opportunity. You have to put yourself in uncomfortable situations. There is always a lesson at the end of a challenging road, but you have to take the first step. Get going.

★ **When you die, you can't take your money with you.** Sitting on your nest egg and refusing to use it unless it's an emergency is responsible up to a certain point, but it also prevents you from making new memories. I'm not encouraging you to spend your money foolishly, but I am challenging you to reconsider what you're saying no to. Are you using your finances as an excuse to stay in your comfort zone?

★ **Being stubborn is not a good look on anyone.** Having strong opinions is admirable, but you have to allow yourself some flexibility or you will end up alienating yourself. No one is right about everything all the time—you're not the exception.

QUICK GUIDE TO

TAURUS

PLACEMENTS

If someone in your life has Taurus placements . . .

DO

★ Respect their need for downtime.

★ Engage their sensual side.

★ Gently prod them when they're being too stuck in their ways.

DON'T

★ Comment on how they manage their money.

★ Force them into social situations.

★ Try to convince them they're wrong.

★ 3 ★

GEMINI

When you meet a Gemini, believe me, you will know it. Geminis embody their sign loud and proud, whether or not they're into astrology. This is one of the easiest signs to spot in others. While they are undoubtedly friendly, Geminis are also known for their two sides. This friendliness can quickly turn into moodiness.

At their best, Geminis are outgoing and bubbly. They can talk to anyone about anything without making it awkward. Communication is something they pride themselves on, and they enjoy expressing themselves, verbally or in writing or both! Geminis make excellent newscasters, journalists, and writers.

While their charisma is definitely their best trait, they have some less-than-favorable qualities too. Geminis are bouncers: They're constantly moving from subject to subject, interest to interest, and person to person. It can be hard to keep up. If you're introverted, you may get exhausted by their constant chatter. Geminis don't often daydream about serious commitments or long-term relationships. If they do settle down, they may feel restricted by the monotony of monogamy.

As the third sign of the zodiac, Gemini rules the third house, the house of communication (and sibling relationships, among other things). If Aries is the child of the zodiac and Taurus is the preteen, Gemini is the teenager finding their place in the world and preparing to leave home for the first time. Everything is exciting. Everyone is a potential friend. There is so much to see and so much to do! Like a butterfly, Gemini doesn't rest in one place for long.

Gemini's symbol is the twins. They're known for having two very distinct sides to their personality. The stereotypical sides are the happy twin and the moody twin, the smile and the frown. I don't consider Gemini to be the moodiest sign of the zodiac—Cancer and Scorpio have that down pat—so this stereotype has never clicked for me. Instead, I like to think of the Gemini twins more as the Gemini Friend and the Gemini Acquaintance: Neither is inherently negative, but different people will see different sides of Gemini. Geminis embrace some people while holding others at an arm's length.

Gemini is an air sign. Air signs (Gemini, Libra, and Aquarius) are social, good with words, sharp, and curious. They are naturally charming. Most Geminis talk a mile a minute because they just have so much they want to say! Their mind is constantly going, racing from one thought to the next. If you encounter a quieter Gemini, rest assured there is a lot going on under the surface.

Gemini is a mutable sign, which essentially means changeable. Mutable signs (Gemini, Virgo, Sagittarius, and Pisces) adapt and go with the flow, which are great qualities to have. One of their more challenging traits is that they push themselves to evolve constantly. Mutable signs are not content to stay the same for their whole life, and they are always on the hunt for that "one thing" that will change their life. They may flit around from place to place in pursuit of elusive eternal bliss.

☉

GEMINI SUN

The Sun is in Gemini between May 21 and June 21, though the exact dates may vary a bit year by year. Individuals born under the Gemini Sun are energetic and charismatic. Growing up, they had plenty to say, and as an adult, they have an opinion on just about everything, though they may prefer to keep their opinions under wraps.

For those with a Gemini Sun, every section in this chapter will apply to some degree. The Sun is the most powerful planetary force, so it has a huge impact on personality. While a Gemini Sun may not have a Gemini Mercury, for example, they will undoubtedly find something in that section that they relate to.

Pure Gemini Energy

Gemini Suns are extroverts to the extreme. Introverted Geminis are likely hiding behind a demure rising sign, though they are very friendly once you get to know them. There is always something to talk about with a Gemini.

★ **Gemini Suns love to talk and regularly tell their loved ones what's been going on in their life**, which creates a feeling of closeness. But it is important to find a healthy give-and-take, and others may feel frustrated by an imbalanced conversation with a Gemini. Geminis should work on becoming better listeners—*actually* listening, which is not the same thing as being quiet.

★ **Geminis are messengers.** If they have something to share, they absolutely will. If you've ever been browsing at a store when a stranger comes up to you to tell you why you should or should not buy the product you're looking at, they're a Gemini. Because Geminis like to spread information as well as absorb it, they know a little about a lot. They have a wealth of knowledge. Ask a Gemini about almost anything, and they will probably have a relevant personal anecdote or a memorized fun fact they can share.

★ **Geminis seem to have a limitless social battery.** Geminis are the perfect people to bring to a party or another social event, even if they don't know anyone there—it's like the word *shy* isn't even in their vocabulary! They can run from event to event and have weeks full of activities without needing much time to recharge. When they do get burned out, they're back on their feet in no time. Being around other people supplies Geminis with an endless energy reserve.

★ **Geminis have a fascinating memory.** They remember every detail about some things but totally forget others. It's hard to know exactly what Gemini's photographic memory will latch on to. For example, a Gemini Sun might remember exactly what a person was wearing the first time they met, but they may struggle to remember your birthday, even if you've been friends for years.

Gifts for a Gemini Sun

Geminis are practical people, so sentimental gifts, while appreciated, may not touch a Gemini as deeply as the gifter hoped. With that being said, it is hard to go wrong when it comes to buying a gift for a Gemini. They have plenty of interests and are always open to discovering a new one.

★ **Buy tickets to a comedy show.** Geminis are witty and quick on their feet, so comedians are right up their alley. Most Geminis are natural comedians themselves, so maybe they'll end up on stage before the night's end!

★ **Go to an amusement park.** Geminis have short attention spans, which means trying out a bunch of different rides will be great fun for them. They don't have the patience to wait in long lines, though, so if you really want to spoil them, buy the expensive tickets that let you jump to the front of the line.

★ **Buy them copies of your favorite books, or visit a bookstore together.** Geminis love to learn, so they like having books on hand, though they often get distracted by something else before they can finish reading them. Similarly, Geminis are drawn to oracle cards, crossword puzzles, poetry chapbooks, and other literary-adjacent items you can find at large bookstores.

★ **When in doubt, buy them something versatile.** Geminis like to change it up, so buy them something that will prove useful in multiple scenarios. Perhaps this is a nice ring, a guitar, or a pressure cooker.

★ **Because Geminis are natural hosts, you could also buy them something with that in mind:** A bar cart, wine rack, fancy serving tray, or set of marble coasters would be a great gift.

So Your Boss Is a Gemini Sun . . .

What a sparkly, charismatic boss you have! Anything you say and do must pale in comparison. On the one hand, it's nice to have a boss who is witty and bright because it's easy to admire them and trust their leadership. On the other hand, their changeable nature and absent-mindedness could lead to some sticky situations.

★ **Don't expect your boss to remember everything you tell them.** You might have to tell them something multiple times for the information to stick. Get in the routine of creating a paper trail that you can refer back to. This will keep you from getting blamed if something goes awry; you'll have evidence that you had, in fact, told them before.

★ **Make a habit of engaging in office chitchat.** Even if you prefer to keep to yourself at work, you need to make an effort to socialize with your boss. Your Gemini Sun boss is higher up the ladder than you, sure, but they want nothing more than to feel like a friend; hierarchy is the least of their concerns. Ask them what they did over the weekend, how working with that tricky client is going, or if they heard about the new exhibit coming to town.

★ **Prepare to be the unsung hero of the office.** It's not that your Gemini Sun boss doesn't appreciate the work you do—it's more so that they're not even aware of it most of the time. Gemini Sun bosses are very hands-off. They are way too busy to worry about what you're up to, and even during slower periods at work, they tend to be in their own little world. Receiving praise from your Gemini Sun boss is a rare occurrence.

★ **Let them shine.** Your Gemini Sun boss lights up the room when they walk in, and this is how it should be. Laugh at their jokes and smile when you pass them in the hallway. Always ask them how they're doing. While some signs prefer to fly under the radar in leadership positions (like Libra), Gemini thrives on social encouragement. Don't worry, they won't think you're sucking up—this kind of behavior is how you get your Gemini Sun boss to remember you exist.

So Your Coworker Is a Gemini Sun . . .

Let me guess—they're the office socialite. Gemini Sun coworkers are always flitting about, having lunch with one coworker and chatting over coffee with another. You might find yourself wondering when they have time to get any work done!

★ **All hail the office gossip!** Because Gemini coworkers are easy to talk to, they are guaranteed to have the best gossip. But beware: This gossipy nature can go both ways. It's hard for a Gemini Sun to keep a secret because they love sparking interesting conversations, witnessing people's reactions, and being in the know. Don't tell your Gemini coworker anything top-secret—better safe than sorry.

★ **Next time you need to send a Gemini Sun an email, deliver your message in person instead.** Gemini prefers face-to-face contact, and this way, you can strike up a conversation after you're done talking about work. They'll appreciate the chat.

★ **Never underestimate the power of asking "How's it going?"** With a little prompting, this question can lead to a lengthy convo. If you haven't picked up on it by now, the best way to get close to a Gemini coworker is by talking to them. This open-ended question lets them steer the conversation wherever they want it to go. Buckle up!

So Your Partner Is a Gemini Sun . . .

How did you manage to pin Gemini down? Kudos to you! Gemini is not a very committed sign, though of course other placements can stabilize their flighty tendencies. If you're dating a Gemini right now, enjoy it—you never know how long they'll stick around.

★ **Get comfortable with the fact that your partner likes to do the talking.** You might have to do a little bit of extra work to elicit the back-and-forth of healthy conversation. By this I mean, when your Gemini Sun partner comes home after work and you ask, "How was your day?" they will launch into a lengthy narrative. Rarely will Gemini remember to ask how *your* day was. Instead of getting offended and assuming they don't care, just tell them how your day was. Nine times out of ten, they didn't even realize they forgot to ask.

★ **Understand that they naturally become the center of attention.** At family get-togethers, they won't stay by your side; they'll sidle up to people they haven't seen in months, though you're more than welcome to tag along! By the end of the night, everyone will be eating out of the palm of their hand. Don't be surprised if your siblings eventually like your Gemini Sun partner more than they like you.

★ **Tell them how much they mean to you.** Words of affirmation jump-start Gemini's emotional side, which is often overlooked in day-to-day life since they are very mental people, and their emotions flow underneath a stream of constant mental chatter. When you combine language and emotion via words of affirmation, you're reminding Gemini that the two are not mutually exclusive.

★ **Don't be afraid to tell them when you need some peace and quiet.** Most people don't have the social battery that your Gemini Sun partner does. They won't be offended; they'll go find someone else to talk to.

☽
GEMINI MOON

When the Moon, which rules emotion, is in an air sign, individuals are very cerebral. Sharing their feelings doesn't come naturally to them because most of the time, how they feel isn't even on their radar. The emotions are there, of course, but they're buried under the million other things on Gemini's mind. Once an emotion rises to the surface, though, Gemini Moon must talk about it, often at length.

Gemini Moons are most compatible with other air Moons (Gemini, Libra, and Aquarius) because they also keep things light. All air Moons process their emotions by talking about them, and a fellow air Moon partner will stay up until the wee hours of the morning chatting. Gemini Moons are also compatible with fire Moons (Aries, Leo, and Sagittarius) because they move through emotions quickly instead of wallowing in them.

Gemini Moons are least compatible with water Moons (Cancer, Scorpio, and Pisces) because they will never be able to meet each other's needs on a deep level. Water Moons will find Gemini Moons too surface-level for their liking, while Gemini Moons will find water signs to be unrelatable and overly emotional.

Gemini Moons may be compatible with earth Moons (Taurus, Virgo, and Capricorn), though true compatibility will depend on other placements. Because Gemini and Virgo are both ruled by Mercury, this combination is a slightly more favorable one.

Restorative Activities for a Gemini Moon

Gemini Moons bounce back from adversity pretty quickly, so if you have this placement, you likely do not need to spend as much time engaging in restorative activities as other Moon signs.

★ **Set aside time to catch up with loved ones.** Social engagement is crucial to your well-being. No one is an island, and especially not a Gemini Moon. Call a close friend, send a family member a card, or text the person who's been on your mind lately. If your social network feels lacking, commit to making new friends either in person or online.

★ **Practice energy work.** When you begin to feel heavy or bogged down, lie down and devote a few minutes to your breath. Breathe in deeply, imagining a white light filling you. Then breathe out and imagine all the heaviness leaving your body through the soles of your feet.

Repeat this exercise until you feel that your body is filled with nothing but white light. Visualization can be challenging for beginners, so do not be discouraged if you struggle with this at first!

★ **Share something you've written.** Whether it is an excerpt from your journal, a poem you wrote while healing from heartache, or an article you wrote for a website or your blog, you find a sense of purpose in sharing your words. If you feel comfortable sharing with people you know, post a link or upload a photo on social media. If that feels too vulnerable, there are countless ways to share this work anonymously online with communities willing to offer you whatever you need, whether it's feedback or a listening ear.

Journal Prompts for a Gemini Moon

If you have a Gemini Moon, your mind is always racing. It can be hard for you to sink into moments of contemplation. Force yourself to settle for a moment by journaling. The act of putting pen to paper will fulfill your need for movement while allowing you to spend a bit more time thinking about yourself than you normally do. It's important to make time to self-reflect.

★ What are some things you won't talk about? Why are these conversation topics off-limits? Have you ever shared this information with someone? If yes, how did they respond? If no, why not?

★ When was the last time you had a deep conversation? Who was it with? Does this person often bring out your innermost thoughts? Looking back, how do you feel about that conversation now? Do you want to have more deep conversations with this person in the future?

★ Think of a recent situation that raised a strong emotion in you. What was the situation? What emotion did you feel? How did you react in the moment? How would you choose to react if you got a do-over?

So Your Partner Is a Gemini Moon . . .

This is a challenging placement for both parties. You likely have a hard time connecting to your Gemini Moon partner emotionally, and if you do connect, it won't be as deeply as some folks would like. Additionally, if your Gemini Moon partner has a hard time relating to what you're going through, they may be supportive one moment and detached the next. This is their symbol, the twins, peeking through.

★ **Keep things interesting.** Gemini Moons are easily bored; variety is the spice of life. Perhaps this means trying a new restaurant instead of going to your tried-and-true pick or bringing a new toy into the bedroom. Even if the experience flops, Gemini Moon will be happy they tried something new.

★ **Casually talk about your future together.** Geminis have a hard time putting down roots, and talking about what things could look like in the long term helps Gemini visualize the future of the relationship. Don't put pressure on your Gemini Moon partner by setting a timeline—this will backfire. Instead, use this opportunity to see if your future goals are aligned. If it seems like you want different things right now, don't fret; Gemini changes their mind all the time.

★ **Be aware that if you feel your emotions strongly, this will push away your Gemini Moon partner.** This doesn't mean they don't care about you—they just have no idea what to do. Gemini Moons aren't prone to yelling or crying, so when they see others reacting that way, they don't know how to handle the situation. Tell your Gemini Moon partner what you need from them when you're upset.

↑
GEMINI RISING

Gemini risings can talk to anyone about anything. Everyone pegs them as extroverts, but they may be a lot more reserved than they initially appear. They have fears and anxieties just like everyone else, but this may surprise others because they come across as very confident.

Gemini risings gravitate toward people with Sagittarius energy. They may have many Sagittarius Sun friends, a partner with Sagittarius placements, or

Sag loved ones whom they naturally click with. Like Gemini rising, Sagittarius likes to keep things light and fun. The two of them can talk all night long, and it truly feels like they'll never run out of things to say. Single Gemini risings should keep their eyes peeled for a Sagittarius. There will never be a dull moment.

Ways to Spot a Gemini Rising

Gemini risings are easy to identify—just find the person talking in a quiet room. Even in solitary situations, they're almost never alone, either because they bring friends with them everywhere or because others are naturally drawn to them.

★ **Gemini risings have a lot to say, especially if they just met you.** Once they've gotten to know someone, the mask slides off and they are less inclined to talk 24/7, but new friends will be inundated with details about Gemini's life.

★ **Gemini risings are often found out and about.** They are the sort of people who love hosting parties or social gatherings, and they rarely turn down an invite. You can count on Gemini rising to RSVP *yes* to every company get-together and every wedding.

★ **You may be surprised by how quickly a Gemini rising opens up to you.** No conversation topic is off-limits for a Gemini rising; they'll say whatever is on their mind.

Downsides of Being a Gemini Rising

Because Gemini risings are so chatty right off the bat, others expect you to be charismatic at all times. But you are typically at your friendliest when you first meet someone, which means that those who try to form a lasting connection with a Gemini rising may ultimately feel confused, jilted, or misled.

★ **Loved ones may feel like you care more about strangers than you do about them.** This couldn't be further from the truth. When you are comfortable with someone, you let the mask drop, so your calmer, quieter personality underneath the mask should not be mistaken for a lack of interest.

★ **You may feel like you have to put on a show in your relationships.** When you first meet someone, your Gemini rising energy is bubbly and over the top; potential partners are drawn to your confidence and happiness. Over time, your true personality is revealed, and it may be difficult for your partner to accept that the characteristics they fell in love with were temporary.

★ **It is hard to form lifelong relationships because loved ones get jealous.** When out in public, they wonder why you aren't as warm and friendly with them as you are with a complete stranger. Naturally, this breeds feelings of resentment, and it is likely the impetus of many arguments. Others should remember that the demeanor of a Gemini rising is only a mask instead of taking these behavioral shifts as a personal attack. Getting to see the real person underneath the Gemini rising mask is the ultimate show of trust.

Using Your Gemini Rising to Your Advantage

This is one of the most beneficial rising signs to have because so much of a person's success in life is tied to how likable they are, and you are *very* likable.

★ **People have a very hard time saying no to you.** This is because Gemini risings are incredibly charismatic. You know exactly what to say at exactly the right time, usually without even trying. When you really want something and turn on the charm, others are dazzled.

★ **You rarely appear to be in a bad mood.** Even if something is getting you down, you are able to put on your mask and interact with the world in such a way that people are none the wiser. You always appear more genial than you feel, which allows you to keep your personal struggles private. This is a fantastic skill to have if you work in customer service.

★ **You climb the ranks at work faster than your colleagues.** Your boss would trust you to serve as the face of the organization because they know you represent the company in a positive light. Because of this, you may be introduced to people that most of your coworkers have only heard of. There is a good possibility that you will be assigned high-stakes clients because you treat everyone with the same level of friendliness, whether they are a celebrity or a stranger.

☿

GEMINI MERCURY

Mercury, the planet of communication, rules Gemini, so this pairing makes for an eloquent person indeed! Gemini Mercury is witty and sharp. They have an easy time stringing words and sentences together, and others are intimidated by their natural confidence. They make excellent public speakers.

Communicating with a Gemini Mercury

Can it really be called *communicating* if you're not getting a word in edgewise? Expect most conversations with a Gemini Mercury to be one-sided.

★ **Do your best to follow along.** Gemini Mercury changes subjects so quickly that it could make anyone's head spin. The conversation's twists and turns all make sense to them, though.

★ **Smile and nod.** You likely won't be allowed to contribute much to the conversation, so these simple gestures go a long way.

★ **Take notes if you need to.** This way, you can double back to something Gemini Mercury said earlier in the conversation if you have questions. If you don't take notes, you're unlikely to remember what it was you wanted to say when they finally come up for air.

Questions to Ask a Gemini Mercury

Honestly, you can ask a Gemini Mercury anything and still get an earful. Underneath all that chatter, they have a lot of interests. Work with Gemini Mercury to home in on their true passions.

★ What do you do for fun?

★ What is something I might not know about you?

★ How do you recharge?

★ If you could have dinner with anyone, living or dead, who would you choose? Why?

★ What's been going on with you? (This is the golden question to ask a Gemini.)

♀
GEMINI VENUS

The planet Venus dictates how we love and want to be loved. It also rules sensuality, pleasure, and beauty. Gemini is the most communicative zodiac sign, so nothing makes Gemini Venus feel loved like riveting conversation. They must be mentally stimulated by their loved ones.

Self-Love for a Gemini Venus

While some signs, like Taurus, are best suited to insular activities, you feel your best when you're out and about.

★ **Change your mind about something, and do so unapologetically.** You don't owe anyone an explanation. Remember, only you are qualified to make choices about your life. Take this advice with a grain of salt; if you rarely offer people an explanation for unexpected behavior, they will grow frustrated.

★ **Wander around a bookstore and find a nonfiction book that will teach you something.** Read a little bit before bed each night or, if you have a longer attention span, set aside time to read during the day. Learning new things excites you and sparks your curiosity—there is so much out there to discover!

★ **Find new friends.** You can never have too many! Join a team, download Bumble BFF, or become a regular at a local establishment. The larger your social network, the more people you can rely on when you need support.

Seducing a Gemini Venus

All I have to say is I hope you're witty. If you're not, well, good luck.

★ **Gemini Venuses aren't turned on by the physical—they're turned on by the mental.** If you're attractive, all the better, but it's really what's in your head that gets them going. Lead with your intelligence instead of your body. Once they're fascinated by you, that's when the physical connection begins to bloom.

★ **Make sure your dates intellectually stimulate both of you.** Visit a museum, participate in bar trivia, or watch *Jeopardy!* Going on dinner dates is fine from time to time, but Gemini Venus quickly gets bored of the same old, same old.

★ **Don't worry about being humble.** Gemini Venus is attracted to accomplishments! Constantly brushing off your achievements is the fastest way to turn off a Gemini Venus. On the flip side, if you want to turn on a Gemini Venus, make sure to tell them all about that impressive thing you did.

★ **Tell them what's on your mind.** Gemini Venus loves hearing about what's going on under the surface. What makes you tick? What keeps you up at night? These are the kinds of things a Gemini Venus wants to discover.

★ **Give them your undivided attention.** Venus in Gemini is better at listening than most Gemini placements, but in true Gemini fashion, they do enjoy talking about themselves. Ask them questions. Make them feel important. Don't hide your interest. If all else fails, find out what makes them laugh and incorporate more of that.

So Your Partner Has a Gemini Venus . . .

Long-term relationships with a Gemini Venus are difficult. For the relationship to withstand the test of time, it will have to morph and adapt as Gemini Venus's desires change.

★ **Monogamy might be challenging for Gemini Venuses.** This doesn't mean they don't love their partner. Rather, once they've learned everything about a person, it just isn't as fun for them anymore. Most Gemini Venuses are better suited for ethical nonmonogamy, polyamory, or relationship anarchy. If you want to keep a Gemini Venus interested in a monogamous relationship, it can't be predictable.

★ **Never underestimate the power of banter.** Some signs like talking dirty, and others like to flirt—Gemini Venus likes rapport. You should be able to go back and forth for hours. Gemini Venus needs a partner whom they never run out of things to talk about with. If you can't keep up a conversation, you won't be able to keep a Gemini Venus.

★ **Don't expect them to be romantic.** It's tough for Gemini Venuses to tap into their romantic side—most of them don't really have one. Unless they have strong water placements, they will not buy you flowers, write poetry about you, or bring you breakfast in bed. If those gestures are important to you, you'll likely feel unfulfilled and underappreciated in a relationship with a Gemini Venus.

♂

GEMINI MARS

The planet Mars rules passion, drive, and aggression. When Mars is in bouncy Gemini, people have a hard time making up their mind. In fact, it may be impossible.

Gemini Mars Behind Closed Doors

Gemini Mars will switch things up at a moment's notice, always keeping you on your toes.

★ **You never know what you're going to get with a Gemini Mars.** Sometimes they want to be dominant, but sometimes they're incredibly submissive; most identify as a switch or vers. They're up for anything, so you should be too, but they won't force you outside your comfort zone. More often than not, Gemini Mars will follow your lead.

★ **Gemini Mars struggles to make a decision and stick to it,** which can make living with them (or spending a lot of time with them) very frustrating. For this reason, they do best with roommates or partners who are decisive. Even when Gemini Mars does trust someone else to call the shots, they may suddenly reject the plan. The fact of the matter is sometimes it takes hearing something they don't want to realize what they *do* want.

★ **This placement is a flight risk**—Gemini Mars may end relationships out of the blue. Even worse, they will probably go back and forth on their decision, creating an on-again, off-again relationship. It will be the other party's responsibility to break the toxic cycle.

★ **Gemini Mars loses focus easily.** For example, while cleaning their room, they may find a memento that inspires them to call a friend, and as they talk and pace around their home, they may see the fridge and realize that they're hungry, and so on and so forth. It's hard to keep a Gemini Mars on track. This is just how they are—it's not a character flaw that can be "fixed." Get in the habit of writing things down for Gemini Mars or embrace the chaos.

Things *Not* to Do to a Gemini Mars

The good news is Gemini Mars isn't easily offended. They move through everything quickly: thoughts, emotions, connections. They're pretty ambivalent about most things.

★ **Don't pigeonhole them.** Gemini Mars needs room to change their mind. Sometimes they even change their personality! There are two sides to every Gemini, and they are constantly switching between them. Trying to force them to pick one will only lead to frustration.

★ **Don't expect them to live life on a fixed schedule.** *Routine* is a four-letter word to a Gemini Mars. They'd rather experience things on a whim. Life is most enjoyable when it's spontaneous and unplanned.

★ **Don't suppress their social side.** Gemini Mars loves talking to others—it's crucial for their well-being. Their social circle is large, and they need time to cultivate it in order to feel fulfilled. If someone invites Gemini Mars to an event, they'll want to go, and it's best if you let them.

Things a Gemini Mars Probably Needs to Hear (But Definitely Doesn't Want To)

The best advice I can give a Gemini Mars is to follow through.

★ **Sometimes you need to stand up for something.** You can keep bouncing around when situations get tense, but all things will eventually come to a breaking point. You can't avoid conflict forever.

★ **When you feel strongly about something, defend it.** When you are ready for a fresh start, end it.

★ **Eventually, you're going to have to make that decision you've been avoiding.** Yes, I know, you hate endings—you're much more comfortable with beginnings, or with that ambiguous in-between space—but some things in life just run their course. Get it over with.

★ **Your loved ones want to know how you're feeling.** Usually, you're not keeping it inside on purpose; you just need to tune in to your emotions more often. Sharing emotions, even the uncomfortable ones, is an integral part of a long-lasting relationship.

★ **Get out of your head and into your body.** When was the last time you hugged a loved one? Kissed your partner just because? High-fived a friend who got good news? Go do it.

QUICK GUIDE TO

GEMINI

PLACEMENTS

If someone in your life has Gemini placements . . .

DO

★ Listen to what they're saying, whether it's thoughtful or stream-of-consciousness.

★ Allow them to change their mind without making them feel bad about it.

★ Engage in banter—Geminis love wit.

DON'T

★ Try to silence or shrink them.

★ Expect them to behave a certain way all the time.

★ Wait for them to ask you a question if you have something you want to share.

When I think of the sign of Cancer, I think of teddy bears. There is something about them that appeals to the inner child. They have a comforting presence that makes every emotion feel supported and validated. Healthy Cancer energy makes you feel like you just ate a freshly baked cookie or put on still-warm laundry. If you have a loved one who is a Cancer, you know what I'm talking about.

At their best, Cancers are selfless, empathetic, tender, and benevolent. They are in tune with their emotions and feel deeply. They hold space for others' emotions too, offering a listening ear and a shoulder to cry on. There is nothing more important to them than the people they love, and their love is unconditional. When a loved one needs help, Cancer will drop everything, and they leave no stone unturned.

At the other end of the spectrum, unhealthy Cancer energy is relentless. At their worst, they will make you wonder if you imagined all the warm and fuzzy memories you had together. Surely this can't be the same person? Cancer is ruled by the Moon, and their mood is just as turbulent and unpredictable as the ocean. Their emotions come in waves, gripping your ankle and pulling you out to sea when you least expect it.

Cancer is the fourth sign of the zodiac, so it rules the fourth house, the house of home and family. If Aries is the child of the zodiac, Taurus is the preteen learning the value of money, and Gemini is the teenager tasting freedom, then Cancer is the young adult who is settling into their own home. Their most wild and reckless days are in the rearview mirror. Instead of thinking about which bar to go to, they're thinking about marriage and kids. People with strong Cancer placements may have felt this way their whole lives, not seeing the appeal of "sowing their wild oats" or other youthful indiscretions. As children, Cancers were likely told they were wise beyond their years or called an old soul.

Cancer's symbol is the crab. They have a soft underbelly, meaning they're sensitive indeed, and they retreat into their protective shell when provoked. Many things trigger a Cancer to hide in their shell, whether it's their own strong emotion, another person's, or a situation that made Cancer feel attacked. And once they're in their shell, watch out! They have pincers, and they know how to use them. A jilted Cancer knows exactly what to say and do to hurt the people around them. They are masters of passive-aggressive behavior. When they're upset, Cancer wants to watch the world burn; think of the phrase "Hurt people hurt people." They'll feel terrible about it all afterward, when they come out of their shell and take in the damage they've caused, but they'll have a hard time apologizing for their actions because they felt justified in the moment. While you may not get an apology, rest assured Cancer knows they were in the wrong; honestly, Cancers are harder on themselves than anyone else ever could be.

Cancer is a water sign. Water signs (Cancer, Scorpio, and Pisces) are highly emotional, sensitive, intuitive people. They are naturally loving and have a demeanor that instantly makes others feel safe and accepted. Having a water sign in your life almost guarantees unyielding devotion, but keep in mind that still waters run deep. Water has the power to give life *and* to take it away. An angry water sign is just as destructive as an angry fire sign—water is just better at hiding it.

Surprisingly, Cancer is a cardinal sign. Like Aries, they don't hesitate to act. When they feel a strong emotion, they do something about it, for better or for worse. This energized modality pumps its brakes when it comes to home and family, though. Above all else, Cancer craves a stable, rewarding home life, so while they're usually quick to move on, they have a hard time extricating themselves from their chosen family.

⊙

CANCER SUN

The Sun is in Cancer from June 22 to July 22, give or take a few days depending on the year. When people are born under the Cancer Sun, they are fantastic friends and acquaintances. It can be challenging to sustain lifelong relationships with them because of their somewhat volatile emotions, but aside from the occasional bit of drama, Cancer Suns are delightful individuals.

For those with a Cancer Sun, every section in this chapter will apply to some degree. The Sun is the most powerful planetary force, so it has a huge impact on personality. While a Cancer Sun may not have a Cancer Moon, for example, they will undoubtedly find something in that section that they relate to.

Pure Cancer Energy

When I think of something that encapsulates Cancer energy, I immediately picture the emoji with the big, round, sparkling eyes or the scene from *Shrek 2* where Puss in Boots gazes up at Shrek with pleading eyes. Actually, Cancer energy can be found in anything with "puppy dog eyes."

★ **Cancer Suns are selfless.** When you're not feeling well, Cancer is the person who brings you homemade soup and checks in on you every few hours. If you live with a Cancer, they'll go above and beyond to take care of you. They'll even tuck in your blankets! With that being said, Cancer will expect the same superstar treatment the next time they are sick.

★ **Empathy comes naturally to a Cancer.** They can't go to animal shelters without wanting to take a new pet home with them. Whenever they see an animal in need of a home, they have an overwhelming urge to help.

★ **Cancer Suns are observant and thoughtful.** When it is their loved one's birthday, Cancer goes above and beyond. They will post a carefully crafted photo collage online, complete with a meaningful, moving caption about your relationship. Make sure to thank them!

★ **Cancers don't hold grudges, per se, but they are incapable of forgetting when they have been slighted.** Don't be surprised if Cancer brings up a situation you've long since forgotten about. They tend to do this by making snide comments that sting.

★ **A Cancer's biggest craving is validation.** They long for someone to love them the way they love others. Because they have so much love to give, they leave sweet comments online, scribble handwritten words of thanks on the restaurant bill, and compliment others freely. But in a self-fulfilling prophecy, they ultimately end up hurt because so few people are capable of giving that kind of love in return.

★ **Every so often, Cancers retreat into their shell and spiral.** They decide that no one truly cares about them, so they lash out. They might post passive-aggressive messages online or share catty memes. Don't take it personally. Wait a few days, then text them to check in. By then, Cancer's mood swing will likely have passed.

Gifts for a Cancer Sun

To a Cancer, gift-giving is an opportunity to show the other person how much you care. So, when trying to think of a gift, tap into your sentimental side. Gifts are supposed to be meaningful, as far as Cancer is concerned.

★ **If you gift them an experience, make sure it's something the two of you can do together.** Sign up for a sip-and-paint class, settle in for a pedicure, or create a custom fragrance at a candle-making class. A custom candle might be the best gift ever, actually, because every time they light their candle, Cancer will think fondly of you. Aww.

★ **Think of something the two of you do together that makes you feel warm and fuzzy inside, then find a way to incorporate that into your gift.** For example, if you bond over loving the same musical artists, buy them some limited-edition merch, splurge on something signed, or spend time curating the perfect playlist.

★ **Most Cancers are collectors.** They're very sentimental people, and they easily form attachments to items. If you know what they collect, buy them something they don't already have so they can add to their collection.

★ **Make them a custom stuffed animal** at a store like Build-A-Bear Workshop. Cancers love cute, cuddly things, and stuffed animals appeal to their inner child.

★ **Pour your heart out when you sign their birthday card**—bonus points if you do so on a separate sheet of paper that they can hold on to forever. Love letters are Cancer's kryptonite.

So Your Boss Is a Cancer Sun . . .

Having a Cancer Sun boss is a blessing and a curse. The good news: Your Cancer Sun boss longs for close relationships at work, so it will be relatively easy to befriend them. The bad news: A jilted Cancer Sun boss will put you through the wringer with their emotions, often unintentionally.

★ **The smallest things have the biggest impact for Cancer.** Pay attention when your boss talks about their weekend plans, then make a point to follow up. Remember their birthday and send them a kind email or leave a card on their desk. Simple gestures of thoughtfulness have a profound impact on Cancer.

★ **Don't be afraid to talk about your personal life.** This is advice that should be taken with a grain of salt, of course, because some things will never be work appropriate. (Your boss doesn't need to know about that risqué DM you got, for example.) As in every relationship, opening up should happen slowly, naturally, and consensually. But Cancers like being in the know; hearing details about your life outside of work makes Cancer feel included and important.

★ **If there is a problem brewing, nip it in the bud and talk to your Cancer Sun boss right away.** It's better to be safe than sorry. Because Cancers are so emotional, if you wait too long to ask for their advice, they might be insulted, or the problem may feel overwhelming to them. And if you bring up a problem that later ends up being a nonissue, your Cancer Sun boss will appreciate your transparency and foresight.

So Your Coworker Is a Cancer Sun . . .

Odds are that your Cancer Sun coworker is the mother hen of the office, regardless of their gender identity. They have a way of caring for others that makes everyone feel safe and protected. Cancer Sun coworkers are always there when you need moral support.

★ **Because Cancers are sentimental, phrases like "This made me think of you" hit them right in the sweet spot.** Most of us see and do things that remind us of other people on a regular basis, but we often don't share that information because we think it's embarrassing or irrelevant. But as far as a Cancer is concerned, there is no greater compliment than being on someone's mind.

★ **Be honest about your struggles.** Whether you're having a tough time with a client or feeling extra run down, your Cancer Sun coworker wants to lend a listening ear. Beware that they will often feel obligated to help, so be clear about your needs from the get-go: Do you actually want advice, or do you just need to vent?

★ **Share recommendations with each other.** If there's a great new restaurant in town, let them know. If you're stumped about what to do over the weekend, ask Cancer if they have any suggestions—they'll be flattered you asked. Cancers enjoy feeling useful.

★ **If you're both open to it, invite them to spend time together outside of work.** Grab dinner, wander through a farmer's market, or meet for coffee. Some people prefer to keep their personal and professional lives separate, but most Cancers would rather blur that boundary.

★ **Smile every time you cross paths with your Cancer coworker,** whether that's in the hallway or while microwaving your lunch. This small act of kindness will mean a lot to them.

So Your Partner Is a Cancer Sun . . .

You'd be hard-pressed to find a more loving partner. While they might not always be the best at communicating it, Cancer Suns have a deep, profound love for their significant others. This may make you feel like previous partners have never come close to their level of intimacy. But Cancer's powerful emotions go both ways; calm waters can have a deadly undertow.

★ **Do your best to hold your tongue when you're upset.** Careless words or phrases tossed out in the heat of the moment will sting Cancer for months, maybe years. Just when you think you've finally moved past that disagreement you had last year, Cancer will dredge it back up. When they do, keep your cool and apologize for the umpteenth time. Maybe in a decade or two they'll finally forgive you.

★ **Your Cancer Sun partner is incredibly devoted to you.** Unless you push them to their absolute limit, they will stand by you for eternity. Do not take them for granted. It is rare to find a true ride-or-die in life, so hold on to yours.

★ **Get in the habit of saying words of affirmation on a daily basis.** Even if words of affirmation isn't your partner's love language, they will greatly appreciate it. Cancers can get stuck in their head, convinced that they are bothering people, and words of affirmation will bring them back to reality.

★ **Go above and beyond for your partner, especially on their bad days.** The little things in life are big things to Cancer. Send them a random

GIF, refill their water bottle, or tuck a blanket around them when they doze off on the couch. Small, tender moments have a profound impact on your Cancer partner.

☽
CANCER MOON

The Moon rules Cancer, and as you may recall, the Moon governs emotion. When an individual has a Cancer Moon, emotions are amplified. Someone with this placement is much, much deeper than they initially appear. They are constantly ruminating on the past, reliving situations and the emotions that accompanied them. Cancer Moons become so entangled in their own head that they forget to enjoy the world around them.

Cancer Moons are most compatible with other water Moons (Cancer, Scorpio, and Pisces). Fellow water Moons have deep emotional reserves and can empathize with their Cancer Moon partner. If both partners have water Moons, they likely feel seen and understood in an invaluable way. Water Moons love together and weep together. This profound emotional bond has the capacity to create something truly beautiful—but be wary of codependent behaviors.

Cancer Moons are least compatible with fire Moons (Aries, Leo, and Sagittarius) and air Moons (Gemini, Libra, and Aquarius). Fire Moons do not like to wallow in their emotions, and that is where Cancer Moons are most comfortable. Air Moons are happy to talk through what they're feeling, but their emotional attention span is much shorter than Cancer's, and they will quickly lose interest, adding insult to injury. Both fire and air Moons lack the sensitivity required to care for a Cancer Moon. Unless they have strong water placements that enhance their empathy, these are combinations that will leave needs unmet.

Cancer Moons may be compatible with earth Moons (Taurus, Virgo, and Capricorn), who are capable of patiently waiting for Cancer to move through one of their moods. True compatibility will depend on the individuals' Venus and Mars placements, though it is interesting to note that Capricorn is Cancer's cosmic opposite, so these Moon signs would complement each other in a unique way.

Restorative Activities for a Cancer Moon

Cancer Moons experience a myriad of emotions on any given day, and it is exhausting. If you have a Cancer Moon, you will become a bundle of frayed nerves without proper rest and relaxation.

* **Spend time with loved ones.** You are a family-oriented person, and if you're not spending enough quality time with the people you care about, you begin to feel hollow. If it's hard to find time to get together in person, talk on the phone or FaceTime.

* **Seek out feel-good stories.** There are plenty of social media accounts that solely share positive news from around the world. When you are faced with repeated evidence of the good in the world, you feel a renewed sense of hope.

* **Take a walk down memory lane.** Go through old photos or social media posts. What are some of your favorite memories from these periods of your life? Nostalgia is healing because it reminds you that there are plenty of good times still to come.

Journal Prompts for a Cancer Moon

While all Cancer Moons have a large capacity for emotion, the act of processing and working through emotion may not come easily. You crave connection, but you begin the true work of self-development when you process things on your own. Journaling is a fantastic way for you to talk through what's on your mind and, ideally, move past situations.

* What's bothering you right now? Write down everything that comes to mind. Once you've gotten it all out on the paper, reread the list and see what sticks out. Pick two or three issues to reflect on for the rest of this section.

★ What about this situation is less than ideal? If your wildest dreams came true, how would this situation be different? Is there anything you can do to steer the situation in the direction of a happily ever after?

★ Who else is involved in this situation? You are not an island. Is there anyone you can ask for support? What fears do you have about relying on others? Are those fears justified?

★ How would you describe this situation to a stranger? A best friend? A therapist? A younger version of you? Which of those descriptions feels most accurate? Why?

★ What is one thing you can do today to improve the situation or, in some cases, to work toward resolving it? Keep it simple. Small steps are still forward movement.

So Your Partner Is a Cancer Moon . . .

Proceed with caution. It is very easy to deeply wound a Cancer Moon. With that being said, this is a person who will love you unconditionally.

★ **Be prepared for many, many deep talks.** Cancer Moons have a lot of thoughts and emotions churning in their heads, and there is no one they feel safer discussing them with than their partner. At times, you may feel overwhelmed by the sheer volume of things going on inside a Cancer Moon's head. In these moments, try to practice gratitude too. Isn't it wonderful that your partner feels comfortable sharing their true self with you?

★ **Encourage your Cancer Moon partner to find healthy outlets for their emotions.** You cannot be their only source of emotional support. Some great outlets for Cancer Moons are going to therapy on a weekly or bimonthly basis; art, especially painting; reading, specifically feel-good books and sappy love stories; and journaling. Buy your partner a stunning journal and a nice set of pens and witness a new hobby unfold.

★ **Family is incredibly important to your partner.** Make an effort to get to know their loved ones, and share your loved ones with them in return. Talk with your partner about what your own little family looks like, as well as what you both would like it to look like one day. Most Cancer Moons dream of being parents and are incredibly supportive of their children. If children are a future goal, consider adding a furry friend to your dyad in the meantime.

★ **When you set boundaries, do so in a thoughtful way.** If you need space and snap at your partner, for example, they won't respond well to that, nor will they forget it. Cancer Moons are always worried about being a burden to their loved ones, so make sure to emphasize that boundaries are not a punishment, but rather a structure for a happier, healthier relationship.

↑

CANCER RISING

Cancer risings give off such welcoming, pure energy. The first word that comes to mind when I think about Cancer rising is *wholesome*. This is not to say that they're dressed all in white, all the time; rather, they exude a warmth that suggests anything is possible.

Cancer risings tend to be drawn to people with Capricorn placements. There is something soothing about the solidity of a Capricorn. Cancer risings may have Capricorn friends, Capricorn family members that they just love being around, or a partner with Capricorn placements. Cancer is able to bring out the tender side of Capricorn, and Capricorn keeps Cancer focused. Single Cancer risings should look for a partner with Capricorn placements (ideally Sun, Moon, or Venus).

Ways to Spot a Cancer Rising

When out and about, your eyes may glance right over a Cancer rising. They tend to be quiet and unassuming, and they are quite comfortable blending into the background.

★ **Cancer risings are great listeners.** They are very patient and supportive. Complete strangers may feel comfortable baring their souls to a
Cancer rising. And somehow, Cancer risings have a magical ability to
keep the whole thing from being awkward.

★ **A Cancer rising is the sort of person who gives you a gentle smile when
you cross paths on the street.** They are the comforting presence in a
sea of strangers that you would run to if something went awry.

★ **Cancer risings appear innocent.** As children, they tended to click well
with parents and teachers because they seemed inherently trustworthy. This is the sort of person who can get away with pretty much
anything, especially if they bat their eyelashes.

Downsides of Being a Cancer Rising

Cancer rising is a great placement because people will assume the best about
you. You have an aura that is calming and kind, and it makes everyone feel
safe. However, this also means you are likely to be underestimated.

★ **When you're going through a hard time, your loved ones may not
know how to act.** You've always been a steadfast source of support for
them in their trying times, so they are flummoxed when you are not
the strong one. It will be uncomfortable for both of you, but tell them
what you need.

★ **You have a terrible poker face.** You wear your heart on your sleeve,
and this is both a blessing and a curse.

★ **Because you have such a friendly, accepting demeanor, you may
be overlooked when it comes to things that are more competitive
in nature,** like a coveted promotion at work. It's assumed that you
always go with the flow, so if you happen to react negatively, it will
throw everyone for a loop.

Using Your Cancer Rising to Your Advantage

Your warm demeanor is a powerful weapon when utilized skillfully.

★ **People may not take you seriously.** Allow them to mistake your kindness for weakness, then come out on top when the time is right. A Cancer rising always gets the last laugh.

★ **You are a safe space for people.** Even if they don't verbalize it, people feel comfortable around you. It is clear that you are a nurturing and caring person—you radiate graciousness. Something as simple as complimenting your barista has the ability to turn their entire day around.

★ **Because you seem to be so sweet, people refuse to feed into gossip.** Rumors of ill will are met with exclamations of disbelief. Indeed, when people talk about you behind your back, you can rest assured they are saying nice things.

$$\text{☿}$$

CANCER MERCURY

Mercury is the planet of communication. In Cancer, Mercury becomes soft, tender, and intentional. Cancer Mercury is aware that words have consequences. In today's day and age, it's rare to find people who immediately make you feel safe. Hold Cancer Mercury close.

Communicating with a Cancer Mercury

One thing that's important to keep in mind with this placement is that feeling emotions and expressing emotions are two very different experiences. Cancers *feel*—this is unquestionable. But putting words to their complex thoughts and emotions is an entirely different process—one that Cancer Mercury seriously struggles with. They are not natural-born communicators, and this inability to express what's going on inside can cause problems, especially when Cancers erupt after letting too many things fester inside the confines of their mind.

★ **Be careful not to say anything offensive.** Easier said than done, especially when it comes to Cancer Mercury. If you are unsure if what you are about to say will hurt a Cancer Mercury's feelings, you're better off not saying it.

★ **Cancer Mercury says things with love, and you should try to do the same whenever possible.** If you have to deliver difficult feedback to a Cancer Mercury, practice the sandwich approach: Lead with praise, squeeze in the uncomfortable piece, and end on a positive note.

★ **Don't be a buzzkill.** Cancer Mercury prefers to keep things light. This placement has a "Look on the bright side" approach to life. At the other end of the spectrum, a Cancer Mercury who is emotionally overwhelmed may be incredibly doom-and-gloom. Misery loves company, but do your best to lift their spirits.

★ **When Cancer Mercury has been pushed to their limit, they may lash out verbally.** They will know exactly what to say to slice you to your core. Try not to reduce Cancer Mercury to their harshest words— they didn't mean what they said when they felt threatened.

Questions to Ask a Cancer Mercury

Conversation with Cancer Mercury is either effortless or a little bit like pulling teeth. The secret to flowing conversation is to appeal to their sensitive side. Bonus points if you can bring up something nostalgic.

★ What's one of your favorite memories from childhood?

★ If you could go back in time and talk to younger you, what would you say?

★ Who do you look up to? Why?

★ What does family mean to you?

★ If your house was burning down and you only had time to save three things, what would you choose? (This question could upset a Cancer Mercury, or it could get them talking about their most prized possessions. Proceed with caution.)

♀
CANCER VENUS

Venus is the planet of love, beauty, pleasure, and sensuality. Cancer, ruled by the emotional Moon, is deeply sentimental when paired with loving Venus. This placement adores everything lovey-dovey. There is no such thing as "too cheesy" to a Cancer Venus. However, tread lightly. Cancer Venus is also capable of being deeply wounded by the simplest slights.

Self-Love for a Cancer Venus

Feeling loved is essential to your well-being. You care for others so naturally, but you can't pour from an empty cup.

★ **Write a love letter to yourself.** What qualities do you admire in yourself? What are some things you have done that make you proud? How have your actions left a lasting positive effect on others? Really hype yourself up—you deserve the same admiration you so freely share with others.

★ **Wrap yourself in a blanket, get comfy, and turn on healing sounds** such as singing bowls, spa music, or chakra healing songs. Close your eyes and let yourself really feel the music. Absorb it. Notice how it feels in your body. Pay attention to what thoughts, memories, or sensations capture your attention. If at any point a song feels unsettling or unpleasant, fast-forward to a new one. Allow yourself at least fifteen minutes to rest and enjoy your homemade sound bath.

★ **Consume content that makes you feel warm and fuzzy inside.** Watch a wholesome TV series like *The Great British Baking Show* or a YouTube compilation of happily married couples talking about how they met, for example. The simple joys of everyday life may move you to tears.

Seducing a Cancer Venus

Many Cancer Venuses suffer from Disney princess syndrome: From a young age, they have dreamt of their happily ever after. This means they are easier to seduce than most Venus placements, because at their core, they believe they need a loving relationship to feel complete.

★ **Be affectionate with a Cancer Venus.** This placement loves consensual physical touch, especially subtle gestures like hand-holding, forehead kisses, or tucking their hair behind their ear. Keep in mind that Cancer Venus may be shy; be sure to ask their comfort level with public displays of affection before trying any of this at the supermarket.

★ **Sprinkle some romance into everything you do.** This may sound daunting, but it is easy to swoon a Cancer Venus. Leave a sweet sticky note on the bathroom mirror, dance around the kitchen, or play them your new favorite song. These small moments of tenderness are everything to a Cancer Venus.

★ **The most sure-fire way to love a Cancer Venus is to first love everyone around them.** Befriend their companions, win over their pets, and, once you're introduced, butter up their family members. The key here is to be genuine in your approach. Nothing fulfills a Cancer Venus more than seeing their loved ones get along.

So Your Partner Has a Cancer Venus . . .

A Cancer Venus is the epitome of devotion. This placement is unlikely to so much as glance at another once they have promised themselves to you. You hold their heart in the palm of your hand, so treat it with care.

★ **There is nothing a Cancer Venus is more attracted to than safety.** Cancer Venus craves a feeling of complete and total trust in their partner. This means that you must keep your promises. Answer the phone when they call. Tell them the truth, even if it's a little uncomfortable. Never, *ever* let your Cancer Venus partner catch you in a lie. These small acts build a rock-solid foundation over time.

★ **Your Cancer Venus partner wants to be told that they are important to you, and often.** If you have a hard time verbalizing your affection, find other ways to show them that you care, and name this as best you can: "I know I have a hard time telling you how much I love you, so I made you this instead . . ."

★ **While a Cancer Venus will always have your back, this doesn't mean they're immune to overwhelm.** If you sense your Cancer Venus partner is reaching their breaking point, make an effort to alleviate some of their stress. Rub their shoulders and ask what you can do to help, and then do it. Teamwork makes the dream work, after all.

♂
CANCER MARS

When Mars, the planet of passion and aggression, is in tender Cancer, its hot-and-fast energy fizzles out. It's like trying to light a fire using waterlogged wood. Cancer Mars may have good intentions, but they're not going to lead any revolutions.

Cancer Mars Behind Closed Doors

Cancer Mars is an interesting placement. These individuals are all bark and no bite. In fact, their ego is quite fragile. And yet, Cancer is a cardinal sign, which gives them a bit of an edge.

★ **Cancer Mars tends to be submissive.** They prefer having a more dominant partner but will do just about anything to keep their partner happy. Without proper self-awareness, this dynamic can be easily abused. Partners should retain a healthy dose of gratitude for Cancer Mars's selflessness, and Cancer Mars should remember that "No" is a complete sentence.

★ **Cancer Mars takes everything personally.** They know they are overly sensitive sometimes, but they can't help it. As an attempt at self-preservation, they carefully observe what people say and how they behave. However, they overlook the fact that many people don't consider how their actions might affect others. Cancer Mars needs to remember that not everything is a personal attack, and the world does not revolve around them.

★ **Cancer Mars pouts when things don't go their way.** They take on a bit of Aries's childishness, wallowing and moping around. People are shocked the first time they see this side of Cancer Mars—it seems so out of character! But really, this is Cancer's response to their tender underbelly being poked and prodded. They have retreated into their shell to feel sorry for themselves. Don't worry, they'll come out eventually!

Things *Not* to Do to a Cancer Mars

Like all of us, Cancer Mars has a few sore spots, especially when it comes to friends and family. It's not uncommon for people to overlook the ways a Cancer Mars enhances their life, but remember: You don't know what you've got until it's gone.

★ **Don't mention an event they weren't invited to.** Cancer Mars wants to feel important to their loved ones, and being excluded—no matter how insignificant the event—is a personal offense to a Cancer Mars. You're better off inviting a Cancer Mars to everything, even if you know they're not interested or busy that day. Regardless of whether or not they show up, they appreciate the invite.

★ **Don't point out a flaw.** This could be something as minute as spinach in their teeth or something more abstract, like an inability to be on time. Cancer Mars is their own worst critic, and when others point out something they could improve on, it makes them incredibly self-conscious. Whereas some signs thrive on feedback, an offhand comment has the potential to totally destroy a Cancer Mars.

★ **Don't take advantage of them.** Cancer Mars freely offers unyielding, unconditional love, and it can be easy to take this for granted. Reflect on how much support a Cancer Mars offers you and make an effort to acknowledge it. Most importantly, do your best to show up for Cancer Mars just as they consistently show up for you. Reciprocity will lay the foundation for a lifelong relationship.

★ **Don't underestimate their grit.** Remember, Cancer is a cardinal sign. Sure, a Cancer Mars may be naturally gentle, but they also refuse to quit. Like the tortoise, a slow and steady Cancer Mars will win the race.

Things a Cancer Mars Probably Needs to Hear (But Definitely Doesn't Want To)

You appear to be a delicate flower—and you are, for the most part. But Cancer is a cardinal sign, so there is an inner fire that keeps you going, even when the odds are stacked against you.

★ **You have to stand up for yourself.** No one is going to have your back 100 percent of the time—it's just not possible. You can't sit around waiting for someone to rescue you. You have to be your own knight in shining armor sometimes.

★ **Stop giving your all to people who wouldn't give you a second glance.** You love hard, I know, but not everyone is deserving of it. You cannot pour from an empty cup. If you are consistently pouring your love into people who don't give you any in return, you're bound to end up high and dry.

★ **Just because you care about someone doesn't mean they need to be in your life.** Sometimes cutting off a relationship is the healthiest choice you can make. You have to prioritize your well-being so you can continue to show up for yourself and others. Ensure that every relationship in your life is mutually beneficial. Reevaluate who has access to you.

QUICK GUIDE TO
CANCER
PLACEMENTS

If someone in your life has Cancer placements . . .

DO

★ Assure them that their thoughts and feelings are valid.

★ Prioritize quality time, including time with loved ones when possible.

★ Enjoy the little things with them.

DON'T

★ Mistake their kindness for weakness.

★ Take their unconditional love for granted.

★ Speak carelessly—they won't forget it.

There is no sign as captivating as Leo. I have loved many Leos in my life, and each holds a special place in my heart. Leos have a way of charming everyone around them, which means they are not easily forgotten. If you've ever had the pleasure of taking a sip of hot cocoa on a chilly day, then you know what life with a Leo feels like, for Leos have the same heartwarming effect.

At their best, Leos are dazzling. They are confident, kind, and loyal to a fault. Leos will do anything for their family and friends, and they treat their loved ones with care and warmth. Creative and playful, Leos easily tap into their inner child and find plenty of ways to keep life interesting. They see things in a unique way, and others naturally move out of the spotlight so Leo can take center stage.

One surefire way to wound a Leo is to take a stab at their pride. Leos are very proud people, and nothing cuts them to their core like criticism. When the wind is taken out of their sails, they flatten. As their natural charisma withers away or they withdraw their affection, Leos become quite cold. Much like lying in the rays of the sun only for it to become shrouded by clouds, a Leo's bad temperament sends a shiver down the spine.

Leo rules the fifth house, the house of creativity, children, and infidelity. (No, this does not mean all Leos are unfaithful.) If Aries is the child of the zodiac, Taurus is the preteen learning the value of money, Gemini is the teenager venturing into the world, and Cancer is the young adult focused on a home of their own, Leo is the new parent. But let me be very clear: Leos are not like regular parents—they're cool parents. Leos are youthful at heart, and they are always happy to roll down a hill, construct a blanket fort in the middle of the day, or have a dance party in the kitchen. They delight in the little things.

Leo's symbol is the lion. Like the lion, Leos are strong and bold, and they charge forward in even the most daunting of circumstances. At times, they sneak under the radar, but when they want you to be aware of their presence, they'll surely get your attention. Leos are sharp observers who know when to unleash their roar. They will fight tooth and nail for what they believe in.

Leo is a fire sign. All fire signs (Aries, Leo, and Sagittarius) are funny, energetic, and down for a good time. More so than any other fire sign, though, Leo is effervescent. If you observe a Leo when they are in their element, you will see their eyes twinkling. While this twinkle inside Leo's eye may dim at times, it never fades away completely. Even when they are at their lowest, Leos are able to poke fun or crack a joke. Somehow, they can always bring levity to a situation.

In addition to being a fire sign, Leo has a fixed modality. Like the other fixed signs (Taurus, Scorpio, and Aquarius), Leos can be terribly stubborn. They believe they know the best way to handle life's challenges, and to be quite honest, they're probably right. Doubt is a four-letter word to a fixed sign, but others' disbelief becomes their biggest motivator. There is a steadfast determination in fixed signs that keeps them laser-focused on their goals. If you're willing to walk alongside a fixed sign, they will reward you with unyielding devotion. However, disagreeing with a fixed sign is like talking to a brick wall.

☉

LEO SUN

The Sun is in Leo from July 23 to August 22, though the exact dates may vary a bit depending on the year. If you have loved ones in your life who were born under the Leo Sun, I'm willing to bet their presence is a powerful one. The Sun, the most influential planet in a birth chart, rules the sign of Leo. The only thing more impactful than a Leo's presence is their absence. It is obvious when a Leo Sun isn't around. They truly are the life of the party. Without them, life has a noticeable damper.

For those with a Leo Sun, every section in this chapter will apply to some degree. The Sun is the most powerful planetary force, so it has a huge impact on personality. While a Leo Sun may not have a Leo Venus, for example, they will undoubtedly find something in that section that they relate to.

Pure Leo Energy

Because Leos have such warm personalities, it is pretty easy to identify them. People are drawn to Leos like a moth to a flame.

★ **Leos are very proud.** They soak up compliments like a sponge. In fact, Leos will outright fish for compliments if they are not receiving the praise they think they deserve. Because they know their worth, Leos are their own biggest fan. Don't be surprised if you catch them checking out their reflection or hyping themselves up.

★ **Leos never turn down an opportunity to bask in the spotlight.** Take a Leo to a karaoke bar and they'll be on stage in no time. (Shyer Leos might need a bit of encouragement!) Once they're in front of an audience, Leo will put on a performance that captures the hearts of everyone in attendance. Sit back and watch them shine.

★ **No matter where they go, Leos are simply adored.** Complete strangers will go out of their way to compliment them. People they have never met suddenly feel like friends. They quickly become the staff favorite

at restaurants and local businesses. All of that is to say, when you're
out and about with a Leo, prepare to be a sidekick.

★ **Leos like to be in the know.** They are often up to date on work gossip
and pop culture. Whether they're watching the new series everyone
is bingeing, reading about the latest celebrity breakup, or using the
meme template of the month, Leos stay current—there is nothing as
horrifying as being out of touch.

★ **No one is as committed to the bit as a Leo.** They have a bevy of running jokes with family and friends. While some think there is a time
and place for silly behavior, Leos don't mind momentary embarrass-
ment if it has a humorous payoff. They will stop at nothing to bring a
smile to your face.

★ **Leos exude childlike joy.** They are incredibly playful people, so they
have no problem postponing their responsibilities to simply enjoy the
moment. This makes them a natural with children, though they bring
this energy to every setting. When they are around other adults, Leo
is the first to suggest a party game like charades or another way to
lighten the mood. And when it comes to animals, Leos shower them
with attention and praise.

★ **Leos are very protective of their family.** They are loyal, caring children, siblings, and parents. Nothing is as sacred to them as their loved
ones, so they may be uncharacteristically private about this aspect
of their life. If a Leo welcomes you into their inner circle, this is the
ultimate display of trust.

Gifts for a Leo Sun

Leos love receiving gifts because gifts are physical proof that they are valued.
Though a compliment is the fastest way to flatter a Leo, gift-giving takes second place.

★ **Give a Leo a gift card to a place where their only priority is themselves.**
Most likely, Leo spends a lot of time taking care of their friends and

family. When they are able to focus solely on themselves for a few hours—whether that is at a spa, a salon, or something similar—they return to everyday life recharged and ready to share the love.

★ **Artistic gifts are a great option for Leos.** Most Leos are incredibly creative, and hobbies like painting or sculpting offer wonderful catharsis. If the Leo in your life hasn't expressed an interest in art, I recommend starting with something simple, like a coloring book or a paint-by-numbers kit. A paper roll and washable paints would offer Leo the ability to create art in an accessible way. For Leos who prefer to create something more tangible, consider a beginner's wood-carving kit, a build-your-own LEGO kit, or a DIY miniature kit.

★ **Leos love anything that involves a stage**, whether that be dance, theater, or music. If the Leo in your life is a performer, buy them a gift that supports their craft. If they are more of an observer, buy them tickets to a concert or a show. Make sure to buy more than one ticket so they can bring along the plus-one of their choice.

★ **A once-a-year splurge is sure to be appreciated** by the Leo in your life. Go on a brief vacation or browse an elegant boutique. Alternatively, give them a high-quality accessory, like a gold-plated necklace or a designer watch. At their core, Leos love feeling like royalty.

★ **Give a Leo a gift that enhances their appearance.** They might not admit it, but they care about how they look, and there's nothing wrong with that! Decide if you want their gift to be luxury or drugstore, then pick up a moisturizer, dark-spot serum, or frizz-fighting gel.

So Your Boss Is a Leo Sun . . .

Because Leos are natural leaders, it's not unusual to have a supervisor with this placement. At their best, Leo bosses are encouraging, uplifting, and funny. At their worst, Leo bosses are self-absorbed, entitled, and phony. Odds are, you have one of the good ones.

★ **Leos are born performers, so if your boss has this placement, you will never truly know how they feel about a situation.** Is their reaction genuine, or are they acting? Leos like to keep it professional, but after hours, you may see a totally different side of them.

★ **One of Leo's greatest strengths is that they appear unflappable.** In moments of pressure or tension, Leos are able to remain calm (and maybe even crack a joke or two). This makes them a superb person to have around in moments of stress. Of course, they have their weaknesses, just like everyone else, but with their acting skills, you'll be none the wiser.

★ **Compliment your boss, and often.** While some signs are uncomfortable being praised, Leos thrive on it. Keep in mind that it's important to be genuine with your compliments. Do you actually like your boss's haircut, or are you just saying that? Your boss will start to get suspicious if you're constantly praising them, and a supervisor doubting your sincerity is never a good thing.

★ **Leo bosses prefer to keep things casual**, at least on the surface. They will chat with you like a friend, but don't lose sight of the fact that they are, in fact, your superior. While Leo would never ask for respect, they expect it, so deferring to their wisdom is always a good idea.

So Your Coworker Is a Leo Sun . . .

I love having Leo coworkers. They feel more like a buddy than someone you're being paid to collaborate with. Stay in their good graces and you'll have an on-demand mood booster.

★ **Ever the jokester, Leos find a way to brighten up even the dullest meeting.** This is the person to sit next to if you want to laugh, but choose wisely—do you really want to be snickering during a budget review?

★ **Rarely will you outshine your Leo coworker in any context.** They are headstrong and innovative, and their charisma has everyone eating out of the palm of their hand. At times, you may compare yourself to your Leo coworker and become filled with doubt or envy. In those moments, remember: Comparison is the thief of joy.

★ **Leos strive to be the best at everything they do.** They are deeply competitive, and they do not like to be challenged. Pointing out a mistake is the fastest way to turn your Leo coworker into an enemy. Keep things positive and they will gladly return that energy.

★ **Having a Leo coworker that you can turn to in stressful times is a godsend.** Not only will loyal Leo do everything they can to cheer you up, but they will offer you steadfast support until things improve. And if you need help, all you have to do is ask.

So Your Partner Is a Leo Sun . . .

You are lucky to have secured a Leo partner! While they may struggle to express it verbally, Leo Suns are deeply devoted to their loved ones.

★ **Shower your partner with affection,** both physical and verbal. Leos do not take this for granted. They are very loyal people, and they thrive when they receive the same love they give. Keep in mind that your Leo partner is probably more comfortable showing you affection physically; often, Leos have a hard time verbalizing heartfelt emotion. To a Leo, actions speak louder than words.

★ **Embrace the chaos.** There is rarely a dull moment with a Leo partner. From sunup to sundown, Leo is laughing, making friends and capturing hearts, or sharing their unique perspective with the world. What a gift to see the world through Leo's eyes!

★ **Allow them at least an hour to get ready.** As you probably know, Leos take immense pride in their appearance! For some Leos, their point of pride is their hair. For others, it's their sense of style; many Leos have a passion for fashion. No matter how much you primp and preen, your Leo partner will outshine you. *C'est la vie.*

★ **Be their number one fan.** All of us forget to praise our partner from time to time, but if this oversight becomes a habit, it will have a deleterious effect on Leos. Your Leo partner needs to know that you are proud of them. No matter their age, Leos crave the approval of their loved ones.

★ **Engage in childlike play.** Leos are in touch with their inner child, and allowing themselves to be goofy is one way they self-regulate. In fact, silliness is crucial to their well-being. There are countless opportunities for play in everyday life: Split the grocery list in half and see who can finish getting their half of the groceries first. Place bets on how long you'll be stuck in a waiting room, with the winner getting a reward of some kind. Have a sleepover in your living room. Be open-minded and allow Leo's creativity to flourish.

★ **Make an effort to get to know their loved ones.** Since Leos are protective of their family and friends, it may take some time to be introduced. Once you are finally invited into Leo's inner circle, the work has just begun. If you are rejected by Leo's loved ones, it will cause an irreparable rift in your relationship.

☽
LEO MOON

The Moon is the planet of emotion. Because Leos are such energetic, optimistic people, they don't dwell in their emotions for long. They are much more comfortable with high-energy emotions like joy and anger than with heavy emotions like sadness or loneliness.

Leo Moons are most compatible with air Moons (Gemini, Libra, and Aquarius). This pairing would rather focus on enjoying the present moment than spend hours talking about their feelings.

Leo Moons are least compatible with water Moons (Cancer, Scorpio, and Pisces). Water Moons are incapable of taking it easy. They're also prone to sadness, and this emotion is anathema to a Leo Moon.

Leo Moons would do all right with earth Moons (Taurus, Virgo, and Capricorn) or other fire Moons (Aries, Leo, and Sagittarius). However, they may find earth Moons to be a bit dull, overly practical, and lacking in spontaneity. Other fire Moons will bring out their chaotic side, which may be fun for a while, but chaos often has consequences. Who is going to put out the fire if they're both holding a match?

Restorative Activities for a Leo Moon

Creativity is an incredibly healing practice for Leo Moons, and the word *creativity* can mean a lot more than picking up a paintbrush (though that's a good idea too, if that floats your boat!).

★ **Use your hands in a meditative way.** By this, I mean participate in an activity that allows you to fall into soothing, repetitive movement. Think crocheting, diamond painting, making jewelry, knitting, or even arm pedal exercise.

★ **Leo rules the heart, so seek out heart-centered practices.** For example, when you are feeling overwhelmed or overstimulated, take a moment to sit up straight and close your eyes. Begin rubbing your hands together, increasing the speed until you can feel heat rising between your palms. After a few moments, rest your warm palms on your chest, over your heart space. Take deep breaths until the warmth dissipates, then open your eyes and reorient with your surroundings.

★ **Spend an afternoon indulging your inner child.** What brought you the most joy as a child? Perhaps you should eat ice cream for breakfast, buy something you've had your eye on, or play one of your favorite childhood games. When was the last time you played hopscotch or jumped rope? For just a few hours, postpone adult responsibilities and honor the younger version of you.

★ **Consume content that makes you laugh.** You can do this with others if you prefer, but it will be most restorative if done solo. Stream a comedy special, browse YouTube, or watch a sitcom. Laughter truly is the best medicine for a Leo Moon.

Journal Prompts for a Leo Moon

While it's possible that you already have a healthy journaling practice, I doubt it—you prefer to work through things actively or not at all. Sitting down to write about your innermost thoughts and feelings probably doesn't sound appealing, but it is a great way for you to work through pervasive issues.

★ What do you love about yourself? Try to come up with five to ten qualities or traits that you admire in yourself. If you're struggling to think of that many, reflect on what loved ones have praised you for in the past, and use that as inspiration.

★ How would you draw yourself? Do it now. Doodle an image of yourself in the margins, taking no longer than five minutes. Then, set your journal aside and come back to it in a few days. From a fresh perspective, what stands out to you about the doodle? What doesn't it capture? How do you feel when you look at this mini self-portrait?

★ When you read the word *proud*, what comes to mind? When was the last time you felt proud of a loved one? When was the last time you felt proud of yourself? Do you think you have a healthy relationship with pride? Why or why not?

So Your Partner Is a Leo Moon . . .

Leo Moons are goofy, well-intentioned, and original, and your partner is surely the light of your life. Leo Moons keep the rest of us young. Though you may get irritated by their stubbornness from time to time, don't lose sight of the fact that your partner would do anything for you.

★ **Thank your partner often.** We usually remember to thank our significant other for the big things in life, but the small things get overlooked. If you notice your partner took the garbage out or loaded the dishwasher, taking a moment to express your appreciation goes a long way.

★ **Plan interactive dates.** Leo Moons would much rather be taken to a mini golf course than a sit-down restaurant. If you can find a way to combine a nice meal and a fun activity, go for it! Check out immersive dining experiences near you. Or you can leave food out of the equation altogether and buy tickets to an indoor trampoline park or visit an arcade. Leo Moons enjoy a friendly competition, but don't forget to cheer for your partner!

★ **Have an at-home spa night a few times a year.** Play relaxing music as you apply face masks, file your partner's nails, and take turns massaging each other's shoulders. This is an affordable date night that will leave you feeling refreshed and reconnected. (It also has the potential to get pretty steamy, if you want it to! Try adding wax play candles to the mix.)

★ **Do your best not to criticize your partner's hopes and dreams.** Leo Moons are idealistic, and they find solace in daydreams. Your Leo Moon partner may not have the most realistic ideas, but this is how they regulate. Smile, nod, and offer words of encouragement. Most importantly, listen. Your partner likely won't remember these whims in a few weeks, but they *will* remember if you didn't support them.

★ **Integrate more consensual physical touch into your relationship.** This does not have to be sexual. Rest your hand on your partner's leg while driving, brush their hair back from their face, or rub circles on their back while they're on the phone. Leo Moons are physical people, so these small gestures of tenderness warm their heart.

↑
LEO RISING

The rising sign is how we come across to people we do not know well. Leo risings have bold personalities. When they walk into a room, they do so with confidence. Often, a leadership role is naturally established, with others deferring to their wisdom. Leo risings have a sense of surety that people inherently trust, whether or not they know what they're talking about. This power should be used for good.

Leo risings click with folks who have Aquarius in their chart. Friends, family members, and partners with Aquarius placements like to have fun, so they will humor even the most ridiculous ideas. Similarly, Leo rising's faith in others encourages Aquarius to believe in themselves. This is a mutually supportive pairing. If a Leo rising is single, they may have luck dating someone with Aquarius placements.

Ways to Spot a Leo Rising

Nine times out of ten, it is easy to identify the Leo rising in the room. They seem to have a glow about them that attracts admirers of all ages. Regardless of their age, Leo risings seem youthful and full of life.

★ When I think of a lion, I picture a flowing mane. Accordingly, **Leo risings usually have great hair.** Their hair is a point of pride for them and, for some, a hobby. Bad hair days have the potential to upend even the best-laid plans.

★ **Leo risings have mastered the art of the accessory.** At least one component of a Leo's outfit will be attention-grabbing, whether that is a funky pair of earrings, polished loafers, or an impeccable manicure. Make sure to compliment Leo's style. Nothing brings them more joy.

★ **Leo risings effortlessly lighten the mood.** They are wonderful at tossing in quips that make people roar with laughter. For this reason, they are invited to lots of parties, and if they don't have anything better to do, they will make an appearance. From the second a Leo rising steps through the door, old friends and new friends drift to their side, unconsciously orbiting Leo's sunny demeanor.

★ **Praise is something all Leo risings seek,** whether or not they're aware they are doing it. You see, Leos crave adoration, so a Leo rising who is not being given a modicum of attention can become petulant. If you notice a storm cloud passing across Leo rising's face, a simple compliment can turn their mood around.

Downsides of Being a Leo Rising

Because Leo risings are charismatic, warm, and playful, people go out of their way to help you, and life may feel like smooth sailing. But being the center of attention all the time isn't ideal.

★ **Leo risings cannot fly under the radar.** If you ever want to be left alone, whether at work or at the grocery store, it is all but guaranteed that someone will strike up a conversation with you. Anonymity is few and far between for a Leo rising.

★ **It's not uncommon for Leo risings to be well-known.** Behind a Leo rising stands a legion of adoring fans, from your dentist to the strangers who like your posts on social media.

★ **On the rare days when you are off your game, "Is everything okay?" will become a refrain.** Because you are so friendly, others grow to expect a sunshiny demeanor, and anything less raises alarm bells. Whether you are under the weather, sleep-deprived, or just having a bad day, prepare to field many inquiries about your well-being.

★ **Jealousy follows you like a shadow.** *How is it possible for one person to be so charming?* strangers and acquaintances wonder. Those who truly know you have gotten to see your flaws and follies, but your exterior is so vibrant it is hard for others to understand its transience. Before welcoming someone new into your life, ask yourself, *Does this person want to get to know me, or does this person want to be me?* This simple question can save you a lot of heartache.

Using Your Leo Rising to Your Advantage

There are far more advantages than disadvantages when it comes to having a Leo rising.

★ **Though it is taboo to acknowledge, being likable sets you leaps and bounds ahead of the competition.** Whether or not you are aware of it, doors open for you with little to no effort. You easily get what you're after, and your achievements are plentiful. Pursue your wildest dreams, as they are certainly within reach.

★ **For whatever reason, people have a very hard time saying no to you.** If you ask nicely, even complete strangers become putty in your hands. Others will go out of their way to come to your aid. This is a cosmic blessing—use it wisely.

★ **Your charisma makes you appear capable and sure, though you may not feel that way on the inside.** Even if you are ridiculously under-qualified for something on paper, people tend to overlook this once they are in your presence. Use this to your advantage by putting on a brave face, and don't pay any attention to niggling insecurities. With enough confidence, you can do anything. Fake it 'til you make it.

★ **People assume the best about you.** Because you tend to be on everyone's good side, others give you the benefit of the doubt. Even when you have made a terrible mistake, people are quick to forgive and forget. Go ahead, charm your way out of a speeding ticket.

★ **You leave a memorable first impression.** Those who cross your path will think fondly of you for quite some time. This is a wonderful benefit when applying for jobs, dating, or pursuing a leadership position.

☿

LEO MERCURY

Mercury is the planet of communication, and Leo is one of the most charismatic signs of the zodiac. So do not be surprised if you feel enraptured in conversation with a Leo Mercury. There is something magnetic about the way Leo Mercury expresses themselves; they exude confidence and are naturally eloquent. This is a fantastic placement for people who have careers that involve public speaking in any capacity.

Communicating with a Leo Mercury

People with a Leo Mercury are easy to talk to. They can keep just about any conversation afloat. Goodbye, awkward silences!

★ **All Leo Mercuries like to talk about themselves.** This is not a bad thing; Leo is an accomplished person, with a bevy of talents, and they're not shy about acknowledging it! Keep in mind that if you want a Leo Mercury to shift the focus of the conversation, they may need to be prompted.

★ **People with a Leo Mercury like to joke around.** They are not fans of heavy conversations, and when faced with one, they often make quips that are insensitive or inappropriate. Depending on their Moon sign, you may become frustrated by their inability to have a serious talk.

★ **Leo Mercury doesn't do it intentionally, but they like to dramatize their storytelling.** In their mind, a little flair can make even the dullest story captivating. When they spin you a yarn, retain a healthy dose of skepticism, for they may not be telling the full truth.

★ **Because Leo is a fire sign, Leo Mercury easily gets loud.** At a football game or a concert, this is no problem, and at a house party, it's part of their attraction. But, depending on the location, this trait may be a bit embarrassing—at the movie theater, for example. It may be better to stream at home.

Questions to Ask a Leo Mercury

Leo Mercury has an opinion on just about everything, and they're happy to share! And if conversation fizzles, all you have to do is ask them a question about themselves.

★ What's your greatest achievement in life thus far? Why do you consider this your greatest achievement? Do you think it can be topped?

★ Do you have a favorite childhood memory? What makes it stand out?

★ What have you been watching lately? Would you recommend it?

♀
LEO VENUS

When Venus, the planet of love, beauty, and pleasure, is in Leo, the sign of creativity, joy, and play, partners are good-natured and eternally youthful. Leos are known for being incredibly loyal, so this is a placement that is committed to their relationships. If they do stray, it will be a spur-of-the-moment decision, fueled by flirtation. They don't always think things through.

Self-Love for a Leo Venus

Leo Venus has a lot of love to give, but they don't necessarily carve out time to turn that love inward. A self-care practice is transformative for this placement.

★ **You need pure, unbridled fun to recharge your batteries.** Be as goofy as possible, and forget about how you "should" behave. Some people may think you're a bit immature, but that just goes to show how disconnected they are from their own inner child.

★ **There is nothing wrong with being selfish from time to time.** People know they can rely on you for a pick-me-up, but even you have bad days. When you're not feeling like yourself, put your phone on silent and do whatever you need to do to find your spark again. Your loved ones will understand.

★ **Learn to say no.** You are immensely devoted to the people you love, and you tend to go above and beyond. A minor inconvenience is a small price to pay for a loved one's happiness. But nobody has unlimited energy, and sometimes you have to say no to things. If saying no sounds challenging, start with "I'll let you know."

★ **Set aside an evening to primp and preen to your heart's content.** What makes you feel good in your skin? Find out, and make this an integral part of your routine. Whether it's weekly, monthly, or biannually, dedicate yourself to treating your body like the temple it is.

Seducing a Leo Venus

You have a lot of love to give, but you don't necessarily carve out time to turn that love inward. A self-care practice is transformative for everyone with this placement.

★ **If you are going to take Leo Venus on a date, whatever you do, do something fun.** Going to a restaurant is *not* the move if you're hoping there will be a second date. This is your opportunity to go on the most creative date you can think of. The sillier, the better. Regardless of the outcome, the date will be a lifelong memory for both of you.

★ **Ask Leo Venus questions about themselves.** They will not think you are being nosey—in fact, they probably won't even realize the conversation is centered around them. Those with Leo placements are their own favorite subject, so when you go your separate ways, Leo Venus will walk away thinking, *Wow, we really hit it off.*

★ **Compliments are the fastest way to a Leo Venus's heart.** Not all Leo Venuses are vain, but they still feel a deep satisfaction when praised.

So Your Partner Has a Leo Venus …

Leo Venus has a lot of energy, and when it's being expressed in healthy ways, they are a fun, encouraging partner who always picks up the phone when you call. But when they are holding in too much of that youthful Leo energy, it may seep out in less-than-favorable ways.

★ **Leo Venus is likely to be quite jealous.** This placement would struggle in a nonmonogamous relationship because they expect complete and total adoration from their partner. If a Leo Venus catches you even so much as looking at someone else, it will ruffle their feathers. They want your undivided attention.

★ **Ironically, Leo Venus will like to look at others, and they will love being looked at themselves.** Your partner needs to be allowed the freedom to express themselves, and flirtation is their mother tongue. It's usually harmless. Besides, keeping your Leo Venus partner on a short leash will only push them away.

★ **Your partner loves with their whole heart.** In fact, the sign of Leo rules the heart, so they know no other way! This a placement that naturally transitions from "me" to "we" when they fall in love with someone. At times, your relationship may feel too good to be true. Enjoy being the apple of Leo's eye and bask in the glow of their love.

★ **Leo Venus will fight tooth and nail for their relationship unless their pride is deeply wounded.** Words said carelessly in the heat of an argument will deeply damage Leo Venus for weeks, if not months, to come. In moments of tension, it is best to take a pause lest you say something that cannot be taken back.

★ **Ensure that laughter is the foundation of your relationship.** Leo is a youthful sign, and when it meets with the planet of love, individuals flourish in goofy, lighthearted relationships that nurture their inner child. What do both of you find funny? Integrate humor into your relationship as much as possible. This way, laughter will keep you connected in times of happiness and in times of strife.

♂
LEO MARS

Mars is the planet of passion, aggression, sex, and drive. There is more passion in a Leo Mars's pinky finger than most people have in their entire body. Buckle up.

Leo Mars Behind Closed Doors

Leo Mars only has two speeds: zero and one hundred.

★ **Leo Mars expects to take charge.** They are a dominant personality, and this extends to every area of life, including the bedroom. If this appeals to you, lean into that dichotomy.

★ **Unless they have Aquarius placements, Leo Mars will not share their partner.** They feel a sense of ownership over the people they date— their partner is their prize! Though not as controlling as Scorpio placements, Leo Mars will expect complete and total devotion from the people they are sleeping with.

★ **Leo Mars likes things done their way.** Leo is a fixed sign, and this stubbornness definitely shows up behind closed doors. They have certain preferences for who they date, how their home looks, what they wear, and their morning routine. People who have never lived with a Leo Mars may be shocked to discover just how particular they are.

Things *Not* to Do to a Leo Mars

Leo Mars is a wonderful person to have in your corner, but if you say something that makes them feel insecure, it will send them into a tailspin.

★ **Do not damage their pride.** (Easier said than done.) Leos do not respond well to criticism, especially if it has anything to do with their character. A truly wounded Leo has no problem cutting people loose. So, before you make an offhand comment, ask yourself: Is it really worth it?

★ **Do not try to put them in a box.** Just because they are a certain age does not mean they have to behave like everyone else. Leo Mars uses their creativity to get what they want in life, so they may travel an unconventional path. This is part of their journey.

★ **Do not minimize their accomplishments.** Leo Mars is a proud person, and that means the smallest steps forward are deemed worthy of celebration. Whereas some people only celebrate after they've reached their goals, Leo prefers to acknowledge any and all triumphs.

Things a Leo Mars Probably Needs to Hear
(But Definitely Doesn't Want To)

In general, Leo Mars has good intentions. But behavior can have unintended consequences, and Leo's tendency toward selfishness can leave others feeling burned.

★ **Feedback is not a personal attack.** We all make mistakes, and we all have room for improvement. If you notice yourself having a negative response to feedback, assume the person had positive intent. Then, take time to delineate between what you heard and what they likely meant.

★ **When you're excited about something, you go full-steam ahead and don't bother waiting for others to catch up.** Yes, you are a natural leader, *and* a leader is nothing without their followers. Take a moment to slow down and check in with the people around you. Are their needs being met?

★ **Once in a while, you have to do the boring, nitty-gritty stuff.** Life is not all fun and games. Life is also doctor appointments and taxes and oil changes. Be a team player and take on some of the grunt work.

QUICK GUIDE TO
LEO
PLACEMENTS

If someone in your life has Leo placements . . .

DO

★ Goof around with them.

★ Be their biggest fan.

★ Remember that they are a natural leader.

DON'T

★ Criticize them or provide unsolicited feedback.

★ Skip out on an event—whether it's a work party or an art show, they want you there.

★ Take them too seriously.

★ 6 ★

VIRGO

As a Virgo Sun, I could tell you that this is the best sign of the zodiac, but to be honest, Virgo is a challenging sign. While Virgos have many admirable traits, they can also be incredibly persnickety. However, this is one of the most well-intentioned signs, and if unevolved Virgos are willing to turn their gaze inward, engage in meaningful self-reflection, and actively work toward becoming the best version of themselves, this is a wonderful sign to have in your corner.

At their best, Virgos are diligent, hard-working, reliable, and organized. If you ask a Virgo to do you a favor, they will be happy to oblige, and they will execute the task to the best of their ability. Others feel comfortable coming to Virgo for help, and their steadfastness is one of their most-recognized personality traits. They keep their word and are trustworthy to a fault. Like the sign of Leo, Virgos are deeply loyal to their loved ones, and almost everything they do is done out of love, though it isn't always received that way.

At their worst, Virgo's worry and hypochondria consumes them. They can be uptight, petty, controlling, and neurotic. Virgo is a sign that likes things done a certain way—*their* way, to be exact. They need structure in every situation, even ones that are supposed to be spontaneous. Tell a Virgo you'll check in later, and they'll say, "Okay, great! But . . . what time later?" Virgos are also prone to judgment, which can make them difficult to get along with.

Virgo rules the sixth house, the house of service and health, among other things. If Aries is the child of the zodiac, Taurus is the preteen learning the value of money, Gemini is the teenager on the cusp of leaving the nest, Cancer is the young adult who is creating their own home, and Leo is the new (cool) parent, then Virgo is the adult settling into their early thirties. Most of their ducks are in a row, and that's the way they like it. Structure has been established after trial and error, and that structure is sacred. Few things bring as much comfort as the humdrum monotony of day-to-day life.

Virgo's symbol is the maiden. This may seem like a random symbol at first, but I think the maiden does a wonderful job of representing Virgo's stability and quiet nurturance. Like the unencumbered maiden, Virgo is always ready and willing to assist. The symbol of the maiden is tied to Persephone, the maiden goddess of spring; Persephone values fruitfulness, integrity, and autonomy, as does Virgo. Both Persephone and Virgo are well aware of the joys and sorrows of being human.

Elementally, Virgo is an earth sign. Like the other earth signs (Taurus and Capricorn), Virgo is driven, practical, and rooted. Virgos aren't fond of change, nor are they particularly fast-acting. There is a slow, deliberate quality to earth signs that other elements find infuriating. Additionally, an earth sign's favorite place to be is at home. Most Virgos would like to have a family to come home to, but they can navigate life on their own just fine if need be.

Like Gemini, Sagittarius, and Pisces, Virgo is a mutable sign, which means they are able to adjust to redirection more easily than most. Mutable signs expertly bounce back from adversity and adapt to challenges. Contrary to popular belief, Virgos *are* capable of going with the flow. Yes, Virgos like things done a certain way, but their mutable qualities teach them to bend rather than break.

⊙

VIRGO SUN

The Sun is in Virgo from August 23 to September 22, give or take a few days depending on the year. When the Sun, the planet of personality, is in the sign of Virgo, individuals are self-sustaining, helpful, and orderly. Aaaaand a little fussy. Think of a Virgo you know (and if you don't know any Virgos personally, think of Beyoncé). That Virgo is probably a pretty polarizing person—you either love 'em or you hate 'em.

For those with a Virgo Sun, every section in this chapter will apply to some degree. The Sun is the most powerful planetary force, so it has a huge impact on personality. While a Virgo Sun may not have a Virgo Mars, for example, they will undoubtedly find something in that section that they relate to.

Pure Virgo Energy

Virgos are pretty reserved and proper. They give off a neutral yet stern energy, sort of like a librarian keeping a watchful eye on you from across the stacks.

★ **Thanks to their love of cleanliness, Virgos can be found picking lint off their partner's clothing.** A stray fuzz, string, hair, or tuft is no match for Virgo's fastidious attention to detail.

★ **Like a worker bee, Virgo rarely sits still for long.** There is always something else to be doing, whether that's scrubbing the grout in the bathroom or trimming a hangnail. Even when a Virgo does sit down, they may not rest; their mind constantly thinks up new tasks, or their hands stay occupied by one hobby or another. It's very difficult for this sign to truly relax.

★ **Virgos have mastered the art of the to-do list**, and tech-savvy Virgos have moved on to the spreadsheet. The smallest tasks can benefit from the structure lists and spreadsheets provide, plus Virgos get a delightful sense of achievement once everything is squared away. Grocery shopping benefits from a grocery list, traveling benefits from a packing list, and so on and so forth. Go on, ask the Virgo in your life how many lists they currently have, either on paper or in their Notes app.

★ **There is always something for a Virgo to complain about.** In their mind, though, it's less of a complaint and more of a critique. Virgo means well. After all, there is always room for improvement! However, this finicky behavior may wear away at lighthearted or sensitive individuals.

★ **Virgos become uncomfortable when certain standards aren't met.** For example, some Virgos detest lying on the bed in "outside" clothes; others won't even climb into bed without first rinsing off in the shower. Less-germophobic Virgos may have constructed "rules" about wearing shoes in the house, placing a coaster under a cup or glass, or alphabetizing their bookcase. These rules bring harmony to Virgo's inner life, and when their rules are disregarded, Virgos may become tense or snippy, sometimes unconsciously.

Gifts for a Virgo Sun

Virgos are hard to buy for because they have everything they need, and they're reticent to ask for anything more. Gift cards are a fantastic option, though if you do decide to give Virgo a present, make sure to include a gift receipt.

★ **Virgos love gifts that stimulate their mind.** Buy them a puzzle or a mind-teaser, like a crossword puzzle book or sudoku collection. In the twenty-first century, this may be a gift card to the app store so they can download some new puzzle games.

★ **Virgos enjoy learning new things and keeping their hands busy.** To that end, reserve them a spot in a cooking class, a bartender training, or another course where they can walk away with something useful.

★ **Virgo is the sign of service, so individuals like taking care of people, pets, and plants.** Buy the Virgo in your life a houseplant or two. To take this gift to the next level, buy them some high-quality, well-draining pots—they probably have a tendency to overwater.

★ **Make a donation to a charitable foundation in Virgo's name.** Make sure to choose a cause that is near and dear to their heart. Virgos feel guilty keeping too many resources for themselves, and knowing that positive change is being made in their honor is a deeply meaningful gift.

★ **A simple gift that will always be appreciated by a Virgo is a copy of one of your favorite books.** For one thing, most Virgos love to read, but there's also a sense of curiosity about what sorts of books others like and why. Virgos will feel like they understand you on a deeper level after reading a book you recommended, and they may even want to engage in a discussion about it!

So Your Boss Is a Virgo Sun . . .

It is not surprising when Virgos ascend to leadership roles. They put their nose to the grindstone and, eventually, reap the rewards. However, it wasn't their people skills that got them to the top—it was their work ethic. Accordingly, this can be a challenging sign to have as a boss.

★ **Develop a thick skin.** Your boss will be prone to criticism, with praise making a rare appearance. Most of the time, your boss won't even realize that they forgot to tell you what they liked about a project you spent months working on. Their greatest skills are catching small things that others may overlook and pointing out areas for improvement. When this gets to be disheartening, remind yourself that your boss has faith in you and your abilities—they would've fired you a long time ago if they didn't.

★ **Write things down.** There is nothing more frustrating to a Virgo than having to repeat themselves. If they ask you do something once, they better not have to ask you twice. You see, if you consistently forget things, Virgo will stop relying on you, and if a Virgo cannot rely on you, they cannot trust you. Trust is the foundation of a positive working relationship.

★ **For most Virgos, there is a fine line when it comes to oversharing.** Sure, you can tell your Virgo boss that you're taking time off to visit family, but you don't need to go into any more detail. Virgos like to keep their working relationships professional, and when the line between employee and friend becomes blurred, it unsettles them.

★ **The absolute best way to get on your boss's good side is to remain a cog in the wheel.** Get your work done on time, do it to the best of your ability, and move on to the next project. Show up on time and leave when the day is done. Respond to emails in a timely manner. In other words, the less a Virgo boss has to think about your work, the more they like you.

★ **Virgo bosses tend to fall on extreme ends of the busybody spectrum:** They are either incredibly hands-off or micromanagers. If your Virgo boss is hands-off, this is a good thing—it means they trust you. If your boss is a micromanager, something has damaged your reputation. The best way to restore your honor is to produce quality work. This will not be an overnight process. In the meantime, let their inquiries roll off you like water off a duck's back.

So Your Coworker Is a Virgo Sun . . .

Virgo Suns are known for being put-together, so if you don't know your coworkers' zodiac signs, you can probably find a Virgo by looking for the most organized cubicle.

★ **When you need help, your Virgo coworker should be the first person you ask.** Virgos *love* being of service to others, and they will complete any tasks to the absolute best of their ability. Who knows, they may even upstage you!

★ **Virgo coworkers are sensitive to stimuli like light, noise, and odor.** Something as mundane as a flickering fluorescent bulb has the potential to upend their day. If you work close by a Virgo, you don't need to walk on eggshells, but you should try to be conscientious. If you're going to be making a lot of noise or eating something particularly fragrant, check in first. Your coworker will really appreciate it.

★ **Your coworker is probably friendlier than they appear,** though it may take some time to wear through their restrained exterior to get to that heart of gold. If you want to befriend your Virgo coworker, expect to put in a little effort. Small gestures of kindness will add up over time.

★ **Virgos are critical people, but ironically, they are sensitive to criticism themselves.** This is not the coworker to give unsolicited feedback to, nor do they respond well to ribbing. The most innocent comment about their work will wound a Virgo, and they will remember it for months—if not years—to come.

So Your Partner Is a Virgo Sun . . .

Having a Virgo Sun as a partner is an achievement indeed. Virgos have incredibly high standards, especially for their romantic partners. You may not realize it, but you have likely passed dozens of subtle tests.

★ **From time to time, your partner needs to let their freak flag fly.** Virgos spend a lot of time acting like they have all their ducks in a row, but perfection is always an illusion. To balance out their high-strung nature, they need to release. Often, this is done through sex, especially kink, or another form of escapism. Do not let their buttoned-up demeanor fool you!

★ **Your partner will often worry that there is something terribly wrong with them.** You see, Virgos are hypochondriacs, and mortality is one of Virgo's greatest fears. They will do everything they can to stay healthy: meticulous meal plans, gym schedules, annual doctor's visits, biannual dentist cleanings, apple cider vinegar tinctures. Still, mysterious aches and pains send them into a tizzy. Become skilled at calming them down and deciding together if their newest ailment is worthy of a trip to the hospital.

★ **Learn your partner's rules.** Every Virgo has things they like done a certain way. Perhaps they always load the dishwasher with the utensils facing down, or they organize their closet by color or season. While your Virgo may not tell you what their rules are verbatim—they may not even realize other people don't think the same way they do—paying attention to their quirks and acting accordingly will be a huge stress reliever for them.

★ **Know that your partner will rarely, if ever, ask for help.** This does not mean they don't need help, however. Because Virgos are hard-working and self-sufficient, asking for help feels shameful, embarrassing even. It is their last resort. If you notice that your partner has a lot on their plate or seems overwhelmed, simply say, "Is there anything I can do?" This phrase alone alleviates some of their stress, as it reminds them that you're in this together.

★ **A Virgo's greatest weapon is their mind, and they are known to have a sharp tongue.** Try to remember that what they say in the heat of the moment is not how they truly feel. Next time your partner gets snippy with you, take a deep breath before responding. This brief pause should help deescalate things.

★ **Small, thoughtful gestures have significant meaning to Virgo.** Take them to the restaurant they mentioned once in passing, remember the names of their distant relatives, or return the library book they just finished on your way home from work. It's rare for Virgos to be spoiled with the same level of care and attention that they give to others.

☽

VIRGO MOON

When Virgo, a logical earth sign, meets the Moon, which rules emotion, an individual is reserved and rational. They seem unnervingly calm in stressful situations, though this is a façade. Virgo Moons feel emotion just like the rest of us, but they are zipped up tight.

Virgo Moons are most compatible with other earth Moons (Taurus, Virgo, and Capricorn) because they will also take a slightly detached approach to emotion. When a situation arises, earth Moons are quick to problem-solve. Their practical, even-keeled responses complement each other and make them a formidable team.

Virgo Moons are least compatible with fire Moons (Aries, Leo, and Sagittarius). Fire Moons are much too feisty for a Virgo Moon's taste. Virgo Moon will encounter a challenge and think, *Okay, let's get this figured out*, whereas a fire Moon will encounter a challenge and think, *Let's burn it to the ground*. Anger is not an emotion Virgo Moon likes to sit with; sure, Virgo Moon may dance with contempt from time to time, but full-blown rage is not in their nature.

A Virgo Moon would do all right with an air Moon (Gemini, Libra, and Aquarius), especially in the sign of Gemini, which is also ruled by Mercury. Air Moons don't wallow for long, and they are quick to problem-solve and move forward, just like a Virgo Moon. Virgo Moons may also be compatible with water Moons (Cancer, Scorpio, and Pisces), especially Pisces Moons, because Pisces is Virgo's cosmic opposite and loosens up this uptight sign.

Restorative Activities for a Virgo Moon

Virgo Moons have a tough time actually relaxing. A trip to the spa or a day of pampering are nice ideas in theory, but in practice, your mind will be racing with all the things you have to do when you get home. Here are some ideas that are rejuvenating *and* productive—the best of both worlds.

★ **Organize an area of your life.** This can be literal (tidying up the kitchen) or figurative (sorting emails into appropriate folders, making that phone call you've been dreading for days, etc.). Taking action on a task that you've been putting off will leave you feeling confident and in charge.

★ **On a blank piece of paper, write down every negative thought plaguing you.** Be as detailed or as vague as you'd like. Perhaps write a letter to a person who has upset you. Scratch, scribble, or doodle if it feels right. Once you've written down everything on your mind, tear the paper into scraps and throw it in the garbage, shred it, or (safely) burn pieces of it. Leave those frustrations behind.

★ **Go shopping for a new houseplant.** Plants satisfy so many aspects of life for a Virgo Moon: They purify the environment they're in, they add a beautiful burst of green to a space, *and* they're something you can care for that doesn't cost an arm and a leg. Take some time researching what sort of plant you'd like to bring home, or pick one that catches your eye. Set your new plant somewhere you'll see it regularly, and consider it a reminder to nurture yourself too.

Journal Prompts for a Virgo Moon

As a Virgo Moon, you may already have a journaling routine, as you like sorting through your thoughts and the catharsis of letting things out. If you don't already journal, consider utilizing this resource.

★ If you could snap your fingers and have the perfect life, what would it be like? Where would you live? Who would surround you? What would you do for work and for pleasure? How would you be different? Write it all down, and then reflect on what the word *perfect* means to you. Is perfection attainable?

★ What are your pet peeves? Think about things that make you cringe when others do them. What purpose do these pet peeves serve in your life? Do you want to work on your relationship to any of your pet peeves? What steps could you take?

★ When was the last time someone disappointed you? What happened? How did you respond? Do you wish you had done anything differently? What will your relationship look like going forward? Are there any takeaways from this situation that may come in handy in the future?

★ Think about someone in your life who recently made a choice that you disagree with. What do you think they should have done instead? Why? Is it possible they made that choice for good reasons that you are not privy to? What could those reasons be? How can you best support this person going forward?

So Your Partner Is a Virgo Moon . . .

Kudos to you for sticking out your partner's snippy side. You clearly understand that the things they say in the heat of the moment are not how they truly feel. Virgo Moons really do have pure intentions, though their delivery can leave much to be desired.

★ **Allow them to be in control more often than not.** When your partner does not have control over a situation, they will feel fearful. Even a false illusion of control soothes their frayed nerves. Something as simple as letting them decide what's for dinner acts like a balm for a frazzled Virgo Moon.

★ **Recognize that fixing things for you is how they show they care.** Your partner's response to stressful situations is to begin problem-solving. It's not that they are unfeeling—it's just that there is a time and a place for emotion, and that is *after* they start rectifying the situation. They are likely experts at compartmentalizing.

★ **Find physical hobbies that you can engage in together as a catharsis for your partner's pent-up emotions.** Go for long walks, join a pickleball league, or become gym buddies. Yardwork and gardening are also great activities for Virgo Moons. If none of those activities appeal, consider something more X-rated.

★ **Above all else, remain calm.** Virgo Moons are prone to panic and worry, and it's absolutely critical for you to be a source of support when their anxiety gets the best of them. The same goes for those moments when Virgo's anxiety manifests as brusqueness. Protect your peace by taking a quick breather. Adding fuel to the fire will not end well for either of you.

↑
VIRGO RISING

Have you ever met someone who seemed so put together that you instantly trusted them? Virgo rising energy. The rising sign is how we come across to people we have just met. Virgo risings are quiet and sure, and there's a sense of solidity to them that is incredibly alluring—or incredibly off-putting, depending on who you ask. Remember that no one is perfect, though Virgo risings do a really good job of seeming like they are.

Virgo risings are naturally drawn to people with Pisces placements. Pisces is dreamy and ethereal. Virgos cannot relate to their go-with-the-flow approach to life, but man, is there something appealing about it! Pisces placements keep Virgo risings from becoming too set in their ways, and Virgo risings will help Pisces add some much-needed structure to their life. If a Virgo rising is single, they may have luck dating someone with Pisces placements.

Ways to Spot a Virgo Rising

Virgo risings are easy to spot—if you know what to look for. They tend to be wallflowers, so you may glance right over them initially. If you attended a party and took a poll of the people who quietly lined the outskirts of a room, you'd meet several Virgo risings.

★ **Virgo risings look impeccable.** They may be fastidious about their makeup, hair, or nails, or they may dress in polished, lint-free clothing. There is never a hair out of place, literally or figuratively.

★ **Virgo risings may be easily overstimulated by loud noises, bright or flashing lights, or crowds.** They're much better suited for quaint coffee shops and quiet corners of the library. Unless they have other, more outgoing planetary placements, Virgo risings would rather stay home than go out.

★ **Virgo risings rarely raise their voice.** They are prone to silence, though when they do talk, it will be at a reasonable level. They may even adopt a "phone call voice" that sounds markedly different from their everyday voice. This isn't intentional—they simply can't help being professional!

★ **Virgo risings are the quintessential "mom friend."** You know the type—the person whose purse or bag is well-stocked with bandages, hand sanitizer, and lip balm. If you ask a Virgo rising for an aspirin, they've probably got Tylenol *and* ibuprofen for you to choose from. They may even carry a snack or two!

Downsides of Being a Virgo Rising

Others hold you to a high standard, which is a blessing and a curse. When excellence is expected, there are plenty of opportunities to disappoint.

★ **You are fallible just like everyone else, but others don't see you that way.** You have an austere, bulletproof quality. When you do slip up, it will be a big deal. "Can you believe so-and-so made that mistake?" people will whisper. Of course you made a mistake—you're human. Try not to let these comments get to you.

★ **When you are just getting to know someone, you may seem quite dull.** Virgo risings are sensible and selective, which may make others think you are unfriendly or uptight. If you have fiery Sun or Moon placements, try to lean into this energy when meeting new people.

★ **People may siphon their workload onto you.** You seem so capable that surely you can handle a little more on your plate. And the thing is, you will do your best to juggle everything. But just because you *can* doesn't mean you *should*. Learn to say no when necessary.

Using Your Virgo Rising to Your Advantage

Having a Virgo rising will naturally open doors for you. You have a quiet strength that others appreciate. Not all Virgo risings have earned this treatment, though—some Virgo risings are wolves in sheep's clothing, especially if they have Scorpio placements.

★ **You appear trustworthy, so lean into that energy to secure what you're after.** Are you looking for a new job? Great! You are more than capable of handling whatever life throws at you. Do you have a favor to ask? No problem! Others will be flattered you asked.

★ **People tend to assume the best about you.** Your solid, placid demeanor is like a blank canvas, and they project their most favorable thoughts onto it. Subsequently, your reputation is pristine. If someone has a problem with you, others are quick to rush to your defense. And if you do need to apologize for something, others will easily accept your apology and let bygones be bygones.

★ **When someone needs feedback, they will come to you.** Others think highly of you and value your thoughts and opinions. This puts you in a unique position of power, where your word holds sway. You may even be the deciding factor on an important decision. Use this power wisely.

$$\text{☿}$$

VIRGO MERCURY

Mercury, the planet of communication, rules the sign of Virgo, which means a Virgo Mercury is a harmonious placement indeed. Virgo Mercuries are excellent communicators, and they especially excel at written communication. Virgo Mercuries are the sort of people whose skills make them well suited to writing technical manuals or detailed web copy.

Communicating with a Virgo Mercury

Talking to a Virgo Mercury should be a pretty painless process, though they may be a bit socially awkward at first.

★ **Virgo Mercuries prefer written communication.** Emails are better than phone calls, and detailed instructions are more helpful than verbally delivered ones. When Virgos communicate via writing, they have time to get their thoughts perfectly worded, and they are able to process at their own speed.

★ **In moments of crisis, this placement can keep their cool and take control of the situation.** Virgos gamely step up to the plate no matter what life throws at them, and their durability immediately puts others at ease. They are fantastic human resources and public relations representatives. If you are experiencing something incredibly stressful, ask a Virgo Mercury for help.

★ **Virgo Mercuries are excellent delegators.** This is a good placement for a supervisor or an individual in some sort of leadership role to have. In a more personal relationship, Virgo Mercuries may be perceived as bossy or controlling. They automatically step up and take charge, even when it's not necessary.

★ **Directions will always be clear and easy to follow when a Virgo Mercury is explaining things.** This straightforward approach may make them seem a little dull, but don't let it mislead you—Virgo Mercuries are some of the wittiest people you will ever meet. Plus, they can roast people like no other.

Questions to Ask a Virgo Mercury

Getting to know a Virgo Mercury may happen in fits and starts, especially if you're trying to get to know them professionally *and* personally, as Virgo Mercury communicates differently depending on the setting.

★ What are some of your biggest pet peeves?

★ If they made a movie about your life, who would be your cast of characters? Which actors would you hire to play them?

★ What's something that you think is unnecessarily complicated?

★ I have this problem [at work/at home/in my relationship]. What do you think I should do?

♀
VIRGO VENUS

When Virgo, the sign of structure, service, and hard work, meets Venus, the planet of love and pleasure, individuals are intensely devoted to making their relationships work, even if they should've let go a long time ago. They're unlikely to end a relationship, though Virgo's mutable quality means that if their partner ends things, they will begrudgingly course correct.

Self-Love for a Virgo Venus

Your Venus sign probably sees self-care as another thing to check off your to-do list. And if that list had a hierarchy, it would be near the bottom. Carving out time to give yourself the devotion you so freely give to others is a necessity.

★ **Refresh your space.** Nothing heals a Virgo Venus like a reset. Move some furniture around, light a candle that is a different scent than you usually buy, or reorganize your kitchen cabinets. As you physically shift objects, you may subconsciously begin to process your thoughts and emotions. At the very least, you'll return to your problems with a new perspective.

★ **Take yourself on a date.** What are you in the mood to do today? Perhaps you should get a haircut, go to the library, or swing by your favorite coffee shop. You work so hard to take care of others' needs that you often neglect your own. For just a few hours, focus solely on what brings *you* happiness.

★ **Solve a problem.** This may be a problem you've been facing for quite some time or a problem a loved one has brought to you. Minor problems like slow Wi-Fi, miscommunications, and an unbalanced checkbook are just as valuable as large-scale problems. The relief you will feel helps mitigate other stressors.

★ **Lose yourself in a good book.** Words are comforting for a Virgo Venus, and nothing whisks you away from the headaches of the real world like literature. Sure, your issues will still be waiting for you when you close the book, but you'll feel more prepared to face them.

Seducing a Virgo Venus

Virgo Venus is not a person who is easily wooed. Their rational brain is much more active than their emotional brain, and they likely have a long list of "icks." They will do their best to talk themselves out of falling in love. If you're in it for the long haul, prepare to put your best foot forward.

★ **Take Virgo Venus on dates where they can showcase their skills or develop new ones.** Virgos love to learn, and hands-on dates give them something tangible to take away even if the relationship doesn't work out. Alternatively, you could ask Virgo Venus to plan the date and give them a few parameters, sort of like a Choose-Your-Own-Adventure situation. For example, "I'm in the mood for a good burger, ideally somewhere near a park so we can get the food to go and have a picnic." Virgo Venus will love scouring the web for the perfect location.

★ **Watch a movie neither of you have seen before, then go out for dinner after and unpack everything.** What did you like? What bugged you? What plot holes did you find? Virgos love to analyze and point out flaws. Being an amateur film critic is fun for them.

★ **Don't be too critical of Virgo Venus, even if it is in good fun.** Virgos are hypersensitive to criticism. While they love to dish it out, they can't take it. If you notice Virgo Venus ribbing you and you want to roast them back, make a conscious effort to bite your tongue, especially if you just started dating.

★ **Be decisive.** If a Virgo Venus asks when you're available, say "Friday at six o'clock" rather than "My weekend is pretty free." Likewise, be straightforward with your communication. If they text, "What's up?" the absolute worst thing you could respond is "Nothing much, what's up with you?" Dry, uninterested responses turn off a Virgo, as do people who take too long to respond. Text Virgo Venus back in a reasonable time frame.

So Your Partner Has a Virgo Venus . . .

People who have a Virgo Venus tend to find themselves in stable, committed relationships. Situationships and on-again, off-again relationships bring out their worst qualities. If your partner has a Virgo Venus, they will be dedicated to your relationship. Be careful not to become enmeshed, because if it was up to your partner, you would do *everything* the exact same way.

★ **Virgo is the sign of service, and your partner will demonstrate their love for you through beautifully mundane tasks.** This is a placement that will wake up early just to surprise you with breakfast in bed. If Virgo Venus knows you've had a long day, they will have a cold beverage and a warm hug waiting for you when you get home. And if you have to go on a work trip, don't be surprised if you find sweet sticky notes from Virgo Venus inside your suitcase. Virgo Venus is devoted to infusing everyday tasks with love, and their actions make you feel cherished.

★ **If you want your relationship to last, you must be willing to accept your partner's peculiarities.** Virgo Venus has certain preferences and stands behind them with steadfast resolve. These preferences may drive you crazy or seem illogical. Take some time to reflect on the following: If your partner stayed exactly the same, would you still want to be with them in ten years? Twenty? Fifty? Because the fact of the matter is they probably *will* still have these peculiarities, and they'll pick up a few more as time goes on. Do you really love them, quirks and all?

★ **Your partner likes things done a certain way, and when their plans go awry, they become distressed.** Some plans go awry through no fault of your own—delayed flights, missing luggage, bad weather. But if you deliberately allow plans to go awry, your partner will grow resentful. If you know you are not going to make a dinner reservation, tell Virgo Venus right away. Your partner understands things happen, but they have no patience for last-minute disruptions.

★ **Control is a *huge* part of Virgo Venus's love life.** Virgo Venus will want to know where you are and what you are doing at all times. This may be a source of friction for more free-spirited partners. Do not be surprised if you find them snooping through your phone or combing your social media likes. These are opportunities to have conversations about boundaries and trust. Virgo Venus can respect your boundaries, though they will certainly grumble about having to do so.

♂

VIRGO MARS

Virgo, the sign of practicality, is a force to be reckoned with when it meets the planet Mars, known for passion, aggression, sex, and drive. Have you ever heard the phrase *organized chaos*? That's Virgo Mars in a nutshell.

I will say, Virgo Mars has a lot of positive qualities. For one, they are great to vacation with because they'll handle all the itinerary planning. But they're also terrifying, because when a Virgo Mars decides to get revenge, they will plan every last detail of the punishment, and they don't mind waiting for the right opportunity to strike.

Virgo Mars Behind Closed Doors

Behind every well-oiled machine are a million moving parts. Virgo Mars orchestrates the million moving parts of their life, ensuring that everything appears perfect. However, their need for control manifests in healthy and unhealthy ways.

★ **Sexually, most Virgo Mars are dominant and enjoy having control over their partner in some capacity.** Power and control dynamics arouse a Virgo Mars; think handcuffs, bondage, and sensory play. This is one of the kinkiest signs in the zodiac, second only to Scorpio.

★ **Virgo Mars is incredibly headstrong.** They don't like to be bossed around and don't respond well to people telling them what to do. If loved ones want Virgo Mars to do something, it's best to phrase it as having a favor to ask. And always remember to say please and thank you.

★ **Virgo Mars is controlling.** If this need is met in the bedroom, they may be more easygoing in everyday life. Typically, though, Virgo Mars has rigid expectations for how things must be done. They will not go anywhere without making a plan, usually with a minute-by-minute breakdown. For organized folks, this is a breath of fresh air, but for more spontaneous individuals, Virgo Mars's rigidity can be a point of frustration.

★ **Virgo Mars has very high expectations.** When others cannot meet their unrealistic expectations, they become disappointed or irritated. While lowering expectations is never fun, it is one way for Virgo Mars to live a more balanced life.

Things *Not* to Do to a Virgo Mars

Virgo Mars holds themselves to an incredibly high standard, and as such, they are their own worst critic. There is no such thing as a harmless jab to a Virgo Mars.

★ **Do not try to micromanage them.** Virgo Mars can handle themselves, thank you very much. They like to tackle things their own way, and the more you poke at them, the more surly they become.

★ **Do not "joke" about their behavior.** Anything you say will be taken personally, and Virgo Mars will become very self-conscious. When a Virgo Mars's feathers are ruffled, they lash out.

★ **Do not feel embarrassed about coming to them for help.** Virgo Mars would rather roll up their sleeves and get to work immediately than have to fix your mistake in the future. Their know-it-all attitude can be intimidating, but they really don't mind showing you the ropes as long as you pay attention.

Things a Virgo Mars Probably Needs to Hear
(But Definitely Doesn't Want To)

This is a prickly placement because all feedback is viewed as criticism.

★ **Control is an illusion.** You can plan and plan to your heart's content, but the Universe has a way of upending even the best-laid plans. Find other (healthy) ways to satiate your craving for control. Perhaps you become very particular about how you make your bed in the morning, or you do not go to sleep until you've read a chapter of the book on your bedside table.

★ **Other people have to be allowed to make their own mistakes.** Sometimes, from an outside perspective, it's easy to assume we know the best way to handle a situation. But mistakes and successes are subjective, and it is really up to the individual how they want to proceed. You may not agree with their choices, but that's okay—you are not the one who has to live with the consequences.

★ **Your way is not the only way.** You make a plan of attack and follow it to a *T*, but others can reach the same end result by way of a different route. Nine times out of ten, your approach will be smoother and faster, but that doesn't mean someone else's bumpy, meandering journey is less valuable.

QUICK GUIDE TO

VIRGO

PLACEMENTS

If someone in your life has Virgo placements . . .

DO

★ Ask them for help, then thank them for a job well done.

★ Honor their need for routine.

★ Defer to their eye for detail.

DON'T

★ Boss them around, because they'll do the opposite just to spite you.

★ Change plans at the last minute.

★ Deliberately disrupt the order they have established.

★ 7 ★
LIBRA

Libra is the ultimate peacekeeper. No sign is more devoted to tranquility. Libras do everything in their power to make sure their loved ones are well cared for, their surroundings are serene, and their work makes the world a better place. If Libras ruled the world, we would all live in harmony, everyone's needs would be met, and conflict would cease to exist. Sounds nice, huh?

At their best, Libras are fair, kind, loving, and calm. They are a safe space for everyone around them, and they bring harmony to tense situations. Libras fight for the underdog and are committed to making sure everyone's voice is heard. For this reason, they are staunch advocates for equality. Those who are loved by a Libra are showered with unconditional positive regard, an openness to all perspectives, and constant reassurance.

At their worst, Libras are codependent or lack a backbone. They are so focused on making others happy that they neglect their own needs and preferences. If they're not careful, Libras become echoes of the people around them, adopting their loved ones' mannerisms, sayings, and opinions to keep the peace. This is an unconscious habit, one that Libras must actively work to unlearn. Individuality is what makes the world go round, and no matter how hard Libras try to avoid disagreements, they are a part of life.

Libra rules the seventh house, the house of partnership (both romantic and platonic). If Aries is the temperamental child, Taurus is the preteen realizing the value of money, Gemini is the teenager preparing to leave the nest, Cancer is the young adult constructing their *own* nest, Leo is the hip parent, and Virgo is the thirty-something who finally knows what works for them, then Libra is the adult approaching forty who is realizing how important their close relationships are. It takes a village, and it's easy to forget that in the midst of young adulthood's chaos. Libra knows they cannot get by on their own, so they deliberately nurture their relationships.

Libra's symbol is the scales. Scales make an appearance in most courts in the United States, representing a balanced society where wrongdoing is made right. Libra is passionate about justice, and for this reason, you will find many lawyers with Libra placements. (Libras excel in any career where they are able to mediate, though, so they may be drawn to fields such as counseling as well.) The symbol of the scales also embodies Libra's commitment to harmony: When a scale is perfectly balanced, both sides have what they need, and all is right in the world.

Libra is an air sign. Like the other air signs (Gemini and Aquarius), Libra dislikes arguments, heavy conversations, and being stifled. While most air signs are tough to pin down—especially romantically—Libra is ruled by the planet Venus, which is the planet of love. For this reason, Libras are more comfortable in a relationship than the other air signs. They are not averse to the idea of a happily ever after.

Like the other cardinal signs (Aries, Cancer, and Capricorn), Libras are used to being knocked down. They get back up again, dust themselves off, and keep moving. Others assume Libra is a pushover because they want everyone to be happy, but Libra has a core of steel that their benevolent demeanor conceals. They will do whatever it takes to get what they're after, and they aren't going to wait around for someone to hand it to them.

⊙

LIBRA SUN

The Sun is in Libra between September 23 and October 23, though the exact dates may vary slightly depending on the year. Libra Suns are some of the most gentle, placid people. They seek harmony in every aspect of their life, so they surround themselves with positive energy. Libra's aversion to conflict makes their closest relationships pretty painless, and family and friends appreciate Libra's good nature. If this sign has any faults, it is that they are *too* good-natured.

For those with a Libra Sun, every section in this chapter will apply to some degree. The Sun is the most powerful planetary force, so it has a huge impact on personality. While a Libra Sun may not have a Libra rising, for example, they will undoubtedly find something in that section that they relate to.

Pure Libra Energy

The Libras of the world are some of the nicest people to interact with and look at. Ruled by Venus, Libras are notorious for their beauty, either physically or aesthetically.

★ **The saying "If you can't say something nice, don't say anything at all" sums up Libra's communication style.** There is a lot of negative energy in the world, and they don't feel the need to add to it.

★ **Libras have no interest in conflict, disagreement, or debate.** They don't understand why everyone can't just get along. They will avoid people with strong opinions, especially those who want to discuss politics and current affairs. Libras have opinions too, of course, but they don't feel the need to make a big show about it.

★ **When you ask a Libra what they want for dinner or what they want to watch on TV, they'll say, "Whatever you want! I don't care."** Other signs may have similar responses, but Libra is the one sign that actually means it. Nothing makes a Libra happier than seeing their loved ones happy.

★ **Because they want everyone to get along, Libras adopt whatever traits will keep the peace,** but if they're not careful, this coping mechanism can quickly become a habitual response. If left unchecked, Libras become mirrors. They lose track of which emotions and reactions are truly theirs and which they have picked up from someone else.

★ **Libras tend to go with the flow.** They rarely, if ever, say no to anyone or anything. The scales become imbalanced when they take on too much for others, though Libra will soldier on until it becomes impossible to continue doing so. Somehow, Libras appear totally in control the entire time, even when they are on the edge of burnout.

★ **Libras are docile people,** and raising their voice is reserved for the direst circumstances. If you hear a Libra yelling, that is a dead giveaway that something is seriously wrong.

Gifts for a Libra Sun

Libras are content with any gift you give them because they believe it is the thought that counts. Whether you gift them a tangible item, quality time, or a compliment, Libras will hold your kindness near and dear to their heart.

★ **Gift a Libra something that is thoughtful yet practical.** Consider their hobbies, then try to think of something they could use on a regular basis. For example, if you have a Libra friend who loves to bake, a set of quality mixing bowls and a personalized dishtowel could be good gifts. Every time Libra uses the gift you gave them, they will think of you and be filled with warmth.

★ **Libra appreciates the finer things in life.** After all, the planet of love and luxury rules this sign. Like the sign of Taurus, Think sumptuous chocolates, silky fabrics, and plush cushions. With that being said, Libra is not as discerning as Taurus; they cannot tell the difference between a five-dollar bottle of wine and a fifty-dollar one. A nice sweater from TJ Maxx will be just as well-received as a cashmere one.

★ **If you and Libra have friends or family members in common, consider gifting them something that involves the group.** Libras thrive in a group setting, and being surrounded by everyone they love is the ultimate gift. So invite everyone to dinner, take a group paint 'n sip class, or meet at a brewery and play some board games. If someone in the group likes to host, consider suggesting an intimate gathering.

★ **There is no need to spend hundreds of dollars on a gift for Libra.** Something homemade has just as much—if not more—value. Get creative. What skills do you have that could be gifted? If you're handy, you could offer to help around the house; if you're a musician, write or memorize a song, then give Libra a private concert; if you're a skilled writer, offer to revamp Libra's résumé. We all have unique talents that can benefit others.

So Your Boss Is a Libra Sun . . .

There are more Libras in power than you'd think. While Libras tend to be placid and content with their lot in life, this is a cardinal sign, and cardinal signs are ambitious and unrelenting. So if Libra senses that being promoted would have a positive impact on others' lives, they won't let anything stand in their way. Slowly but surely, they will climb the ladder, extending their influence with each rung.

★ **Your boss will always have your back.** When you ask them for help, they will do their best to provide guidance or resolve a situation. And if your Libra boss can't fix things, they will try to put you in contact with the person who can.

★ **Libras don't get worked up very often.** This is a blessing and a curse—your boss will not snap at you or abuse their power, but they will expect you to fight your own battles. You may hope your boss will use their position of power to create change, but nine times out of ten, Libra would rather not get their hands dirty.

★ **More than likely, you are in your boss's good graces.** Libras naturally see the best in people, and if you slip up, they are quick to forgive and forget. Libras believe in second chances, and third chances, and fourth chances—their tolerance is endless. One downside of their limitless compassion is that Libras will absolve colleagues long after others have grown fatigued of their shenanigans.

So Your Coworker Is a Libra Sun . . .

Libras go out of their way to get to know the people they work with. They deliberately learn people's names and backgrounds. When it comes to work relationships, Libra embodies the phrase "Never met a stranger." Though they may not be friends with everyone they work with, they will at least be friend*ly*.

★ **Everyone needs a coworker they can go to for advice,** whether personal or professional. Your Libra coworker will listen calmly, then offer a few thoughts. They will never pick sides or assign blame; no matter what, Libras remain totally neutral and unbiased. They may not offer a solution to your problem, but hopefully talking things out takes a weight off your chest.

★ **Libra coworkers appreciate deep, meaningful relationships with their colleagues.** While some signs would recoil at the concept of a workplace being like a family, Libra thinks that actually sounds kind of nice. This is a sign that aims to develop close bonds with select coworkers. Libras are happiest with a "work spouse." They may even have more than one!

★ **Your coworker can get along with just about anyone.** At company events, make the rounds with your Libra coworker because they can easily strike up friendly conversation. All you have to do is smile and nod, maybe throwing in a quip now and then, and every interaction will be smooth sailing. Awkward silences and tension evaporate when Libra is around.

So Your Partner Is a Libra Sun . . .

Sweet, sweet Libra Sun. Your partner rolls with life's punches and keeps you sane. More than likely, they are the calm, reasonable one in the relationship.

★ **Libras are happiest when partnered, so they will bend over backward if it benefits the relationship.** On the one hand, it is great that your partner is so committed to the longevity of the relationship. On the other hand, neglecting their own wants and needs ultimately helps no one. Get in the habit of asking your partner how they're doing, and then dig deeper. How are they *really* doing?

★ **Your partner must feel included in your life.** Introduce them to your friends and family, yes, but also to your coworkers and acquaintances. Invite them to company happy hours and your distant cousin's birthday party. While some signs may consider these sorts of invites to be a tedious inconvenience, Libras value connection, so every invitation is appreciated.

★ **The opinions of Libra's family and friends hold a lot of weight.** If their inner circle does not approve of something—whether it be Libra's choices or the company they keep—it will cause Libra a lot of heartache. They want everyone to be happy, so they may sacrifice their own happiness for the benefit of the collective.

★ **It will be hard to have a productive argument with a Libra.** While this sounds counterintuitive, disagreements in relationships are opportunities for positive change; arguments may lead to renegotiating an imbalanced relationship dynamic or interrupting an unhealthy pattern. However, Libras are so quick to acquiesce that these conversations stop before they really get started, so things remain unchanged. If you have a serious problem that needs resolving, look into couples therapy, where an unbiased third party can help you dig into the issue.

★ **Be your partner's support system.** Libras are used to biting off more than they can chew, though you wouldn't know it, since they will not utter a single complaint. But all of us need help from time to time, and Libra is no exception. For Libra to feel safe asking you for help, you must prove that you are a person they can lean on. This means consistently checking in, keeping your promises, and offering encouragement. Simply lending a hand now and then is not enough to earn the role of Libra's confidant.

☽
LIBRA MOON

When Libra, the sign of compromise and harmony, meets the Moon, the planet of emotion, individuals are level-headed and able to see both sides of a situation. Because of this, they often play devil's advocate, though they may do so silently to avoid ruffling any feathers. Rarely will Libra Moons burst into tears; their emotions are like a calm pond, gently rippling when disturbed but quickly leveling back out.

Libra Moons are most compatible with other air Moons (Gemini, Libra, and Aquarius) because they are quick to talk things out and move forward. Libra Moons don't like to dwell—they are a cardinal sign, so they're always on to the next. They would do all right with fire Moons (Aries, Leo, and Sagittarius) because these signs operate at a similar speed.

Libra Moons are least compatible with water Moons (Cancer, Scorpio, and Pisces). Think of how far apart these elements are—the sky stretches up and up, while the ocean plummets to unfathomable depths. Similarly, air Moons and water Moons cannot reach each other. In a relationship, Libra Moons will feel overwhelmed by their partner's seemingly never-ending emotions, and water Moons will feel completely invalidated by their partner's cerebral approach to everything.

Libra Moons may be compatible with earth Moons (Taurus, Virgo, and Capricorn), though true compatibility will depend on other placements, like Venus and Mars. Of the earth signs, Libra is most compatible with Taurus, because both are ruled by the planet Venus, so these signs understand each other on an intrinsic level.

Restorative Activities for a Libra Moon

You don't need as much time to emotionally recharge as other Moon signs if you are doing a relatively good job of keeping yourself balanced in day-to-day life. Of course, we all benefit from regular self-care.

* ★ **Practice saying no.** You like to lend a helping hand, but you may be overextending yourself. How much of your energy is devoted to others' thoughts, feelings, or problems? What would happen if you declined the next time someone asked you for a favor? Saying no is a superpower, but it will take some time to feel comfortable with this word.

* ★ **Go somewhere on your own.** It is easy for you to get swept up in other people's problems, but returning to yourself is a crucial component of executive functioning. Settle down in a serene location, perhaps near a body of water or in a park, and spend some time in quiet contemplation. Make sure your phone is on silent. For a set period of time, your only responsibility is to be an individual.

* ★ **Schedule time with loved ones.** Nothing replenishes your soul like being around people who get you. If you're feeling stressed, consider coming clean about what's going on. Maybe you should ask someone for advice for a change. No matter what, work on co-regulating with those you trust.

* ★ **Visit a museum.** You like looking at beautiful things, and you like being around other people, so a trip to the museum is the best of both worlds. Allow the art to soothe you as the pleasant hum of other museumgoers provides ambient background noise.

Journal Prompts for a Libra Moon

Air Moons prefer to communicate about emotions rather than actively feel them; they like to talk something out and then move along. Journaling is an excellent practice for Libra Moons because you can release your emotions and not hurt anyone's feelings in the process.

★ When was the last time you were very upset? What was the situation? How long did it take for you to feel okay again? What did you do to return to a regulated headspace? As you reflect on the situation, are any lingering emotions or thoughts coming up for you?

★ Which relationship in your life is causing you the most stress right now? How would you describe your current relationship with this person? What would you like it to be in the future? Are there any steps you can take to guide the relationship in that direction?

★ What are some of your passions, morals, and values? When was the last time you stood up for something you believed in? How did it go? How did you feel? Do you think you are living in accordance with your belief system? What are three small ways you can honor your passions, morals, or values in the next month?

So Your Partner Is a Libra Moon . . .

Libra Moons are wonderful partners because they stay calm, cool, and collected in the midst of turmoil. However, that baseline is where they are most comfortable. Heart-to-heart conversations are not their forte; strong emotions of any kind are not their jam, including lust.

★ **Libra Moons will say and do just about anything to end a disagreement.** Was it genuine, or were they just trying to please you? Actions speak louder than words, so see if something shifts after a tough conversation. If things stay the same, you've been Libra'd. Think of another way to bring up the issue—ideally one that doesn't involve raised voices—and try again.

★ **Your partner is the epitome of compromise.** They like delegation and clear role descriptions. This partnership will do well with household division of labor (e.g., one partner always does the dishes, while the other always does the laundry). Likewise, it will be important to your partner to split time evenly between your families; for example, celebrating Christmas Eve with one side of the family is fine as long as you're planning on spending Christmas Day with the other.

★ **At times, you may feel frustrated with the lack of emotional intimacy your partner can give you.** Unless your partner has water placements, they struggle to express strong emotions of any kind. While this can be great mid-argument, it also causes excited conversations about the future of your relationship to fizzle. Words of affirmation are not your partner's strong suit; while they may be flirty, you will not be on the receiving end of a heartfelt poem, song, or love letter. Try to appreciate the way your partner *does* show their love, which is most likely via quality time.

↑
LIBRA RISING

The rising sign is how we come across to people we've just met. Because Libra is ruled by Venus, the planet of love and beauty, they are known for being easy on the eyes. At least, that is the stereotype. Beyond that ethereal, attractive quality, Libra risings are benevolent peacekeepers.

Libra risings are naturally drawn to people with Aries placements. They admire Aries's ability to be unfailingly themselves. Libra risings wish they embodied more of that "Ask for forgiveness rather than permission" energy that accompanies so many Aries. They may surround themselves with Aries friends, lovers, or colleagues. Single Libra risings would benefit from pursuing a partner with Aries placements.

Ways to Spot a Libra Rising

Have you ever met someone and immediately felt at ease in their presence? They might have been a Libra rising!

★ **Libra risings have a gentle, calming demeanor.** They usually have a smile on their face and use that smile to relieve tension. Libra risings know the power of a friendly face, so they readily become that for others. They make excellent counselors, office managers, and receptionists—they do wonderfully anywhere they come face-to-face with distressed folks.

★ **It can be easy to overlook a Libra rising because they will never be the center of attention.** Introverted Libra risings are wallflowers who are more comfortable observing than engaging. Extroverted Libra risings can make small talk with just about anybody, but they do so in an understated way; they prefer intimate conversations to florid introductions.

★ **When Libra risings are faced with an uncomfortable situation, they escape as quickly as possible.** Around loved ones, Libra risings have a bit more staying power. We adopt our rising sign characteristics when we are around unfamiliar people, so when it comes to strangers, Libra risings won't stay in imbalanced environments for long. They have no desire to mediate discordance or soothe upset, especially if they're not personally invested in the matter.

Downsides of Being a Libra Rising

When it comes to being a Libra rising, there are more positives than negatives. However, there are a few common pitfalls.

★ **Libra risings need to be liked.** Sometimes, this longing for acceptance can be interpreted as desperation. For this reason, your attempts to fit in may have the opposite effect: Others may shut you out, perceiving you as clingy. Try to be your authentic self when meeting someone new; this is the surest way to make real connections.

★ **Some may perceive you as weak.** In reality, they are picking up on the fact that you are gentle, which is a marvelous quality. Remember that kindness and strength are not mutually exclusive.

★ **Others may look to you to solve disputes.** It can be exhausting, constantly being asked to weigh in on situations, especially if you have no skin in the game. Plus, you prefer to keep your opinions to yourself, so being put on the spot makes you uncomfortable. Memorize these words: "Thanks, but I'm at capacity right now. Best of luck!"

Using Your Libra Rising to Your Advantage

There are numerous benefits to being a Libra rising. In fact, if I could pick my own rising sign, I think I'd want this one!

★ **With a little bit of effort, you can charm anyone.** On a first date, during a job interview, or at the DMV, you know exactly what to say to shift things in your favor. This is a priceless gift. However, it's hard to turn your charisma off—while you may be on the worst date of your life, the person across from you thinks you're clicking effortlessly. A blessing and a curse.

★ **Your calming presence has the ability to change people's lives.** This is not an exaggeration! Imagine being at your lowest and meeting someone who makes you feel held, seen, and safe. For this reason, you would be an asset to an emergency room or a crisis center.

★ **Others want to be around you.** You don't attract drama or chaos, and your serenity is like an oasis amid the chaos of everyday life. For this reason, you will never be lonely, except by choice—you can easily find community anywhere you go.

☿

LIBRA MERCURY

Mercury is the planet of communication, and air signs (Gemini, Libra, and Aquarius) are known for their communicative prowess. When the planet of conversation is in an air sign, individuals are loquacious. And, because Libra is concerned with peace and harmony, they will be powerful mediators.

Communicating with a Libra Mercury

Striking up a conversation with a Libra Mercury will be a pleasant experience. They are able to make fluid small talk and easily fill awkward lulls in conversation.

★ **Libra Mercury abhors conflict.** Raised voices, arguments, and debates are the bane of their existence, and they never intentionally start a disagreement. Libra Mercury does not start a fight—or finish one.

★ **Silence is uncomfortable for a Libra Mercury**, especially when they are around strangers. They may chatter endlessly just to fill the silence with the sound of themselves talking. If you're talking to a Libra Mercury who is going on and on, put them out of their misery: Politely exit the conversation, or change the subject to something both of you find interesting.

★ **Nine times out of ten, Libra Mercury will sprinkle some flirtation into a conversation,** especially if they're talking to someone they find attractive. Venus, the planet of love, has a powerful influence on the way Libra communicates. Flirting is a skill just like any other, and Libra Mercury likes to practice.

Questions to Ask a Libra Mercury

Like all air Mercury placements, Libra can go on for quite a while, especially if they've had a drink or two. Libra Mercuries love to ask questions, which means they aren't often on the receiving end.

★ Who are some of the most important people in your life? Why?

★ If you could snap your fingers and make everything perfect, how would your life have changed?

★ When was the last time someone asked you for advice? What happened?

★ How would you describe your ideal partner?

♀
LIBRA VENUS

Venus, the planet of love, beauty, and pleasure, rules charming Libra. Individuals with a Libra Venus will be lucky in love, as matters of the heart come naturally to them. Intimate relationships are prioritized. Libra Venus likely started fantasizing about meeting their soulmate at a young age; the planet Venus craves a dreamy love affair that blossoms into a happy marriage, though sometimes this results in Libra Venus settling down too quickly.

Self-Love for a Libra Venus

You derive the most pleasure from making your partner happy, so you lose sight of your individualism in a relationship. Whether you're single or part-nered, it's imperative to hold on to what makes you you.

* ★ **As difficult as it may be, stay single for a while.** If you are already in a committed relationship, prioritize alone time. This will be deeply unsettling for you. You prefer to be someone's significant other—after all, a second person helps balance your Libran scale. However, it's important to find wholeness on your own. Remember that you are in control of the scale, and you already have everything you need to find balance. Partners should add to your life without disrupting your inner harmony.

* ★ **Set aside time to reflect on the kind of partner, friend, parent, or child you are.** Grab your journal or open the Notes app and jot down initial thoughts about how you show up for others. You do a lot for the people you love, yet you tend to overlook just how helpful you really are. In fact, thinking about how you care for others may make you feel prideful, egotistical even, but being a martyr benefits no one. Pause to share some kindness with yourself.

* ★ **Pamper yourself.** You are your last priority, but it shouldn't be that way. What makes you feel like a million bucks? Set aside time to do that more often. The more you take care of yourself, the more energy you will have for others. No one can pour from an empty cup!

* ★ **Thoroughly vet the people you are sharing your energy with.** You are a very loving person, and all sorts of people will latch on to that. Spend time with people who give and receive in equal amounts. Above all else, remember that you can end a relationship at any time. It doesn't

matter how long someone has been in your life—if they start taking advantage of your heart, they should no longer have access to it. End one-sided relationships, or if the relationship is one that cannot be easily terminated, reduce the amount of interactions you have with that person.

Seducing a Libra Venus

Romancing a Libra Venus should be pretty easy because they love love. They fall head over heels faster than any other sign because from the moment they meet someone special, they begin picturing a happily ever after. When reality comes crashing down, things can get rocky, so enjoy the honeymoon phase as long as possible.

★ **Before seducing a Libra Venus, watch a few romcoms for inspiration.** Libras are suckers for flirty banter and romantic gestures, as well as anything cheesy. Make them a custom playlist; send them a cute text every once in a while; save the receipt from your first date. And, of course, be prepared to pull out all the stops on Valentine's Day.

★ **Realize that Libra Venus will become attached quickly**; folks who enjoy their alone time might perceive them as clingy. Libra Venus wants to chat all day long via small texts here and there. They can't help it; once you've won their affection, they can think of nothing else. Romance overrides all logical thought for a Libra Venus. They dive headfirst into love—often before checking how shallow the water is.

★ **To leave a lasting impression on a Libra Venus, make them feel special.** They're naturally self-sacrificing, so when you're around, they deserve all your attention. Libras love classic dates (think dinner and a movie), fine dining, and glamour. In public, open doors for Libra Venus and pull out their chair before they sit down. Hold their hand and always, *always* compliment their appearance. In private, remember that candles are phenomenal mood lighting—who needs overhead lights anyway?

So Your Partner Has a Libra Venus . . .

Partners with a Libra Venus are committed to their relationships, for better or for worse. However, they may have a hard time dealing with the unfortunate, complicated realities of life, much preferring to keep their rose-colored glasses on. For this reason, you may feel unsupported by your partner from time to time.

★ **Keep romance front and center.** Libra Venus is a deeply romantic person, and the sensual side of a relationship must be active for them to feel fulfilled. It is not enough to be a stable, reliable partner; you must also flirt, seduce, and tease to keep the spark alive, no matter how long the two of you have been together. Flirtation is Libra's elixir.

★ **Engage in conversations about the health of your relationship often.** Libra Venus is unlikely to bring up what's bothering them on their own, and they may suppress emotions or ignore serious problems until it is too late. Take on the onus of responsibility for regular relationship check-ins if you want the relationship to stand the test of time.

★ **Do not be a jealous partner.** Libra Venus is immensely loyal, though their flirtatious nature and innate warmth may have you fearing otherwise. Others are drawn to Libra like a moth to a flame; they lap up Libra's affectionate nature and positive perspective. Yes, you have to share your partner in a social sense, and being bitter about that will only drive a wedge between the two of you.

♂
LIBRA MARS

This is an interesting placement because in a lot of ways, Libra Mars embodies two ends of a spectrum. They are cardinal, meaning they are strong and driven, and Mars is the planet of passion and aggression. However, they also hesitate to choose a side in life, much preferring neutral ground. For this reason, Libra Mars may appear quite wishy-washy.

Libra Mars Behind Closed Doors

Libra Mars is just as focused on peace and harmony at home as they are in public.

★ **The most important thing to a Libra Mars is pleasing their partner.** For this reason, they will mold themselves into whatever role their partner would like them to take. If their partner is more dominant, they will be submissive; if their partner is submissive, they will take on the role of dominant. Libra Mars will try just about anything for their partner, which may lead to them neglecting their own boundaries. Encourage them to set the tone more often and, in the process, discover their own preferences.

★ **Libra Mars really doesn't want to argue.** Disagreements make them uncomfortable. They would rather dance around a topic than address it point-blank. This can complicate their intimate relationships because they won't bring up an issue until it is too late. It is in the best interest of their relationship to date a partner who has a more direct Mars placement so that conflict can be resolved in a timely manner. Otherwise, relationships may be too avoidant and nonconfrontational.

★ **Libra Mars will carefully weigh the pros and cons of a situation before making a decision.** The forward momentum of Mars and the cardinal aspect of Libra guarantee Libra Mars has drive, but the sign of Libra never makes a rash decision. In other words, it takes them a little bit longer to get started, but once they have made up their mind, they go for the gold.

Things "Not" to Do to a Libra Mars

Libra Mars is quick to forgive, but do not take this for granted—it is a wonderful thing to meet someone who always offers a fresh start.

★ **Do not bury Libra Mars in tasks, favors, or responsibilities.** They are used to being the catch-all for others, though you'd never know it—

they seem cool as a cucumber. However, if most people in Libra's life are asking them to help out with even one thing, your favor may be the straw that breaks the camel's back. Libra Mars is like the Ten of Wands card in tarot: Eventually, the load that they are carrying is going to overwhelm them. You're better off tackling your problems on your own.

★ **Do not expect them to pick a side.** No matter how evident "right" and "wrong" may appear to you, Libra Mars's brain doesn't work that way. If you put pressure on Libra Mars to back you up, you will be unhappy with the result: They'll play devil's advocate, staunchly refuse to engage, or side with the other party simply because they feel sorry for them.

★ **Do not rely on Libra Mars in intense situations.** Libra Mars does not do well under pressure; like the air sign they are, they will simply disappear. Libras hate to disappoint the people they love, so they are more likely to "ghost" than to have an honest conversation about their boundaries or limitations.

Things a Libra Mars Probably Needs to Hear (But Definitely Doesn't Want To)

It's important for a Libra Mars to remember that you can be sweet *and* firm simultaneously. "No" is a complete sentence.

★ **Sometimes, you have to state your opinion and fight for what you believe in.** If you don't, life will chew you up and spit you back out. I'm not saying you have to be at the forefront of a picket line, but you do need to determine what your values are and then stand behind them. Start small with this by internally challenging a viewpoint that opposes your own, then work up the courage to start sharing your thoughts verbally.

★ **Disappointments, conflicts, and platonic and romantic breakups are a part of life.** I know you avoid them at all costs, but they're inevitable. You can try to say all the right things, dance around all the hard topics, and fix everyone's problems, yet you are still going to hurt people and make them angry. The fact of the matter is you could be the most delicious apple in the orchard and there will still be someone who'd prefer a peach. Coming to terms with this now will save you a lot of heartache in the future.

★ **Just because you've committed to something doesn't mean you're bound to it forever.** You have a tendency to form an alliance and then remain loyal to it no matter what. However, you can—and should—change your mind when new information comes to light. If something or someone isn't working for you anymore, cut your losses and respectfully move on. Life is too short to settle.

QUICK GUIDE TO
LIBRA
PLACEMENTS

If someone in your life has Libra placements . . .

DO

★ Seek their expert advice as needed.

★ Ensure the relationship has an equitable give and take.

★ Respect their need for harmony.

DON'T

★ Treat them like your personal therapist.

★ Force them to pick a side.

★ Raise your voice when speaking to them.

* 8 *
SCORPIO

Scorpios are one of the most well-known signs of the zodiac. They are notorious for being dark, powerful, and seductive. Scorpios rarely forgive, and they *never* forget. They are a ride-or-die friend and a terrifying opponent. In my life, I have had more than one best friend who is a Scorpio, and those friendships ended after an irreparable rift—it is almost impossible to move forward after fighting with a Scorpio. But don't be afraid: Scorpios are also wonderfully loyal and supportive, and I know and love many (shout-out to my therapist). Plus, I was raised by one, and I like to think I turned out all right.

At their best, Scorpios are passionate, emotionally intelligent, thoughtful, and intentional. A well-rounded Scorpio is in touch with their emotions and knows how to use them to benefit themselves *and* others. They act with care and staunchly support their loved ones through every situation, even if their loved one may be at fault. No one is as loyal as Scorpio, not even Leo, who is known for their loyalty—Leo only has so much wherewithal, but Scorpio will go to hell and back for those they love.

At their worst, Scorpios are vindictive, temperamental, vicious, and controlling. When pushed to their limit, they are the epitome of an evil villain. Their anger is bone-deep and unyielding. No one gets revenge like a Scorpio, for they wholeheartedly believe revenge is a dish best served cold. They patiently wait for the right moment to strike, which is usually long after the other person has forgotten about their tiff in the first place. Then, Scorpio enacts their revenge, savoring each and every moment. In short: Do everything in your power to stay on Scorpio's good side.

Scorpio rules the eighth house, the house of death and rebirth, among other things. If Aries is the child of the zodiac, Taurus is the preteen learning the value of money, Gemini is the teenager preparing to leave home, Cancer is the twenty-something preparing a home of their own, Leo is the new parent, Virgo is the tried-and-true adult, and Libra is reestablishing their support system, then Scorpio is the adult approaching midlife who is coming to terms with mortality. Wrinkles, health scares, and sick family or friends can spark an existential crisis, and Scorpio is no stranger to existential dread. Their mind naturally wanders toward the worst-case scenario.

Scorpio's symbol is the scorpion. The similarities are more than just alphabetical; scorpions are unassuming yet deadly. Most scorpions are quite small and go through life unnoticed. It is only when one is challenged that others become painfully aware of a scorpion's presence: It sneaks up and stings, and its jab can be fatal. Scorpios have the same attitude in life. They are perfectly pleasant if you bump into them at the grocery store, and for the most part, they are pleasant to their loved ones. But a spurned Scorpio attacks and, in doing so, fights for their life—they never accept defeat. No matter how harmless they may appear, you must remember that the sting awaits.

Scorpio is a water sign, though they are very different from the other two water signs, Cancer and Pisces. Whereas Cancer and Pisces are friendly, warm waters—think a clear Mediterranean Sea or a kiddie pool—Scorpio is the deep ocean. On the surface, Scorpio appears approachable, but if they pull you under, you can get swept up in a deadly undertow. Likewise, Scorpio expertly applies pressure from all angles until you have no choice but to give up. If you remember one thing about Scorpio, let it be this: Still waters run deep.

Scorpio is a fixed sign. Fixed signs (Taurus, Leo, Scorpio, and Aquarius) are stubborn and resistant to change. Unsolicited feedback falls on deaf ears—even solicited feedback may be totally disregarded! Convincing them to change their mind is futile, as they believe they know best. There is no point in arguing with a fixed sign; you won't win.

⊙

SCORPIO SUN

The Sun is in Scorpio between October 24 and November 21, give or take a few days depending on the year. Scorpio Suns may seem like an enigma at first, but once you have earned their trust, some of that mystery lessens. At their core, they are incredibly loyal, intelligent, and purposeful. However, no matter how close you think you are with a Scorpio, there will always be things they keep hidden.

For those with a Scorpio Sun, every section in this chapter will apply to some degree. The Sun is the most powerful planetary force, so it has a huge impact on personality. While a Scorpio Sun may not have a Scorpio Moon, for example, they will undoubtedly find something in that section that they relate to.

Pure Scorpio Energy

Most of us have heard at least one Scorpio stereotype. In mainstream society, they are renowned for being "emo" and intense, but they are so much more than that.

★ Sleepover games like Two Truths and a Lie, Truth or Dare, and Never Have I Ever appeal to Scorpio. They love learning people's deepest, darkest secrets, what makes them tick, what their limitations are. However, when others ask Scorpio to reveal something about *their* inner world, mum's the word.

★ **Stereotypically, Scorpios are dark and moody.** Some reflect this in their appearance (think piercings, tattoos, and dark clothing), others in their taste in decor (skulls, antiques, velvet or gothic furniture), and still others in their special interests (horror movies, violent video games, true crime, or the occult). Regardless of how clean-cut a Scorpio may appear, rest assured they have a dark side.

★ **Scorpios are mysterious.** They keep things under wraps, especially personal information. Privacy is of the utmost importance to them, and they keep secrets from everyone, even their most trusted confidants. This allows them to maintain the upper hand.

★ **This is one of the most open-minded signs, though you might not expect it.** Scorpio's interests are off the beaten path, so they have an appreciation for and an understanding of those who are labeled "different." They are most comfortable with fellow outcasts, those who are misunderstood or deviate from social norms. Similarly, they may have taboo interests, such as reading tarot cards or practicing Wicca.

★ **Scorpios are wildly possessive of everything:** their belongings, their relationships, their innermost thoughts and feelings. They do not share, nor do they play well with others. Don't steal a fry off a Scorpio's plate, borrow their favorite sweater, hang out with their best friend, or pry for more information—these sorts of behaviors are perceived as a threat.

★ **Scorpios are marvelous investigators.** Give them a first name and a blurry photo from 2012 and, in no time, they can dig up the person's full name, occupation, and last known address. Friends often ask Scorpio to uncover more information about the person they are dating, and Scorpio loves every minute of it.

Gifts for a Scorpio Sun

Buying a gift for a Scorpio Sun is challenging because you will never know how they truly feel about it. Whether you've given them the greatest gift of all time or something they will immediately toss in the bin, their reaction will be the same.

★ **The best thing you can give a Scorpio is something you have heard them mention in the past.** For example, if the Scorpio in your life says, "Oh, I want to read that book," make a mental note to buy it another time. Likewise, objects, items of clothing, or experiences that Scorpio Suns point out are excellent future-gift material.

★ **Give them the gift of a solitary experience.** Scorpios value solitude; they need time to process their multitude of thoughts and feelings. Perhaps this is a credit for a massage, a full-service trip to the salon, a day pass to a museum, or a gifted enrollment in a community education class.

★ **If Scorpio has a pet, child, or partner, consider buying a gift that is customized to their loved one(s).** Personalized coffee mugs, jewelry, wall decor, and tchotchkes are meaningful to a Scorpio, even if they do find it all a little cringey.

★ **When all else fails, give Scorpio cash.** The fact of the matter is Scorpios are so much deeper than what we see on the surface, and that makes them hard to buy for. So play it safe. All of us appreciate a little extra dough.

So Your Boss Is a Scorpio Sun . . .

Truthfully, I would be terrified to have a Scorpio boss. Scorpios crave power, and they use a mixture of skill and subtle manipulation to secure it. A Scorpio in a higher-up position is a person who lets nothing get in their way.

★ **Never overtly challenge your boss.** This is not a boss who responds well to constructive criticism. Because your boss is your superior, they expect to be treated as such. If you have feedback you want to share with your boss, make a point to do so in a subtle way; try affirming what is working well instead of drawing attention to what isn't.

★ **Respect your boss's need for privacy.** Questions about their plans for the weekend may be innocent, but to your Scorpio boss, it feels like you're prying. If your boss volunteers personal information, it's okay to ask a follow-up question, but in general, respect work-life separation.

★ **Your boss will either be totally hands-off or a bit of a micromanager.** Scorpio is not good at finding balance between extremes. If your boss is a micromanager, prepare to have your work analyzed under a microscope. The best way to earn their trust is to be consistent and confident in your work. Eventually, when trust is earned, they will let you off the leash.

★ **Know that your boss is a keen observer.** Scorpios fly under the radar but are astutely aware of everything going on around them. If you are faced with a dilemma, your Scorpio Sun boss may have a unique perspective on the situation.

So Your Coworker Is a Scorpio Sun . . .

Scorpio coworkers are a tough nut to crack: They are friendly, but not warm; they care about their work, but they fly under the radar; they seem to be in their own little world, but they are remarkably observant. If you manage to befriend your Scorpio coworker, you should feel quite accomplished.

★ If you want to befriend a Scorpio Sun, there are three simple steps to follow: **Don't pry for details about their personal life, vow to share office gossip and secrets, and appreciate the slow burn.** Friendship with a Scorpio is not built overnight; it takes many interactions to earn their favor.

★ **Respect your Scorpio coworker's need for space.** It's always best to get consent before hugging a coworker or giving unsolicited advice, but especially so for a Scorpio Sun. Scorpios need space literally and figuratively: Respect their bubble, don't touch their stuff, and keep conversations work-related unless they willingly supply personal information.

★ **Scorpios like to be invited to things, though they often decline.** No matter how many times your coworker has shot you down, it's still best practice to invite them to lunch or happy hour. They probably won't go, but they grow resentful if they weren't invited in the first place.

★ **You may feel closer to your Scorpio coworker than you actually are.** Are they your friend, or are they just friendly? Do you know a lot about each other, or do they just listen as you overshare? The true measure of friendship with a Scorpio is how much of their personal life you have access to. Do you follow each other on Instagram? Have you ever been to their house or met up with them outside of work? Do you know the names of their partners, parents, and other loved ones? These are indicators of a true friendship.

So Your Partner Is a Scorpio Sun . . .

Scorpios are challenging partners. Loving a Scorpio is not for the faint of heart; this relationship will have intense highs and lows.

★ **Your partner craves control, and they will satisfy this craving one way or another.** If your partner has a healthy relationship to control, they will find satisfaction in choosing where to have dinner or what to watch on TV. Sometimes your partner's cravings for control are satiated by checking who you follow on social media and knowing your phone's current passcode. If your partner has an unhealthy relationship to control, they may try to dictate who you talk to or how you dress. If you find yourself in this dynamic, please seek professional help.

★ **No matter how well you think you know your partner, there is always more to discover.** Scorpios keep a lot of their thoughts and feelings to themselves. Most of the time, if you don't ask, they won't tell. Ironically, your partner will want to know everything about you. They will have no problem asking probing questions, though they may prickle if you do the same.

★ **Scorpios get jealous very easily.** To some degree, they view their partner as property. When others encroach upon what is "theirs," Scorpio
Suns become incredibly territorial. Your partner will want to vet all
your friends to ensure that none of them are secretly into you. If you
mention a coworker's name consistently, they will want to know what
that person looks like and if they are single. Scorpios expect you to be
totally devoted to them, though they will constantly question if you
are devoted *enough*.

★ **Your partner takes loyalty to the next level.** Once they have committed to a person, they do so with body, mind, and soul. Scorpio knows
the difference between being there *for* someone and being there *with*
someone. They will fight all your battles alongside you and defend
you unwaveringly, even if you are in the wrong.

★ **Your partner is incredibly observant.** Scorpios tend to be quiet and
withdrawn, but don't let this fool you: They are always listening and
analyzing. This doesn't just apply to their partner—Scorpios slowly
gather knowledge about everyone they meet, stockpiling tidbits of
information like a magpie collecting shiny objects for their nest.

☽
SCORPIO MOON

Whew! What a combination. The Moon rules emotion, and water signs are
notorious for being in tune with theirs. Scorpio is the most emotional of
the water signs, though they are incredibly private about their thoughts and
feelings. So, when the Moon is in Scorpio, there are volatile emotions buried
deep beneath the surface.

Scorpio Moons are most compatible with other water Moons (Cancer,
Scorpio, and Pisces). These are the only people who will be able to come
even remotely close to understanding Scorpio's emotional depth. While Cancer Moons are more easily wounded and Pisces Moons are more prone to
sadness, there is still a visceral understanding between fellow water Moons.

Scorpio Moons are least compatible with air Moons (Gemini, Libra, and Aquarius). Air Moons are quick to process and move on from life's highs and lows, which means they move at a breakneck speed compared to Scorpio Moons. Scorpio Moons need time to ruminate, lament, unpack, and sulk—and then they have to decide if they want to talk about it. Air Moons won't have the tolerance or fortitude to handle Scorpio Moon's moods, and Scorpio Moon will be offended by their surface-level passions.

Scorpio Moons may be compatible with earth Moons (Taurus, Virgo, and Capricorn) or fire Moons (Aries, Leo, and Sagittarius), though true compatibility will depend on Venus and Mars placements. Of the earth Moons, Scorpio is most compatible with Taurus, which is its cosmic opposite. Of the fire Moons, Scorpio is most compatible with Aries, as these signs used to share a planetary ruler and understand each other on a subconscious level.

Restorative Activities for a Scorpio Moon

You need a lot of time to process everything on your mind. It's best if this can be done in solitude. When in doubt, sequester yourself in a dark room and lie down to think.

★ **Visit a rage room.** Scorpios aren't prone to anger, per se, but this sign is prone to deep-seated resentment. Think about everyone who has ever done you wrong—or everyone who has done you wrong in the last few weeks—and release that frustration. Alternatively, hitting the gym can have a similar effect.

★ **Do something creative.** This could be tactile, like drawing, playing piano, or building something in the garage, or imaginary, like getting lost in a simulation video game or a guided meditation. More than likely, you are a deeply creative person, though you may not acknowledge this side of yourself. You don't have to share what you create with anyone—immerse yourself in the process.

★ **Go to therapy.** I know, I know—but your mind is always racing, and seeing a professional could really alleviate some of that mental pressure. If one-on-one therapy seems too overwhelming, consider group therapy: The spotlight won't be solely on you, plus you may learn people's deepest, darkest secrets!

★ **Spend time by or in water.** Take a bath, go swimming, sit by a lake, or make your lock screen a picture of the ocean. Water rules Scorpio, and this is a healing element for you.

★ **Tap into your spirituality.** Scorpio is an incredibly spiritual sign, and if you are not aligned with some sort of religious or spiritual belief system, I would encourage you to find one that resonates. A spiritual connection will bring fulfillment to your life, as Scorpio is the sign that dances between life and death. Worship or reflect in ways that resonate with your belief system.

Journal Prompts for a Scorpio Moon

You would benefit from journaling because it allows you to share your thoughts without anyone else having access to them. However, you value privacy, and your journal being leaked would be your worst nightmare, so you need to keep your journal locked away or in a password-protected document.

★ Who are you holding a grudge against? Why? When you read over the name(s) you wrote down, what do you feel in your body? A year from now, do you think you will feel differently?

★ What is one of your biggest regrets in life? When you think back on that moment, how do you feel? If given the chance, would you do anything differently? Can you think of a few ways that this regret actually benefitted you?

★ Write the word *love*. What phrases, memories, people, or objects come to mind? Now, write the word *ownership*. What phrases, memories, people, or objects surface for you? Was there any overlap between the two? If so, why do you think that is? If not, can you think of anything that feels like it belongs in both categories?

★ What is something no one knows about you? Why haven't you shared this with anyone? Do you think this is something you will share someday? Why or why not?

So Your Partner Is a Scorpio Moon . . .

Scorpio Moons aren't interested in flings, so if you're dating a Scorpio Moon, prepare to be in it for the long haul.

★ **Your partner is a very intense person.** They feel deeply, they think deeply, and they love deeply. A relationship with a Scorpio Moon is not for the faint of heart. Something you may consider inconsequential, like an out-of-the-blue text from an ex, is monumental to a Scorpio Moon. They are not overreacting, per se; they just experience life with the volume turned all the way up. While you may not understand it, the passion that Scorpio Moons possess makes life that much richer.

★ **When things get heated, Scorpio Moon may retreat.** They are more likely to ruminate privately than to melt down in front of their partner. It's crucial to allow them this time to reflect at their own pace. While you may be ready to apologize and move on, Scorpio Moon needs time to lick their wounds.

★ **You will be put through tests, either subtly or overtly.** This was especially evident at the beginning of your relationship; Scorpio Moons consider dating an act of trust, which means potential partners will be put through the wringer before a commitment can be established. Even after you have been dating for some time, your partner may test you to ensure that you are the right person for them. Do your best to be patient.

★ **Your partner has a keen eye**, and they pick up on things that the rest of us are totally oblivious to. They are especially sensitive to changes in mood or tone. Your partner may know something is bothering you before you do! Additionally, Scorpio Moons like to use their hidden knowledge to support and spoil their loved ones, making them remarkable and thoughtful gift givers.

★ **Never lie to your partner.** Nothing destroys Scorpio Moon's trust like a lie, even if it's a white lie. If Scorpio suspects you are lying, they will investigate, and the truth will come out one way or another. It is always better to be brutally honest than to stretch the truth.

★ **Patient lovers will be rewarded with the utmost devotion.** As a Scorpio Moon falls in love, they will begin to let their walls down one by one. Eventually, their tough exterior reveals one of the most tender, sensitive souls. Yes, it takes a lot of time to earn a Scorpio Moon's trust, but it is worth it.

↑

SCORPIO RISING

The rising sign is how we come across to people we have just met. Scorpio rising may be the easiest rising sign to identify, with Aquarius rising a close second. There is an air of mystery to Scorpio risings that draws people in, but they're hard to get to know.

Individuals with a Scorpio rising are naturally drawn to people with Taurus placements. Tauruses are equally as stubborn, but they are grounded and peaceable, which brings balance to Scorpio's highs and lows. Scorpio risings may have an inner circle full of Taurus friends and family members. Single Scorpio risings should seek out partners with Taurus placements.

Ways to Spot a Scorpio Rising

There are many stereotypes about Scorpio risings, though of course this sign can present in a multitude of ways. Remember that the "darkness" Scorpio risings embody may not be visible.

★ **Scorpio risings usually have at least one edgy aspect to their appearance:** tattoos, piercings, leather, dark colors (especially black), funky hair, bold makeup, or bold jewelry. But, in true Scorpio fashion, they might prefer to hide their edginess, which only adds to their aura of mystery.

★ **Scorpio risings are pretty quiet around new people and in groups.** They gravitate toward the edge of the room in social settings and are perfectly content to sit in silence. They never volunteer during presentations nor befriend strangers, though if you initiate contact with a Scorpio rising, they will begrudgingly engage in conversation.

★ **This is one of the most intimidating rising signs.** Scorpio risings are the strong and silent type, which can bring out others' insecurities and create internal discomfort. And Scorpio does this without having to lift a finger or say a word! Their power is that palpable.

Downsides of Being a Scorpio Rising

The intensity of a Scorpio rising may turn people off before they get a chance to know you. You may be the sweetest person, but if you glower at strangers, they won't stick around to find out.

★ **Others may see you as standoffish.** You prefer to keep things under wraps, and you don't share information easily. This "my lips are sealed" attitude can be frustrating and may make it especially difficult to develop friendships or secure a romantic partner.

★ **Your resting face is probably pretty unfriendly.** There's nothing wrong with that—you don't owe anyone a friendly face—but it may make you less approachable. This is something worth keeping in mind if you're trying to make a positive first impression.

★ **You are a very serious person at first meet**; it's unlikely that you will strike up a conversation with a stranger, and even less likely that you will start joking around. It's hard for you to let your guard down around new people, so you may come across as disengaged and uninterested. At times, you may have to fake it 'til you make it.

★ **Engaging in small talk is painful for you,** especially if you've been doing it for a while. It requires so much energy to keep small talk going, and you'd rather talk about something meaningful. You dread work events and first dates for this reason.

Using Your Scorpio Rising to Your Advantage

Up until this point, it's sounded like being a Scorpio rising is a bit of a downer, but that couldn't be further from the truth. There are a lot of perks to being a Scorpio rising!

★ **There is something absolutely spellbinding about you.** It's clear that you are much more than meets the eye. Scorpio risings are mysterious, which can be quite seductive. You may draw stares when you go out in public, and the bold may even approach. Use this to your advantage! You are more charming than you think.

★ **People feel safe confiding in you.** You seem trustworthy, and you tend to be quiet around new people, so much so that complete strangers may suddenly bare their soul to you. You have the demeanor of a therapist, listening and thoughtful. While you may not be the easiest person to get to know, this disposition makes it relatively easy for you to get to know others.

★ **No matter how unsure you may feel on the inside, you come across as strong and capable,** with your head held high. Without you even having to say a word, people know that they can rely on you. This is an excellent quality to have when applying for a new job or meeting a new client.

☿

SCORPIO MERCURY

Mercury is the planet of communication, but Scorpio isn't interested in sharing what's on their mind. Getting a Scorpio Mercury to open up is rare, and if they do, they're more likely to spin a yarn than to actually share their genuine thoughts and feelings.

Communicating with a Scorpio Mercury

There's no way around it: Conversation with a Scorpio Mercury will be unpredictable. If your loved ones have this placement, good luck getting a straight answer out of them.

★ **Do your best to balance the conversation.** If Scorpio asks you a question, ask them one in response. Never hog the spotlight, though Scorpio Mercury will repeatedly try to shine it on you. This is because they are more comfortable in the shadows, observing. If it was up to Scorpio Mercury, they wouldn't have to say a word.

★ **Scorpios like alternative methods of communication**—the more cunning, the better. For example, using a code to communicate is something they find intriguing. It's possible that they developed their own language to talk to siblings or close friends. They may have experimented with these alternative forms of communication when they were younger. Scorpio Mercury also enjoys riddles and deliberately vague communication, because if they have to work for it, it feels like it has more merit.

★ **For a Scorpio Mercury, there is much said in silence.** What *isn't* said? This is what they find most interesting. If there is a topic you are dancing around, they will home in on it. Don't bother trying to keep secrets from a Scorpio Mercury, because they will chip away at your resolve until you let the cat out of the bag.

★ **Scorpio Mercuries don't like ambiguous questions.** If you want to know something specific, ask something specific. If you don't ask a specific question, they won't give you the answer you're looking for. This is infuriating for the person asking the question, but for Scorpio, it's a fun little game.

★ **Scorpio Mercury is a formidable debate opponent.** There is no battle they cannot win, as they are predisposed to find others' weak spots. Moreover, they *enjoy* unraveling another's argument, so much so that others may deliberately avoid hot-button topics.

Questions to Ask a Scorpio Mercury

Truthfully, getting Scorpio Mercury to say more than a few words will be challenging. With that being said, it's worth a shot! The more intentional your question, the better your chance of getting a real answer.

★ If you had the power to be a fly on the wall at any point in time, which conversations would you eavesdrop on?

★ Have you heard any rumors about me? What were they? (Alternatively: "Have you heard any rumors about yourself? What were they?" Keep in mind that Scorpios don't really like talking about themselves, though.)

★ Who was your first enemy? (Alternatively: "Who was your first rival?" Not everyone has enemies, but most of us have butted heads with someone, even if it was during childhood.)

★ Where would you go if you woke up and discovered you had the power to read minds?

♀
SCORPIO VENUS

Venus is the planet of love and all things soft and tender. Typically, water Venuses are patient and nurturing. Though it is a water sign, Scorpio is known to be intense, more like a twenty-foot wave than the ebb and flow of the tide. This is because Scorpio is very protective of those they love.

Self-Love for a Scorpio Venus

You spend more time thinking about others than about yourself, whether you're wishing them the best or plotting their demise. What if you were the center of your own attention for a day?

★ **Write a letter to the younger version of yourself.** Before you begin, find a picture of yourself at a young age, ideally between five and eight. What would you tell yourself? What did you need to hear?

Write as long as you feel called to do so, then put the letter someplace safe and take a few minutes to ground your adult self in the present. Rest your hand on your chest and close your eyes. Can you feel the influence of your younger self still with you today? How can you honor your inner child going forward?

★ **Do something that makes you feel sexy.** Your connection to the sensual side of life is an important part of who you are. What makes you feel sexy when no one is around? Perhaps this means going by an alias online, buying and wearing something lacy under your everyday clothes, or sending a risqué text message. Whatever you choose, let it be a reminder that sensuality can be a solo journey.

★ **Release any resentments you are harboring.** Easier said than done, I know. Write down the names of the people who have hurt you, then (safely) set the pieces of paper on fire; make your own version of the *Mean Girls* Burn Book, for your eyes only; rant and rave in an audio message, then delete it. However you choose to release your grudges, keep harmlessness a priority. You don't have to hurt others to heal.

★ **Reestablish your devotion to yourself.** Have you lost sight of who you are underneath all the titles society has assigned to you? How can you restore your individualism? It might be time to pick up a new hobby or devise a harmless secret, something that is just for you—perhaps a tiny tattoo or a piercing in an area that's typically covered?

Seducing a Scorpio Venus

Seduction and Scorpio Venus go hand-in-hand, though Scorpio Venus is typically the one taking the reins. If you want to seduce a Scorpio Venus, you cannot be timid.

★ **Be brutally honest.** Scorpio Venus finds it incredibly attractive when people say what is on their mind—no dancing around topics nor guessing how someone feels. After all, Scorpio wants to be the mysterious one in the relationship. Remember that you can be brutally honest without being cruel. What would you say if you had no fear of being judged?

★ **Embrace your sexuality.** Scorpio Venus is not attracted to shame or insecurity; they are confident and sure of themselves, and they want a partner who can keep up with their desires. So wear the revealing clothing, flirt unabashedly, and don't be shy about saying what you want—Scorpio Venus will eat it up.

★ **Keep things exciting.** Dinner and a movie? Blah. Dates with a Scorpio Venus should be unique and exploratory. Have a picnic in the middle of the night, let the chef decide what meal you're ordering, or get walk-in tattoos. Scorpio Venus thinks life is too short for ordinary experiences.

★ **If you're feeling bold, confess your attraction.** Most of us like to know we are desired, but for Scorpio Venus, this is especially satisfying. Scorpio Venus wants to be lusted after; in fact, they may even want you to be completely obsessed with them. It's okay to be "thirsty" for a Scorpio Venus; behavior that turns off other placements is what turns them on.

So Your Partner Has a Scorpio Venus . . .

If you are partnered with a Scorpio Venus, there will be many emotional highs and lows. It takes a lot of patience to sustain a long-term relationship with a Scorpio Venus, but their devotion makes it all worth it.

★ **Your partner is incredibly possessive.** They adore you and want to make sure you are safe. Most of the time, their possessiveness is pretty mellow; they may bristle when someone expresses too much interest in you, for example. Sometimes, though, their possessiveness can become problematic. Ensure that the two of you have healthy boundaries so that you do not become enmeshed.

★ **Scorpio Venus is a sign that says "'til death do us part" and means it.** When things go awry, they hold on tighter. Tough conversations are not their thing, but they will go there if it's necessary to saving the relationship. They are very unlikely to terminate a relationship, because they have a soul bond with their partner; however, once they decide they're done, there is no convincing them to stay. If you end the relationship, know that they will never forgive you.

★ **Share your deepest, darkest thoughts with them.** Nothing is too shameful to share with Scorpio Venus. They have their own fair share of dark thoughts, so they get it. Similarly, you should never, ever keep secrets from your partner, because they will find out. Scorpio Venus would always prefer to hear the hard truth—they can handle it.

♂

SCORPIO MARS

Mars is the planet of passion, aggression, and sex. Prior to the discovery of Pluto, Mars ruled both Scorpio and Aries. For the last several decades, Scorpio's "official" ruler has been Pluto, but the sign still has strong associations with the planet Mars.[3] As such, Mars is comfortable in the sign of Scorpio and brings out its competitive side, making Scorpio Mars a fierce combination. There is nothing wishy-washy about this placement—they are all in or all out.

Scorpio Mars Behind Closed Doors

All Scorpio placements prefer to keep things hidden, and Scorpio Mars is no exception. There is a side to Scorpio that only comes out when the doors are locked and the lights are off.

★ **Scorpio Mars is aggressive, though not in an obvious way.** They are more subtle with their aggressive tendencies, but this roughness may come out in the way they flirt, joke, or have sex.

....

3   Karen Frazier, "Scorpio's Ruling Planet and How It Affects You," LoveToKnow, February 24, 2020, https://www.lovetoknow.com/life/astrology/scorpios-ruling -planet-how-it-affects-you.

★ *Power* and *control* are a Scorpio Mars's two favorite words. This applies
to every facet of their relationships, but especially to intimacy. Their
sex life is kinky—at least, it would be if it was solely up to Scorpio
Mars. There is nothing vanilla about this placement.

★ **Roleplay is fun for Scorpio Mars.** It's tantalizing to pretend to be
someone else, and it is even *more* tantalizing to watch a partner
pretend to be someone else. This may stay in the bedroom, or it may
not: Scorpio Mars and their partner may pretend to be strangers in
public, possibly even flirting with others before coming back together.
Scorpio Mars does not like to share, but sometimes it's fun to pretend
they do.

★ **Scorpio Mars is passionate about revenge.** If someone has hurt them
or a person they love, they patiently plot their comeuppance. For a
Scorpio, revenge can range from the minute to the catastrophic. This
is not a placement you should knowingly cross. On the flip side, loved
ones should know that Scorpio Mars will always have their back.

Things *Not* to Do to a Scorpio Mars

Scorpio Mars has a few triggers that bring out the worst in them: doubt, disagreement, and disrespect. While these are triggers for many people, they
morph Scorpio Mars into a totally different person.

★ **Don't become an obstacle.** Once Scorpio Mars has set their sights on
something, they will stop at nothing to get it. Whatever is in their
way will be demolished. Let's say you have a friend with a Scorpio
Mars, and you think they are about to make a mistake, so you tell
them so. Instead of appreciating the warning, Scorpio Mars will be
disgusted at your intrusion and will double down on their decision.
They will never admit you were right, and you may lose a friend in
the process.

★ **Don't speak poorly about people they respect.** It's normal to get
defensive when someone disses a friend or family member, but Scorpio's sensitivity extends to colleagues, teachers, and even admired

icons like celebrities. Scorpio Mars takes it all personally and may have a strong reaction—though to Scorpio Mars, their reaction is totally justified.

★ **Don't challenge them.** They are incredibly competitive; there is no such thing as friendly competition. Something as innocuous as "Hey, I bet I can beat you at this game" is equivalent to a declaration of war for a Scorpio Mars. They love to prove people wrong, and they will stop at nothing to do so, so expect them to play dirty in the name of victory.

★ **Don't try to control them.** Scorpio Mars rebels against control in any form, which means that setting boundaries and rules with a Scorpio Mars will be an uphill battle. It is better to focus on what you want them to do rather than on what you don't. For example, the sentence "You need to be home by midnight" will result in deliberate tardiness, whereas the sentence "I'd love it if you were home before I went to bed" will not.

Things a Scorpio Mars Probably Needs to Hear (But Definitely Doesn't Want To)

Getting you to change your behavior is about as likely as finding a needle in a haystack, but stranger things have happened!

★ **You take things too personally.** Most of your "enemies" are going about their lives totally unaware that they have wronged you. Not everything in life is a personal attack. Your life will be easier if you can remember that you are only the main character in *your* narrative.

★ **The tighter you hold on to people, the more they will want to leave.** If you have to force someone to stay, you would be better off without them. Letting go of relationships is hard for you, but not every relationship is meant to last a lifetime.

★ **It's okay to throw in the towel.** If you realize halfway into a fight that you actually agree with the other person, you can admit that you were wrong and move forward. You do not have to fight to the death. Save your passion for when it is truly warranted.

★ It's easy to forget that forgiveness goes both ways—it benefits the other person just as much as it benefits you. Holding grudges drains your energy and makes you bitter. You do not have to forget how someone hurt you, but you can choose to lay down your arms.

QUICK GUIDE TO
SCORPIO
PLACEMENTS

If someone in your life has Scorpio placements . . .

DO

★ Hold space for their dark side.

★ Respect their privacy.

★ Prioritize honesty and loyalty.

DON'T

★ Lie, cheat, or hide things—Scorpio is a world-class investigator.

★ Tell them what to do.

★ Bad-mouth them or anyone they care about.

Sagittarius is unlike any other sign because they embrace life's opposites: They're warm and friendly, yet they cherish their solitude; they're honest to a fault, yet they're lighthearted and goofy; they're down to try anything, though they're ambivalent about leading the charge. Sagittarius is just as comfortable on their own as they are in a group. Clearly, they embody the best of both worlds.

At their best, Sagittarians are honest, adventurous, and open-minded. Laughter is the best medicine, and they aren't afraid to be silly if it makes someone crack a smile. Imposter syndrome does not exist; they know they can be anything and do anything they set their mind to. They love to learn and explore. Sagittarians are world travelers who thrive in unfamiliar surroundings. Those without a passport prefer to travel intellectually and regularly get lost in a good book or a fantasy world of their own design.

At their worst, Sagittarians are flighty, unfocused, and harsh. While they are committed to telling the truth, their delivery can leave much to be desired, and sensitive loved ones may be rubbed the wrong way by Sagittarius's feedback. To some Sagittarians, no commitment is binding. Whether they have been married for decades or just moved to a new state, if they feel a calling to leave, it is only a matter of time before they listen. They are always on to the next adventure, gone before they have to witness the destruction in their wake.

Sagittarius rules the ninth house, which represents travel and higher education, among other things. If Aries is the child of the zodiac, Taurus is the preteen discovering the value of money, Gemini is the teenager preparing to leave home, Cancer is the twenty-something who craves a home of their own, Leo is the new parent, Virgo is the adult who has a tried-and-true routine, Libra is reestablishing their close relationships, and Scorpio is the adult coming to terms with mortality, then Sagittarius is the middle-aged adult who looks forward to all that is yet to come. There is so much more of the world that they haven't seen, so many things they haven't tried, and so many people they haven't met. They have expertise in a few areas of life, but they're also interested in what they don't know.

Sagittarius's symbol is the archer. Half-man, half-horse, the archer stands with his arrow drawn. There's confidence in his stance; he knows that his arrow will hit the mark, whether that's the actual target or something else he never expected. Wherever the arrow goes, the archer follows, trusting the process. Likewise, Sagittarius has patience for life's curveballs; what others may see as an ending, Sagittarius sees as a new beginning. What was an obstacle becomes an opportunity. This outlook on life keeps Sagittarius youthful no matter how many years they have been earthside.

The final fire sign of the zodiac, Sagittarius has much in common with Aries and Leo. All three fire signs are confident and bold, leaving a lasting impression on people they come in contact with. Fire signs chase a good time, so it is no surprise that they are far more comfortable feeling euphoria and rage than sadness and disappointment. Fire signs are hilarious, loving, and a bit scatterbrained, though they have a way of making their short attention span seem endearing. People are drawn to them like a moth to a flame.

Sagittarius is a mutable sign, like Gemini, Virgo, and Pisces. Mutable signs are fine letting others take the reins, but if no one else is stepping up, they'll fill the role of leader. Ultimately, they go with the flow. Mutable signs are not afraid of change and are quick to readjust when plans go awry. However, they have a hard time trusting stability.

⊙

SAGITTARIUS SUN

The Sun is in Sagittarius between November 22 and December 21, though the exact dates may change a bit depending on the year. Sagittarius Suns see life as one grand adventure. They seem fearless, for they are willing to charge headfirst into the unknown. And, for the most part, they *are* fearless. Mistakes are learning opportunities, not setbacks—failure is a state of mind.

For those with a Sagittarius Sun, every section in this chapter will apply to some degree. The Sun is the most powerful planetary force, so it has a huge impact on personality. While a Sagittarius Sun may not have a Sagittarius Mercury, for example, they will undoubtedly find something in that section that they relate to.

Pure Sagittarius Energy

Sagittarians are some of the friendliest, most open-minded people you will ever meet. They believe life has endless opportunities and see themselves as along for the ride.

- ★ **Sagittarius believes that true wealth comes through experience.** Their material possessions have far less value than the memories they have made and the corners of the earth they have explored. Unless they have Taurus or Capricorn placements, Sagittarians are unlikely to put money away for a rainy day—they'd rather use it to buy a plane ticket.

- ★ **Language is a hobby for Sagittarius.** They enjoy watching foreign television shows and movies and reading books translated from other languages. They may study a language other than their mother tongue, either in a higher education setting or via community programs, or they may learn a new language in their downtime.

★ **This is one of the most spontaneous signs of the zodiac.** Sagittarius is willing to try anything once; this is because they suffer from FOMO (fear of missing out). The last thing they want to do is miss out on a memorable experience, so they are far more likely to accept an invitation than to decline.

★ **Sagittarians are hard to pin down.** A nine-to-five job, a white picket fence, and a spouse and kids doesn't sound like the American dream to a Sagittarius—quite frankly, it sounds pretty stifling. Of course, Sagittarians do settle down, but they must have adventure in their life. They may switch jobs frequently, travel for work, or seek unconventional relationships or family structures. Alternatively, they may need plenty of alone time to explore whatever tickles their fancy.

★ **Learning is a lifelong endeavor for Sagittarians.** They feel called to pursue undergraduate, graduate, or doctoral degrees. However, academia may be too restrictive or rigid for them. Whether or not they pursue higher education, Sagittarius is always excited to learn something new. If they don't know the answer to something, they'll find out.

★ **Sagittarians are nonjudgmental listeners with a no-holds-barred attitude to feedback.** Their honesty can be abrasive at times. They don't mean to hurt anyone's feelings; they just don't see any point in beating around the bush. Only ask a Sag for their opinion if you're ready to hear hard truths.

Gifts for a Sagittarius Sun

When it comes to gifts, Sagittarius is not picky—they're simply touched that you thought of them. Keeping track of holidays, birthdays, and anniversaries is not their strong suit, so they're always pleasantly surprised when others remember their special dates.

★ **If you can afford it, book Sag a trip.** It doesn't have to be an all-inclusive stay somewhere exotic; a nearby city that Sagittarius has never explored is just as enticing. To keep costs low, buy them a ticket (or two) to an upcoming event that could easily turn into a day trip.

★ **When it comes to gag gifts, Sagittarius is the perfect recipient.** Sagittarians have a good sense of humor. They like to keep things light. Sometimes, giving and receiving gifts can be intense; there may be pressure to react a certain way or choose the "perfect" gift. But a gag gift is fun and unserious, which is exactly what Sagittarius likes.

★ **If you have an upcoming vacation planned, pick up a gift for the Sagittarius in your life.** Challenge yourself to go beyond traditional tourist gifts, like keychains and T-shirts. Think about cuisines that are popular in the place(s) you're visiting; is there a nonperishable spice, sauce, or seasoning that you could bring back with you? If you're struggling to think of ideas, visit local small businesses to see if you can find a handmade gift.

★ **Buy Sagittarius a book or two.** If you know what they like to read, great! If you don't, that's okay too—they're willing to give anything a chance. Ask a bookseller for recommendations, find a book that is similar to a movie or TV show they enjoy, or give them a copy of a book you liked. Keep in mind that their adventurous nature prefers fast-paced genres (action, fantasy, contemporary fiction, thriller) over "heavier" ones (historical fiction, classics, nonfiction).

So Your Boss Is a Sagittarius Sun . . .

It's uncommon for Sagittarius Suns to secure leadership positions because they don't like to stay in one place for long. If they have worked for the same company for a prolonged period of time, there must be variety in their work. Perhaps they work in a place where the day's tasks aren't predictable, where they can customize their work schedule to match their mood, or where they are promoted internally and acquire additional tasks.

★ **Your boss cherishes work-life balance.** They are more likely than other signs to encourage employees to take vacation time, and they practice what they preach. Don't be surprised if your boss takes weeks off at a time. They may even take a sabbatical.

★ **Develop a thick skin.** Your boss is more likely to deliver feedback in a blunt, honest way than to pair it with praise. Try not to take their delivery personally. They don't see any point in dancing around a topic, but their communication style can be abrasive to less-direct folks.

★ **Your boss has a lot of great ideas, though they may lose interest before seeing them to fruition.** This can impact your work if they are constantly pitching their ideas to you and expecting you to keep up—you may put weeks of work into something only for your boss to forget they brought it up in the first place. Make sure to clarify what your responsibilities are every time your boss shares a stroke of genius; take notes or save emails.

★ **When it comes to keeping your personal and professional life separate, Sagittarius bosses couldn't care less.** Tell them the intimate details of your life—or don't. They have no preference either way.

So Your Coworker Is a Sagittarius Sun . . .

Sagittarians are known to hop from job to job because staying put in one place becomes stifling for them. They thrive in versatile environments where their daily tasks are unpredictable or their hours are flexible. If your job is humdrum, you likely won't have a Sagittarius coworker for long, but if you play your cards right, they could be a friend for life.

★ **Your Sagittarius coworker should be your go-to person when you're having a foul day.** Sagittarians are kindhearted and optimistic, and they know exactly what to say to lighten the mood. Their natural friendliness extends to acquaintances and work besties alike, so don't be shy—say hello!

★ **Sagittarians will happily set work aside if a friend is in need.** Money isn't their motivator, and while they are loyal to the place they work to an extent, they will always choose people over profit. Don't hesitate to reach out if there is something they can do to support you.

★ **Sagittarius easily bounces between their authentic self and their professional persona.** You may not recognize the person sitting across from you when you hear them take a work call, but it's only a matter of time before they're back to their goofball ways. Likewise, relationships with Sagittarians effortlessly move from purely work-related friendship to a real-world connection. If there is a Sagittarius you would like to befriend, start asking them out to lunch and follow them on Instagram; it's smooth sailing from there.

★ **Your coworker may have a temper that flares from time to time.** Usually, they are able to talk themselves down by reminding themselves that it's just a job and it's not something that is worth getting upset about, or they may need to vent to someone outside of work. These heated moments seem very out of character because everyone is used to Sagittarius being a laidback team player—that's their preference too! They'll be back in their comfort zone in no time.

So Your Partner Is a Sagittarius Sun . . .

While some people daydream about their happily ever after, Sagittarians are more likely to fantasize about checking things off their bucket list. The last thing Sagittarius fantasizes about is settling down—there is so much they want to see and do. If you have managed to enter a committed relationship with a Sagittarius, surely it is an adventurous one.

★ **Cherish the fact that your partner is funny.** Sagittarians love to laugh and goof around—life is too short to be taken seriously. Of course, this can become irritating, especially if you're trying to have a somber conversation and your partner won't stop cracking jokes, but this is who they are. Their goofiness really is a gift because even on your worst days, you've got a partner who can make you smile.

★ **Prioritize exploration.** Sagittarius loves to travel and try new things. Take vacations often, even if you have to stay close to home to fit your budget. Visit new restaurants, discover hidden gems in the city you live in, and expand your palate. For a Sagittarius, variety is the spice of life.

★ **Don't take your partner's need for alone time personally.** While Sagittarians are incredibly outgoing, they also need a healthy amount of solitude. They use this time to think, decompress, and find inspiration. If you have space in your home to create a nook for your Sagittarius partner, they will love holing up there—having their own study, library, or office sounds like a dream.

★ **Your partner likely has a decent amount of friends, though they will start to become bored if they haven't socialized with anyone new in a while.** When they were single, they loved meeting new people—it scratched their itch for adventure. There are so many interesting people in the world, and Sagittarius loves being exposed to different ideologies. Encourage your partner to join a club or take up an activity where they will meet groups of people. As a couple, the two of you could join a league, participate in group therapy, or go to a convention.

☽

SAGITTARIUS MOON

When the Moon, the planet of emotion, meets Sagittarius, the explorer of the zodiac, the result is creative problem-solvers who don't like to wallow in one emotion for long. Sagittarius Moons are not the sort of people who feel sorry for themselves for weeks at a time—endings are beginnings, and they are on to the next adventure.

Sagittarius Moons are most compatible with other fire Moons (Aries, Leo, and Sagittarius). Together, fire Moons cycle through emotions quickly and prioritize restoring their happiness. Sagittarius Moons would do all right with air Moons (Gemini, Libra, and Aquarius) because they, too, would rather move on than wallow. However, air Moons won't have much tolerance for a fire Moon's frustrations.

Sagittarius Moons are least compatible with water Moons (Cancer, Scorpio, and Pisces). Water Moons will seem depressing and whiny to Sagittarius, whose utmost desire is to move on; Sagittarius Moon will seem insensitive and brusque to a water Moon, who needs a partner who can provide patient emotional responses.

Connections between Sagittarius Moons and earth Moons (Taurus, Virgo, and Capricorn) are hit-or-miss. Ultimately, compatibility—or lack thereof—will be influenced by other placements.

Restorative Activities for a Sagittarius Moon

The greatest thing you can do for self-care is chase your dreams. You do not benefit from standing still, so get out there!

★ **Go somewhere you have never been before.** This can be as simple or as elaborate as you'd like. Perhaps there is a restaurant down the street that you've been meaning to try, or you've got a free weekend for a quick trip to a new city. Whatever you choose to do, do it alone if possible. You are an adventurer at heart, and while it is nice to have a travel buddy, you learn the most about yourself when you fly solo.

★ **You are a lifelong learner, but you may not have time to satisfy your curiosities—make time.** Set aside a few hours to immerse yourself in something that you don't know much about. Whatever you choose, make sure it interests you. You could pursue something tangible (learning how to knit) or abstract (memorizing the *Game of Thrones* family tree); you could even go a more historical route (studying up on the Haitian Revolution, for example). Once you've selected your subject matter, listen to a podcast, read a book, watch YouTube videos, or reach out to an expert. By the end of the day, you'll feel energized and excited to share what you've learned.

★ **Go out with your friends.** Nothing revitalizes you like laughing with your people. Friendship should trump most of your commitments. The older we get, the harder it is for people's schedules to align, but do not let this deter you. Meet with friends one-on-one in the meantime, but continue to push for a large group get-together. When it finally happens, you will all wonder why you waited so long.

★ **Get your hands dirty.** If you have a yard and the weather is nice, spend several hours interacting with Mother Nature. Mow the lawn, work on your garden, or pull some weeds, then simply enjoy the fresh air. If you do not have a yard or it is the winter season, engage with nature indoors by repotting one of your plants, cleaning your plants' leaves, or fertilizing their soil. If you don't have a green thumb, buy some flowers at the supermarket and keep them in a vase on your kitchen table. Caring for plants is incredibly restorative for a Sagittarius Moon.

Journal Prompts for a Sagittarius Moon

This placement is unlikely to have a robust journaling practice; you are more likely to scrapbook your travels or send hour-long voice memos to a friend. In your mind, these are more efficient ways to reflect. If you are interested in journaling—or if you are one of the rare Sagittarius Moons who already keeps a journal—these prompts are worth exploring.

★ Make two lists. The first should be a realistic list of all the things you would like to do in the next year, factoring in financial limitations and time constraints. The second list does not need to be realistic in the slightest—what would you achieve in the next year if there were no holds barred? When you've finished writing, compare the two lists. What do they have in common? Are there sensible ways you can work toward the second list, the list of your dreams, in the next year?

★ What makes you feel stifled? Are there people, places, or activities that make you feel restricted? Why do you think that is? What makes you feel free? Are there people, places, or activities that feel expansive and full of possibility? How can you prioritize freedom in your everyday life?

★ When do you feel most alive? Why, do you think? Has this always been the case, or is it a recent discovery? Do you share this aliveness with others, or is it a private endeavor? If you shared it with another (or, conversely, pursued it alone), do you think that would make a difference? Try sharing or sequestering what makes you feel alive, then reflect on how it affected you.

★ Imagine that you have just woken up in a new city with no memory of who you were before. Your slate has been wiped clean, and it is impossible to reunite with the life you've left behind. In this new reality, who would you become?

So Your Partner Is a Sagittarius Moon . . .

Sagittarius Moons loathe being bored. They do not want to do the same routine for the rest of their life. Partners with Sagittarius Moons must be allowed to roam, or the relationship will become suffocating.

★ **Your partner is brutally honest.** This is a blessing and a curse. You will always know how they feel, but it will hurt your feelings at times. Sagittarius Moons are not the most sensitive listeners, and they automatically leap into problem-solving mode. Clearly state what you need from your partner before opening up: Do you want feedback, or do you just need to vent?

★ **Plan regular dates, and make sure each one is unique.** Date your partner as long as the two of you are together—never stop pursuing them. Be creative in your pursuit. Sure, dinner and a movie is nice once in a while, but if all your dates are the same, your partner will feel unappreciated and bored senseless. Go camping, visit a farmer's market, or paint pottery.

★ **Save for vacation.** While some people constantly set aside money for a rainy day or a retirement fund, Sagittarius Moons want to see the world *now*. They look forward to leaving behind everyday life for a few days (or weeks, if you've got the budget). Yes, it's smart to have an emergency fund, and bills and home improvements can usurp travel. But even if you are only setting aside twenty dollars a month, it's *something*, and that keeps Sagittarius's fire stoked.

★ **Take a class as a couple.** Learn to salsa dance, join an improv group, or become CPR certified. Sagittarius Moons are eager lifelong learners. They thrive in environments where they are exposed to new things— all the better if they have a partner who is along for the ride! These experiences will bring you closer together.

★ **Ensure laughter is the foundation of your relationship.** Play, explore, and humor your inner child. Surely, your partner has a sense of childlike wonder. Life is too short to be serious all the time! Sagittarius Moons love releasing their inhibitions and remain youthful at all stages of life. They believe you are never "too old" for something, and they flourish when their partner has the same attitude.

↑
SAGITTARIUS RISING

The rising sign is how we appear to people when we first meet them; our rising sign characteristics may have nothing in common with our true personality. Sagittarius risings tend to be extroverted, friendly, and funny. Others find Sagittarius risings easy to talk to. Strangers quickly become acquaintances or friends.

Sagittarius risings should seek out those with Gemini placements. Sag risings are drawn to Gemini's wit and the way they flit through life. There is something exciting about this pairing, and the relationship feels easy, whether it is romantic or platonic. Both signs love to have a good time.

Ways to Spot a Sagittarius Rising

It's usually easy to identify a fire rising sign: They are charismatic, loud, and confident. With that being said, Sagittarius is the quietest of the three fire signs.

★ **Sagittarius risings are always part of the crowd.** They likely won't be the center of attention, but they certainly won't be hiding in the shadows. They like to be in the know, which means they have to be comfortable mingling.

★ **Sagittarius risings laugh often.** They love to add humor to a conversation, with their jokester status only surpassed by Gemini risings. If someone is constantly telling jokes, it's a safe bet that they are either a Gemini or Sag rising. To distinguish between the two, assess the subject matter of the joke: If it's witty or a play on words, the person is likely to be a Gemini rising; if it's blunt or a roast, you've found a Sagittarius rising.

★ **Have you ever gotten feedback that stung? You may have been talking to a Sagittarius rising.** They don't sugarcoat things, which means they tend to forgo niceties. Sag rising tells it like it is, social norms be damned. This brutal honesty can be jarring, but at least you always know what they're thinking.

Downsides of Being a Sagittarius Rising

Every rising sign comes with its own unique set of challenges.

★ **Others may assume you are flaky.** Sagittarius is a mutable sign, which means you may go with the flow but have a hard time following through. Peak Sagittarius rising energy is telling someone, "Yes, we definitely need to catch up soon!" and then never messaging them.

★ **Your humor may rub people the wrong way.** You love to tell jokes, no matter the setting, but not every situation lends itself well to humor. Others may think your jokes are inappropriate or insensitive. To a Sag rising, every conversation topic can be a punchline.

★ **First impressions may be misleading.** Sag risings seem extroverted and adventurous, but in reality, you could be a quiet homebody who is afraid of airplanes. Those who truly get to know you may be shocked to discover you are not nearly as outgoing as you first appeared. Ask someone who knows you well what their first impression of you was and how well their assumptions about you held up as they got to know you.

★ **You can seem like a know-it-all at times.** Sagittarius risings know a little about a lot, meaning they'll chime in with their two cents at any given opportunity. Fun facts keep conversation flowing, but some people may feel insecure about their perceived lack of knowledge.

Using Your Sagittarius Rising to Your Advantage

There are loads of benefits to having a fire rising sign, especially Sagittarius, which is an adaptable sign that appears easygoing.

★ **Others perceive you as fearless.** There is a sense of adventure about you—you don't shy away from the unknown. You aren't afraid to look silly, and you know failure is an opportunity to try again, so you approach new experiences with confidence. In fact, you are so confident that you seem to skip the novice stage entirely. Onlookers will envy your natural fortitude.

★ **You get away with telling it like it is.** While other rising signs think before they speak, you don't, and others have come to accept this about you. You are likely notorious for your bluntness, but you're so charming that this bluntness is seen as an asset rather than a flaw.

★ **Others like being around you.** Sagittarius risings don't take life too seriously; you think small talk should be enjoyable, so you keep conversations light. Others will warm up to you easily, which is a benefit when dating, interviewing for a new job, or giving a presentation. You're quite likable!

★ **You seem very worldly.** Whether or not you've traveled the globe, your knowledge is vast, and others are impressed by it. Your life experiences have shaped you into a well-rounded person, and as such, you come across as intelligent, capable, and experienced, especially to non-peers. Parents see you as a brilliant role model, and children are fascinated by you.

☿

SAGITTARIUS MERCURY

Mercury is the planet of communication, and when it combines with straightforward Sagittarius, individuals are honest to a fault.

Communicating with a Sagittarius Mercury

Sagittarius is a fire sign, and like most fire signs, it is effortlessly charismatic. It's also a mutable sign, meaning it goes with the flow. Thus, conversation with a Sagittarius Mercury should be a breeze.

★ **Nothing is off-limits for a Sagittarius Mercury.** Conversation topics that others might consider taboo are fair game. This is a refreshing quality in a friend or partner because it can lead to deeper conversations and increased intimacy. On the other end of the spectrum, however, Sag Mercury may make inappropriate or off-color comments that are embarrassing at best.

★ **Sagittarius Mercury likes to sprinkle fun facts throughout a conversation.** They are a wealth of knowledge waiting to be shared. Talking to a Sag Mercury is a bit like watching a game of *Jeopardy!*—you can learn so much if you just pay attention.

★ **Humor is a huge part of Sag Mercury's communication style.** They love puns, jokes, and one-liners. While laughter is healing for Sagittarians, most people can only tolerate so much horseplay. If you're going through a tough time, you would be better off finding someone else to confide in, as Sagittarius will be unable to resist finding the humor in the situation.

Questions to Ask a Sagittarius Mercury

It's relatively easy to get to know a Sagittarius Mercury. If conversation stalls, ask them about their travels.

- ★ What is on your bucket list?

- ★ Where is your favorite place you've traveled? Why?

- ★ What do you like to do in your free time? Are there any hobbies you're hoping to pick up in the next few months?

♀
SAGITTARIUS VENUS

When Venus, the planet of love and pleasure, meets spunky Sagittarius, individuals crave freedom in even their most intimate relationships.

Self-Love for a Sagittarius Venus

A key component of feeling balanced as a Sagittarius Venus is spending time on your own. This is a very independent placement.

- ★ **Take yourself on a date.** Where would you go if you didn't have to take anyone else's preferences into account? Perhaps you would like to visit a brewery, browse a local bookstore, or go for a walk. Making time in your schedule for activities that are solely individual pursuits would be healing for you.

- ★ **Read a fantasy book or watch a fantasy television show or movie.** The sign of Sagittarius is curious and idealistic, so the world-building of the fantasy genre sucks you right in, and frequent conflicts hold your attention. Whatever storyline format you choose, allow yourself to become fully immersed in this new world by limiting outside distractions. Even if you only allow yourself to escape the mundane for a few minutes, you will return to everyday life feeling refreshed.

★ **Meditate.** Sagittarius is the most introverted of the fire signs because it knows there is much wisdom to be found in isolation. Get comfortable, close your eyes, and be still. If meditating is challenging, practice in small increments. You may find it easier to meditate with some sort of noise in the background; search for meditative playlists online.

Seducing a Sagittarius Venus

Seducing a Sagittarius Venus is much easier than managing to hold on to one. The sign of Sagittarius is constantly chasing whatever brings them happiness, so they enjoy falling in love—but the hard stuff that comes after? Not so much.

★ **Sagittarians are attracted to novelty.** Dating someone who is predictable is a turnoff. They will not be flattered if you send a good morning text every day—they think these sorts of things lose all meaning if they're expected. You see, they cannot be bothered with routines that build intimacy, like texting or calling regularly. Do not expect to have constant communication with a Sagittarius Venus. If virtual contact is important to you, you will have to be the one initiating it. Keep conversation interesting to increase the likelihood of a reply.

★ **It is difficult to get a Sagittarius Venus to commit to anything**—a conversation, a date, a relationship. This is because Sagittarius Venus is drawn to the chase; they like to play games with prospective partners. Their intentions aren't cruel, though this does not minimize the hurt feelings they can leave in their wake. If you want to seduce a Sag Venus, play hard to get—but not *too* hard to get, because they will eventually lose interest.

★ **Sagittarius Venus is attracted to people who are full of life.** Bubbly, cheerful extroverts are their type. They will have a hard time connecting with people who are quiet, shy, or insecure. Additionally, people who want to talk about heavy, emotional subjects will be avoided. Sag Venus believes dating should be fun, so they will pursue relationships that feel playful and unserious.

So Your Partner Has a Sagittarius Venus . . .

Long-term relationships with a Sagittarius Venus can prove challenging due to their constant need for excitement. However, if you live a hectic life, your relationship may stand the test of time because your love will provide much-needed respite.

★ **Above all else, your relationship should be fun for both of you.** This is harder than it sounds. All relationships go through "slower" seasons, when life is simply not very interesting, but this is complicated by the fact that Sagittarius Venus is easily bored. To a Sag Venus, life is one grand adventure, and if their relationship begins to feel stagnant, they may develop a wandering eye. To counteract boredom, keep the friendship in your relationship alive. If you and your partner are truly best friends, even the slowest season will be filled with love and laughter.

★ **Commit to being lifelong adventure buddies.** Travel often, whether you stay local or go global. Have your partner be your plus-one to every event, even the ones that sound boring—they'll find a way to make it fun. Find new ways to tackle everyday tasks: You could take turns making dinner, or you could do rock-paper-scissors to see who's cooking that night. (Sag Venus prefers the latter.) Capriciousness will deepen your connection and satisfy Sagittarius Venus's wanderlust.

★ **Never lose sight of each other's individualism.** Sagittarius Venus needs to feel like a fully functional person on their own, and they want their partner to as well. It is important for each of you to have your own hobbies, groups of friends, and professional interests. This way, when you reunite, you have plenty to discuss, and you can learn from each other. Sagittarius Venus wants to believe that there is always more to discover about their partner; they crave a multidimensional relationship.

♂
SAGITTARIUS MARS

Mars, the planet of passion, aggression, sex, and chaos, is a fiery planet. When Mars is in a fire sign like Sagittarius, expect sparks to fly.

Sagittarius Mars Behind Closed Doors

The sign of Sagittarius is renowned for its boldness, socially *and* physically.

★ **Sexually, Sagittarius Mars is adventurous.** They are willing to try just about anything at least once. Ideally, their love life is spontaneous and fun; there is potential for voyeurism, exhibitionism, or inviting others into the bedroom. For a Sag Mars, nothing extinguishes desire like sexual routine.

★ **This Mars sign may be prone to bursts of rage, though they simmer down in no time.** Fire signs have a bit of a temper, but Sagittarius is mutable, so their flame quickly fizzles. After all, Sag Mars is self-sufficient—simply give them space to cool off.

★ **It is challenging for a Sagittarius Mars to commit to things.** They like keeping their schedule open in case something better comes along. This applies to more than friendly get-togethers; often, it extends to their love life. Sag Mars requires a flexible, laidback partner who respects the fact that they will always require room to roam.

Things *Not* to Do to a Sagittarius Mars

Though this placement can be intense at times, Sagittarius is the most easygoing of the fire signs.

★ **Do not force them to abide by rules or routines.** Sagittarius Mars likes to get things done on their own time and in their own way. They may follow others' lead to keep the peace, but only for so long—eventually, their patience will run out.

★ **Do not ask too many questions about the future.** Sagittarius Mars prefers to live in the here and now, so being pressured to answer questions about the future frustrates them. They know the future is unpredictable, and that's the way they like it.

★ **Do not take them too seriously.** This Mars placement is fun and feisty, and they live life with a healthy dose of reckless abandon. They enjoy getting a reaction out of others, and they will go to great lengths to do so.

Things a Sagittarius Mars Probably Needs to Hear (But Definitely Doesn't Want To)

Unless you have strong earth sign placements, you will struggle to mitigate feelings of restlessness.

★ **Commitment is a part of life.** Even choosing not to commit to something is a commitment in its own right. So is it actually commitment that is unappealing, or is it the fact that someone, somewhere is depending on you? This is something that can be worked through if you are willing.

★ **There is comfort to be found in predictability.** This may seem anathema to you, but knowing exactly when something is going to happen, or exactly how someone is going to react, can provide respite in an overwhelmingly unpredictable world. Even if you yourself do not need this stability in your life, consider the needs of your loved ones. Being predictable for the ones you love is a worthy sacrifice.

★ **Do not take your loved ones for granted.** No matter how many times you cancel plans, they continue to extend an invitation; no matter how silly you are, they still take you seriously. The wrong people would grow frustrated by your shenanigans, but you have managed to find a real support system. Cherish it.

QUICK GUIDE TO
SAGITTARIUS
PLACEMENTS

If someone in your life has Sagittarius placements . . .

DO

★ Support their need for exploration.

★ Encourage their myriad of interests.

★ Appreciate their sense of humor.

DON'T

★ Threaten their independence.

★ Expect them to adhere to social norms, time constraints, or schedules.

★ Ask them for advice unless you're prepared to hear their honest, unfiltered opinion.

★ 10 ★
CAPRICORN

I have seen dozens of posts online about how Capricorns don't believe in astrology. After going on dates with multiple Capricorns, I can confirm that most of them think astrology is nonsense. Regardless of whether or not a Capricorn believes in the metaphysical, there are key takeaways in this stereotype: This sign prefers to focus on the tangible. Plus, before they make up their mind about something, Capricorn will want to gather their own evidence.

At their best, Capricorns are hard-working, forward-thinking, and practical. They keep their eyes on the prize and rarely let things keep them down. Capricorns have a drive for success that is unmatched. They will work long hours, giving it all they've got, and then go home and work on themselves. Capricorns are high achievers who have set even higher standards for themselves. This sign is also pretty selfless—family-oriented Capricorns work hard with the intention of their loved ones reaping the rewards.

At their worst, Capricorns are close-minded, stern, and somber. In general, Capricorn is the most solemn zodiac sign—it is ruled by Saturn, the "fatherly" planet of responsibility, authority, and discipline—and unsurprisingly, many Capricorns have lost touch with their inner child. They may not know how to be silly or enjoy the simple pleasures in life. Others have a hard time understanding why Capricorn is so serious all the time.

Capricorn rules the tenth house, the house of career. If Aries is the child of the zodiac, Taurus is the preteen discovering the value of money, Gemini is the teenager preparing to leave home, Cancer is the young adult settling down, Leo is the new parent, Virgo is the established adult, Libra is refocusing on their personal relationships, Scorpio is the adult entering middle age and coming to terms with mortality, and Sagittarius is the lifelong learner looking forward to the future, then Capricorn is the adult at the pinnacle of their career. A lifetime of hard work is finally paying off. However, no matter how successful Capricorn becomes, they will always desire more. Anything less than complete and utter mastery is unsatisfactory. Besides, Capricorn is used to having their nose to the grindstone—that is how they are most comfortable.

The symbol for Capricorn is the sea goat. Like this mythical creature, Capricorn adapts to the present circumstance and will make do. When Capricorn's symbol is discussed, it is the goat aspect that is typically highlighted, and there is good reason for this: Goats are notorious for climbing to unprecedented heights, easily navigating surfaces that appear impossible to scale. Goats are undeterred by even the steepest of precipices, and similarly, Capricorns will make their way to the top one way or another—failure is not an option.

This tenaciousness may be due in part to the fact that Capricorn is an earth sign. Earth signs (Taurus, Virgo, and Capricorn) are grounded, solid, and determined. They tend to be family-oriented and committed to their responsibilities and relationships. Capricorn is the most driven of the three earth signs (followed closely by Virgo) and also the most persistent. Whereas Taurus will take a break when confronted by obstacles and Virgo will pause to create a plan, Capricorn does not even slow down. Instead, they blast through an obstacle without so much as a backward glance.

It makes perfect sense that Capricorn is a cardinal sign. Cardinal signs (Aries, Cancer, Libra, and Capricorn) are constantly moving forward. They refuse to let anything stand in their way and are excellent problem-solvers. Cardinal signs bounce back from devastation faster than mutable and fixed signs, and they do so without any assistance. They stand on their own two feet, dust themselves off, and persevere.

⊙

CAPRICORN SUN

The Sun is in Capricorn from December 22 to January 19, give or take a few days depending on the year. Capricorn Suns are incredibly devoted people. Whether they are devoted to their loved ones, their career, or a passion project, they let nothing stand in their way. Capricorns have a grit that most signs can only dream of; they overcome obstacles that would halt most people in their tracks. There is a lot to admire about this Sun sign.

For those with a Capricorn Sun, every section in this chapter will apply to some degree. The Sun is the most powerful planetary force, so it has a huge impact on personality. While a Capricorn Sun may not have a Capricorn Mars, for example, they will undoubtedly find something in that section that they relate to.

Pure Capricorn Energy

Capricorns are easy to identify because they're always busy. Usually, they're working. On holidays, for example, they're more likely to take overtime than attend family get-togethers, especially if they are single.

★ **Capricorns are very sarcastic.** If they like to laugh or goof around, their sense of humor will be dry, so much so that acquaintances will be unable to tell they are joking. Unless they have strong Gemini or Leo placements, Capricorns will rarely be described as "funny"; instead, a plethora of antonyms will come to mind. Because Capricorns are very task-driven, humor is the last thing on their mind.

★ **Capricorns have physical hobbies that others deem arduous.** For example, they may enjoy fixing up cars, repairing broken items, doing yard work, or going for lengthy runs. This is because Capricorns are happiest when they feel productive. Restoring an object to pristine condition or keeping things in tip-top shape satisfies them more than any emotional, intellectual, or social pursuit ever could.

★ **Family is Capricorn's top priority.** They are usually very close to their parents, siblings, or extended family, and this makes them extremely protective. If Capricorns have a family of their own, or if they start one someday, they will deem themselves responsible for everyone else's well-being. They work hard so that they can ensure comfortable lives for their loved ones. Do not be surprised if a single Capricorn regularly talks about their future children—in fact, they may already be saving for their college funds!

★ **Capricorn is a very traditional sign.** They often find themselves in a stable career with a spouse, children, and at least one family pet, in a nice home surrounded by a white picket fence. If they aren't there yet, that is the ideal they are working toward. Whereas some signs daydream about travel or adventure, Capricorn is perfectly fine right where they are, thank you very much.

★ **In accordance with their serious, traditional nature, few Capricorns have tattoos or piercings.** If they do choose to get a tattoo, it will be small and tasteful, and of course easily coverable. Most Capricorns like to look polished, which may make them seem old-fashioned or dull. There is more to them than meets the eye.

★ **It is quite common for a Capricorn to be a small business owner.** They don't want to work for someone else because they are sure they could do a better job. Thus, they become their own boss. Capricorns have the stamina and wherewithal to get their own business up and running. They put in the work necessary to keep a business afloat and have a hard time passing the reins to anyone else. When the time comes to step down, they will keep their foot in the door, for Capricorns never truly retire.

Gifts for a Capricorn Sun

Capricorns rarely spend money on themselves, and many are uncomfortable receiving gifts. However, everyone deserves to be spoiled now and then, so do not let a Capricorn dissuade you from buying them something nice.

★ **Buy Capricorn one of those kits to brew your own beer or, for non-alcoholic Capricorns, kombucha.** Capricorn loves seeing the fruits of their labor pay off, and they will enjoy tweaking their batches until they're just right.

★ **When in doubt, buy Capricorn a practical gift card.** While some signs enjoy receiving gift cards to luxurious destinations, like the spa, Capricorns will balk at such a gift. They are uncomfortable being pampered, even on someone else's dime. Instead, buy them a gift card to a place they go on a regular basis: to the grocery store, perhaps, or the gas station. This sort of thing is deeply appreciated by Capricorn.

★ **Capricorns refuse to spend money unless it is absolutely necessary and tend to keep things until they are totally useless.** Even after something is beyond repair, Cap may hang on to the item in hopes of one day restoring it to its former glory. For this reason, home decor and household items are wonderful gifts for a Capricorn. If you have noticed that their favorite sweater is becoming threadbare, or if they have complained about the suction of their vacuum, buy them a new one.

★ **Acquiring a new skill is great fun for a Capricorn, and they prefer to be self-taught.** If there is a hobby they've expressed interest in, find a way to help support it. Perhaps they have mentioned that they wish they knew how to sew; you could buy them a nice pair of fabric shears or a secondhand sewing machine. If they expressed interest in learning a new language, consider signing them up for a community education course. Carpentry and woodworking are of interest to Capricorn, as they'd rather make everything by hand than buy it from someone else; see if there a local business where they could try their hand at these skills.

★ **Most earth signs love being surrounded by plants.** Capricorns see plants as just another thing to take care of, but most Cap Suns do enjoy having something to nurture, especially if they do not have a family of their own yet. Plus, if Capricorn travels for work or puts in long hours, plants may be the closest thing to a "pet" that they can manage. Buy them a low-maintenance plant, like a pothos, just to be safe, and make sure to include clear care instructions.

So Your Boss Is a Capricorn Sun . . .

I am not surprised in the slightest. Capricorns tend to make their way to the top of an organization because of their strong work ethic and their loyalty to the company. They are perfectly fine working for the same business for most of their life—in fact, that's their preference. With each passing year, they ascend to yet another position of power.

★ **Your boss expects you to work hard.** They will be displeased if they walk past and see you checking your phone, browsing the web, or chitchatting. This is not to say that you should fake productivity for their sake, but you should be mindful of how you come across—your boss is the one conducting your performance review, after all.

★ **Explanations usually fall on deaf ears.** Even if you have a perfectly valid reason for being late, it is all the same to your Capricorn boss: *excuses.* If you need to extend a deadline, take an unexpected day off, or push back a meeting, you should clearly communicate that in writing as soon as you realize there may be an issue. It is better to ask for extra time and complete a job well done than to rush to finish or—worse yet—miss a deadline completely.

★ **Excellent work will be rewarded with curt praise, a reasonable wage increase, and heightened expectations.** No matter how well you perform, your boss will not shower you with positive feedback—to them, that sort of support is unnecessary, coddling even. In fact, most

Capricorn bosses believe that too much praise can lead to laziness, and as such, they are cautious about saying anything that may lower your work performance.

★ **Capricorns rarely take time off.** They will be the first one in the office and the last one to leave. Capricorn bosses forget that most employees clock out at a certain time and take vacations. Work-life balance simply does not apply to a Capricorn. They send emails at 9:00 p.m. and on weekends. Be sure to clarify with your boss whether or not you are expected to check your email after business hours. If your boss expects you to constantly be "on the clock," they should compensate you accordingly.

So Your Coworker Is a Capricorn Sun . . .

Cap Suns often choose careers where there is plenty of opportunity for advancement. They are drawn to fields like business, science, and finance because they are more comfortable working with software, numbers, and spreadsheets than people.

★ **This is a person you should befriend, because you may be working for them someday.** Capricorn Suns climb the career ladder quickly, though they make it look effortless. They will become restless or frustrated if they haven't advanced recently, which will motivate them to ask for a performance review or to seek employment elsewhere.

★ **Your coworker takes their job seriously.** Whereas some signs embody the motto "I do not live to work, I work to live," Capricorn is the polar opposite. Their job is a source of great pride and passion for them. They will become offended if you consistently rag on the company you both work for, as Capricorn Suns think complaints should be taken right to the top. So, if you need to vent, find a different coworker.

★ **Your coworker's office space will be pretty sterile.** They prefer to keep surfaces neutral and uncluttered. Decorating with personal items is the last thing on their mind. They may put up a photo or two, but for the most part, their surroundings will give nothing away. It may be hard to get to know them or learn about their personal life, in part due to their lack of customization.

★ **Capricorn coworkers are willing to get lunch once in a while, but they'll want to head back to work as soon as the lunch hour ends.** Taking a longer break makes them feel uneasy, like they are doing something wrong. Cap Suns hold themselves to an incredibly high standard and are rigid about following the rules, even if your workplace does not uphold them.

So Your Partner Is a Capricorn Sun...

Some signs find Capricorn Sun stuffy or distant. However, there is incomparable stability to be found in a Capricorn partner.

★ **Success will always be your partner's first love.** They find it exhilarating to cash a check that they worked hard for or to surpass a record they set previously. Capricorns are high-achieving individuals. This is something you must learn to love about your partner if you want your relationship to stand the test of time; otherwise, you may grow resentful. Do not discourage their drive. Instead, be an enthusiastic cheerleader. Their work ethic should add to your attraction to them, not detract from it.

★ **Your partner is competitive**—they want to be the best in everything they do. When Capricorn Sun plays a game, they play to win. They also seek to be the best version of themselves. Often, they put pressure on themselves to be more successful than their siblings or parents. For example, if their mother has a master's degree, they'll shoot for a doctorate. Because of this, your partner may become discouraged if they have not met certain goals they set for themselves. Remind them that winning isn't everything, and they have all the time in the world.

★ **Your partner holds themselves to an incredibly high standard, and they may have similar expectations for you.** They prefer to date people who are motivated and driven. In fact, the busier Capricorn's partner, the better, because then Capricorn doesn't have to spend so much time tending to the relationship. Capricorn Sun loves nothing more than chatting about what you've accomplished that day, month, or year. Setting yearly goals for yourselves, both individually and as a couple, is a wonderful bonding activity.

★ **Relaxation does not come naturally to your partner.** You will have to encourage them to take vacation days, to spend money on themselves, and to do things purely for fun. Capricorn Sun's main connection to joy and play is their partner; a relationship should feel safe enough for them to let their hair down. Encourage this as much as you can.

☽
CAPRICORN MOON

The Moon is the planet of emotion, and Capricorn is the sign of rigidity and responsibility. When the Moon is in Capricorn, emotions will be observed rather than felt. Capricorn Moons prefer to handle emotions logically: They assess the situation, problem-solve, and process privately, in that order. Capricorn Moons rarely act on their emotions, and they are unlikely to share how they are feeling unless prompted; even then, they will have a detached response. Regardless of an individual's Sun sign, their Capricorn Moon will dull their emotional reactions. For example, they may seem extraordinarily calm in distressing situations.

Capricorn Moons are most compatible with other earth Moons (Taurus, Virgo, and Capricorn). They appreciate that fellow earth signs take a logical, nonreactive approach to emotion. Earth Moons rarely experience extreme emotions; their responses are blunted. This is because earth signs are able to hold problems at an arm's length. They analyze multiple perspectives, rank potential solutions, and then attempt to resolve the issue rather than dwelling on their emotions.

Capricorn Moons are least compatible with fire Moons (Aries, Leo, and Sagittarius). From a Capricorn Moon's perspective, fire Moons act rashly; they perceive fire Moons as overly dramatic and vengeful.

Capricorn Moons can be compatible with air Moons (Gemini, Libra, and Aquarius) and water Moons (Cancer, Scorpio, and Pisces). Ultimately, compatibility—or lack thereof—will be influenced by other placements. In general, air Moons are too inconsistent for Capricorn, and water Moons are considered overly emotional, possibly weak. With that being said, of the water signs, Capricorn Moons are most compatible with Cancer Moons, because Capricorn and Cancer are cosmic opposites.

Restorative Activities for a Capricorn Moon

To a Capricorn Moon, rest and relaxation are seen as luxuries, not necessities. However, all of us become burned out eventually if we aren't practicing self-care.

★ **Go through your unread emails.** What can be deleted, filtered as spam, or filed away? Are there any mailing lists you can unsubscribe from? Decreasing the number of unread emails in your inbox will take a weight off your shoulders.

★ **Isolate yourself for an hour or two and focus on being in the present moment.** You tend to think about the future and everything you need to get done, but what would happen if you strictly focused on what was right in front of you? Try to abstain from using technology during this time. Meditate, journal, put laundry away, or wash dishes. Focus your attention on things you can touch, smell, and feel.

★ **Spend time outdoors.** Get your hands dirty, if you can. Garden, go for a walk, or rake leaves. If the weather is warm enough, stand barefoot in the grass and feel the sunshine soak into your skin. Nature is healing for you, but you don't spend as much time outside as you should.

Journal Prompts for a Capricorn Moon

I bet the last thing you want to do in your limited free time is journal. Journaling requires you to think about your emotions and what is going on in the present. However, this is a private way to work through things, so it would be beneficial.

★ When you were younger, what did you think your life would look like now? In what ways have you met your expectations? Where have you exceeded them? Failed? Are those hopes and dreams still relevant today? If you described the life of your dreams now, how would it differ from your childhood fantasy?

★ What does happiness feel like in your body? Where can you locate it? What about sadness? Anger? Can you remember the last time you felt these emotions? What was the situation? How was it resolved? Looking back, do you have any new takeaways from these experiences?

★ In a perfect world, how would you leave your mark? What legacy would you leave behind? Are there steps you can take in the next year to work toward your aspiration? Reflect on where you are now and where you would like to be someday. How do you feel?

★ What does the word *family* mean to you? Make a list of ten people that come to mind when you think about family, whether you are related to them or not. Whom do you feel comfortable going to for support or advice? How can you strengthen and prioritize these connections?

So Your Partner Is a Capricorn Moon . . .

Typically, those with a Capricorn Moon only have one or two long-term relationships during their lifetime. They are picky about who they choose to date, and once they have selected a partner, they take the relationship very seriously. Their motives are longevity, stability, and security.

★ **When you are going through a hard time, your partner will leap into problem-solving mode.** This is how they show that they care.

Remember that this is not the most empathetic Moon sign—Capricorns are programmed to resolve emotions rather than process them. If you simply need a hug or a listening ear, clarify that with your partner ahead of time. Even so, the gears in their mind will turn until the situation has been resolved.

★ **Your partner has relatively even-keeled responses to events in life.** Depending on your own Moon sign, you may be disappointed by your partner's responses. Good news and bad news elicit the same level of reaction from a Capricorn Moon. While this may be frustrating when you experience a high, it's a wonderful quality for a partner to have when you're in the midst of a low.

★ **Your partner is focused on the future, so much so that most of your conversations revolve around it.** They will want to build a sizeable nest egg, move into their forever home, establish college funds for children (even if they are not born yet), and regularly contribute to their retirement account. Clearly, money will be a source of great tension for your partner. In fact, most of your disagreements will be around this topic. Consider maintaining separate bank accounts so your partner feels in control of their money.

★ **Your partner does not know how to fully relax.** You may need to bring them back to reality by reminding them that they can leave dirty dishes in the sink or remove their work email account from their phone. If it was up to Capricorn Moon, they would have little to no downtime because resting makes them feel antsy—this is a great indicator that they need to make *more* time for rest. Brainstorm ways the two of you can unwind together.

↑
CAPRICORN RISING

The rising sign is how we come across to people when we are just getting to know them. When their rising sign is in Capricorn, individuals come across as serious and capable. They are unlikely to goof around with strangers, nor will they be overly warm.

Capricorn risings tend to be drawn to those with Cancer placements. Capricorns are fascinated by Cancer's ability to freely express their love and honor their sensitivity. Cancers immediately feel like family, and Capricorns wish they had this quality. When seeking friends, lovers, or business partners, a Cancer could be a good fit.

Ways to Spot a Capricorn Rising

Capricorn risings have an air of responsibility about them. More often than not, they are clean cut: They may wear button-ups or fine jewelry, and if they have tattoos or piercings, these bodily modifications will likely be subtle or easily coverable.

★ **The easiest way to spot a Capricorn rising is to look for the person who is working the hardest.** Capricorn risings don't do anything half-assed—they don't know how to! When they volunteer, they strive to be the most helpful. When they attend a meeting, they take diligent notes. Even when going grocery shopping, they will strut right to the appropriate aisle, cross the item off their list, and beeline to the checkout.

★ **Capricorn rising acts in a very distinguished manner.** The way that they hold themselves and the way that they speak is poised, regal even. Their posture is impressive: They stand tall with their shoulders back. Unless Capricorn rising has inner planets in an earth sign, this austerity likely does not match their true personality.

★ **Friendly yet restrained, Capricorn risings are neither extroverted nor introverted—they fall somewhere in the middle.** Capricorn risings are able to strike up casual conversation, though they could take it or leave it. They are comfortable sitting in the front row, though they would rather be standing in the back of the room.

★ **Capricorn risings are often told that they are an "old soul."** From a young age, others have used this phrase to describe them.

Downsides of Being a Capricorn Rising

Some settings are ideal for your rising sign: a workplace, for example, or a highly professional environment. When others see you at a bar, it's clear you are a fish out of water.

★ **Others may think you are a stick in the mud.** It's hard for you to relax when you're in unfamiliar spaces or around unfamiliar people. You are far more comfortable in small, intimate settings with close family and friends than surrounded by strangers. Because of this, you may come off more unfriendly than you truly are.

★ **You warm up to people slowly.** When chatting with someone you are still getting to know, you prefer to stick to small talk and cordialities; it's hard for you to make jokes or contribute to a personal conversation. On a first date, others may perceive you as disinterested even if that is not the case.

★ **No matter how lighthearted or laidback you are, you come across incredibly serious.** When you talk about your family, career, or ambitions, your passion will be evident, which can be intimidating. People wonder if you ever let your hair down or goof around. As they get to know you more, they will realize that this rigidity is a façade.

Using Your Capricorn Rising to Your Advantage

There are plenty of benefits to being a Capricorn rising. Namely, you are always taken seriously.

★ **You have a quiet confidence that makes you seem trustworthy.** You know your own worth and carry this with you in your day-to-day interactions. Your boss feels comfortable assigning you a challenging task; acquaintances know that you can keep a secret; people who have just met you already believe you can do anything you set your mind to.

★ **Others perceive you as reliable.** There is nothing flaky about a Capricorn rising: If you say you are going to be somewhere, others won't even think to send a follow-up. Your steadfastness attracts people who are looking to build something lasting, which may make it easier for you to find a partner who wants to settle down.

★ **Your ability to succeed is evident.** There is no doubt in anyone's mind that the world is your oyster. This is a wonderful vibe to give off when you are interviewing for a job, fundraising, volunteering, speaking publicly, running an organization, or trying to persuade people. Others naturally have faith in you.

☿

CAPRICORN MERCURY

Mercury, the planet of communication, is restricted in serious Capricorn. Of all the Mercury placements, earth signs (Taurus, Virgo, and Capricorn) are the hardest to have a casual conversation with. They don't want to talk about emotions or anything silly—they want to talk about practicalities: current events, politics, the economy, and other real-world issues. Some signs think they are a bit of a drag.

Communicating with a Capricorn Mercury

Capricorn Mercury is a logical thinker who believes communication should be purposeful, so they choose their words carefully. When they do speak, what they have to say will hold a lot of weight.

★ **It is hard to get a Capricorn Mercury to share personal details.** This is not a Mercury sign who will "spill the tea" or overshare. In fact, they find it a little tasteless when other people divulge information so freely. If Cap Mercury is pressured to open up, it will only make them that much more rigid.

★ **Capricorn Mercury does not joke around very often**, and if they try, they struggle to deliver the punchline. This placement is not comedic, and attempts at humor tend to fall flat. They are much better suited for dry or witty remarks, which require the right audience.

★ **Capricorn Mercury's walls come down when they start talking about what they do for a living.** Whether they love their job or hate it, this is a subject that they could talk about for hours. They become especially fired up when talking about ways their job could be better—if there's one thing an earth sign can do, it's complain.

★ **This is one of the quietest Mercury signs.** Do not let their silence mislead you: Capricorns have a million things on their mind at any given time. As a result, communication falls by the wayside. When Capricorn Mercury does open up, their thoughts will be presented in a coherent, organized manner. In challenging situations, they'll have no trouble orchestrating a plan and delegating action.

Questions to Ask a Capricorn Mercury

Some conversation topics are not Capricorn Mercury's thing—they have no interest in drama, for example, unless they have strong air sign placements. When it comes to communicating with a Capricorn Mercury, pretend you're talking to a distant family member you only see once a year.

★ What do you like about your job? Would you recommend your career field to others?

★ When you hear the word *family*, what memories come to mind?

★ How is your life now different from how it was [number of] years ago?

★ Did you hear about [current event]? (This is a safe bet: Capricorn Mercuries *love* to talk about the news.)

♀
CAPRICORN VENUS

Venus is the planet of love, pleasure, and beauty. Capricorn is the planet of sensibility, predictability, and restraint. As such, Capricorn Venus is not romantic in the traditional sense of the word. They are more likely to randomly fill your tank with gas than to write you a love letter. However, this

Venus sign offers something priceless: Their loved ones will always be well taken care of.

Self-Love for a Capricorn Venus

Self-sacrifice is Capricorn Venus's ultimate expression of love. You are happiest when your loved ones are supported and thriving, even if that means your own needs have to be disregarded. But being a martyr doesn't benefit anyone in the long run—and believe me, those sacrifices *will* catch up to you, one way or another. You must prioritize yourself once in a while.

★ **Taking care of others is how you show them you care, but when was the last time you took care of yourself?** Think of a task or chore on your to-do list that you are dreading, then ask for help. This is not easy for you, I know, but people don't know how to help unless you ask. What have you been putting off, and who can you reach out to? Perhaps your brother-in-law can mow the lawn this weekend, or your friend can pick the kids up from school so you have time to get a haircut.

★ **Try to meditate once in a while.** When your mind is racing with all the things you need to get done, this is a sign that you could benefit from some quiet time. Meditation does not have to be sitting on a cushion with your eyes closed. Going for a walk can be meditative, as can practicing deep breathing or standing outside barefoot. Take time to unplug and bask in the present moment.

★ **Go somewhere and soak up the atmosphere.** I'd recommend the public library, a coffee shop, a nail salon, or a sit-down restaurant. Leave your phone in your pocket and observe your surroundings. Get something to eat or drink, or receive a service, all while letting the environment be your entertainment. Really immerse yourself. What do you notice? How do people interact? Do you hear anything funny or touching? Does anyone acknowledge you? People-watching can be an incredibly intimate experience. It promotes feelings of oneness; when you zoom out from your own problems, you remember that we are all human.

★ **If something has been frustrating you lately, go outside and find a large leaf.** Then, write a summary of what's on your mind on the leaf using a permanent marker. Cover both sides of the leaf if needed. Then, rip the leaf into a bunch of little scraps. Release the scraps in the wind, bury them in the dirt, or blow them out of your cupped palms like confetti. You don't have to carry that frustration with you anymore.

Seducing a Capricorn Venus

Capricorn Venus is picky about whom they hitch their wagon to. They have big plans for themselves, and they want a partner who will add to their life, not complicate it. Put your best foot forward!

★ **Nothing is sexier to a Capricorn Venus than someone who has their shit figured out.** If you have your own place, have a 401k, invest, or go to therapy, find a subtle way to mention that in conversation—it's like talking dirty to a Cap Venus.

★ **Be consistent.** Capricorn Venus is attracted to reliability. If you decide to go on a date, show up on time. Better yet, show up early! If you see that they texted you, text back. Responding "too fast" does not matter to a Cap Venus. This is not a sign that likes to play games—they don't have the patience. Your intent should be clear.

★ **Talk about your future plans—within reason.** You probably shouldn't list your favorite baby names on a first date, but you should share some of your general hopes and dreams. Capricorn Venus finds ambition attractive and needs a relationship where both parties motivate each other to achieve their highest potential.

★ Whereas some signs want to be taken on adventurous dates, Capricorn Venus is just fine with dinner and a movie. Dating doesn't have to be extravagant—in fact, they'd prefer if it wasn't. Cap Venus is uncomfortable spending too much money on a date.

So Your Partner Has a Capricorn Venus . . .

People with a Capricorn Venus like to partner up for life. Some signs think a lifelong commitment sounds stifling, but to Cap Venus, it's the only way to truly build an empire.

★ **Your partner needs to be able to rely on you.** Capricorn Venus finds security to be one of the most attractive things a partner can offer. They need to know that when they call, you will pick up the phone. When they've had a bad day, they want to be able to turn to you for support. Ideally, Capricorn Venus desires a partner who is a safety net, catching them when they fall and gently helping them back up on their feet.

★ **Unless your partner has strong water placements, they will not be very romantic.** Capricorn Venus takes a practical approach to love: They will hold back your hair when you're sick—and they'll do so without a complaint—but they have a hard time flirting or expressing their devotion. Grand gestures are not their thing, nor are surprises. They are perfectly content to have a date night scheduled every other week—they don't understand that for some, this custom is not romantic in the slightest.

★ **Your partner works hard, but they don't play hard.** Their top priority is building a stable foundation and reinforcing it. It will be hard to convince your partner to let things go, especially where the two of you are concerned. Capricorn Venus tends to make mountains out of molehills. If they sense something is awry, they'll immediately start trying to fix it; their hypervigilance is often unwarranted.

★ **Capricorn Venus daydreams about a happily ever after**: marriage, kids, a dog, a nice house with a fenced-in yard, a successful career, a cushy retirement fund, and so on. To that end, their mind is so occupied with the future that they forget to enjoy the present moment. Cap

Venus is focused on their next milestone instead of relishing what they've already built. Encourage your partner to live in the present. Life is a journey, not a destination. They need to live a little.

☌

CAPRICORN MARS

Mars is the planet of passion, chaos, and sex—the total opposite of Saturn, Capricorn's ruler, which is the planet of responsibility, rules and regulation, and restraint. When Mars is in Capricorn, individuals will try to set limitations around passion and chaos, which means they tend to have an all-or-nothing approach.

Capricorn Mars Behind Closed Doors

Capricorn Mars likes to appear as if they have it all figured out, but this is an illusion.

★ If I had to describe this placement in one word, it would be *restrained*. There are two kinds of Capricorn Mars: those whose sex life is formulaic, and those who are very kinky, often incorporating power and control in their sex life. The planet Saturn oversees rigidity, lessons, and rules, and as such, these are critical aspects of sex for a Capricorn Mars.

★ **Capricorn Mars is their own biggest critic.** They have high expectations for themselves, and when they do not meet those expectations, they beat themselves up. Only those closest to Cap Mars see this side of them; they are much harder on themselves than people realize.

★ **There are numerous rules that Capricorn Mars sets and abides by, whether they're subconscious or overt.** This is their attempt to control life's unpredictability. Perhaps they are particular about the way they load the dishwasher or make the bed; they may only allow certain people to cut their hair. At a more extreme level, Capricorn Mars may start to assign rules to others, especially their intimate partners.

These may start out innocent enough: They'd prefer their partner to be home by a certain time, for example. However, this can amplify to the point that they are trying to control how their partner dresses or whom they talk to. If they are not careful, their controlling behavior may become abusive. It's important for Cap Mars to remember that each of us has free will to live life the way we choose, and making mistakes is how most of us learn.

Things *Not* to Do to a Capricorn Mars

Capricorn Mars does not seek revenge when people cross them—instead, they use this as motivation to become an even better version of themselves so that they can outshine the other person.

★ **Don't change plans on short notice.** Capricorn Mars likes things to go a certain way, and when their schedule gets thrown off, it seriously frustrates them. For example, if the two of you scheduled to meet at 7:00 and you text the day of and ask to meet at 6:30 instead, it will imbalance Capricorn Mars's whole day. That half-hour disruption makes them second-guess everything else they had planned, and it puts them in a bad mood. The same goes for rescheduling trips, dates, or reservations. Try to give Capricorn Mars ample warning when plans are going to change.

★ **Don't belittle their drive.** Capricorn Mars has plenty of goals, and they wholeheartedly believe they can achieve whatever they set their mind to. Sometimes their dreams are not realistic, and loved ones may discourage Cap Mars's goals in an effort to protect them. This attempt at "helping" Capricorn Mars has the opposite effect—they will restrain themselves and lose faith in their abilities. Cheer them on, no matter what.

★ **Don't stand in their way.** Capricorn Mars only has two speeds: full stop and full speed ahead. Most of the time, Cap Mars is functioning full steam ahead, charging toward whatever goal they have set for themselves. Any attempts to reroute Capricorn's path will not end well, so fall into step alongside them or get out of their way—Cap Mars is going places.

Things a Capricorn Mars Probably Needs to Hear (But Definitely Doesn't Want To)

You mean well, but sometimes you are so focused on what you want that you neglect others or even trample over them. There is a lack of self-awareness that could be improved upon.

* ★ **There is more to life than what you can achieve.** Success is admirable, but so is being a good person. Making a difference in the community is important, but so is making memories with your loved ones. You have lofty expectations for yourself, so much so that you forget the "little people" around you who love you regardless of your success. Spend more time enjoying what is going on around you right now. As the saying goes, today is a gift—that's why they call it the present.

* ★ **Money is not the only indicator of wealth.** You could have all the riches you've ever dreamed of and still feel hollow and incomplete. True wealth is found in good health, unconditional love, and stability. You may not be as financially wealthy as you'd like, but are you wealthy in other ways? What do you have that money cannot buy?

* ★ **Nothing in life is predictable.** Even the best-laid plans go awry. Becoming comfortable with uncertainty is a superpower. You will be much happier once you accept that life throws us curveballs now and then, and how you respond is the difference between a setback and a course-correct.

* ★ **Loving someone unconditionally means accepting them as they are.** If you have to force someone to change—whether you're trying to change their behavior, appearance, or a personality trait—you do not love that person unconditionally. There will always be things that frustrate us about other people, but differences are opportunities for compromise, growth, and empathy.

QUICK GUIDE TO
CAPRICORN
PLACEMENTS

If someone in your life has Capricorn placements . . .

DO

★ Call on their problem-solving skills as needed.

★ Be consistent and reliable.

★ Understand that they hold themselves to a certain standard.

DON'T

★ Pressure them to overshare.

★ Stand in the way of their hopes, dreams, and plans.

★ Expect them to be emotional or romantic.

★ 11 ★
AQUARIUS

I describe Aquarians as the "lovable weirdos of the zodiac." There is something special about an Aquarian; they are benevolent and good-natured, yet remarkably detached. They approach emotions and behaviors from a place of curiosity rather than judgment or shame, giving them a unique perspective on every situation. Most Aquarians march to the beat of their own drum, as they are totally uninterested in social norms.

At their best, Aquarians are original, hopeful, independent, and good. Their primary motivation is the happiness of everyone they come in contact with. They would give the shirt off their back for a person in need, whether that person is an old friend or a new one. As the saying goes, they never meet a stranger.

At their worst, Aquarians are noncompliant, disorienting, transitory, and aloof. Aquarians know they are different, and they have from a young age. This can manifest as unruliness because they refuse to adhere to society's expectations. They may intentionally go against the grain just to get a reaction, and others may become frustrated by their constant need to challenge. Every time you think you understand an Aquarius, they will switch things up.

Aquarius rules the eleventh house, the house of friendship, community, and humanitarianism, among other things. If Aries is the child of the zodiac, Taurus is the preteen learning the value of money, Gemini is the teenager preparing to enter the world, Cancer is the young adult who has begun nesting, Leo is the new parent, Virgo is the adult with a tried-and-true routine, Libra is refocusing on their close relationships, Scorpio is the middle-aged adult grappling with mortality, Sagittarius is the excited expert, and Capricorn has built a successful legacy, then Aquarius is the adult approaching retirement. They see the world with fresh eyes, and they have accepted the fact that things they've held as truths can be revised with enough experience and reflection.

Aquarius's symbol is the water bearer. For this reason, a lot of astrology novices think this is a water sign. (I, too, struggled to remember Aquarius did not belong to the water element, especially considering it begins with the word *aqua*.) Aquarius brings much-needed charity to the people. In ancient times, the water bearer provided sustenance to the entire community. Aquarius is also associated with the Greek figure Ganymede, a mortal boy who was elevated to the status of immortal after becoming Zeus's cupbearer.[4] From a more metaphysical perspective, you can replace the word *water* with the word *spirit* to highlight Aquarius's humanitarianism.

Aquarius is the third and final air sign of the zodiac. Like Gemini and Libra, Aquarius prefers to be rational rather than emotional, and they think and act quickly. They do not become bogged down by people, places, or things; in fact, they enjoy the ephemerality of life, and they become inspired by the idea of hitting the reset button and starting anew. For this reason, air signs may struggle to find contentment in long-term situations, namely where they live, who they love, and what they do for work.

Aquarius is a fixed sign. Like the other fixed signs of the zodiac (Taurus, Leo, and Scorpio), Aquarius can be quite stubborn. They want to follow their dreams, regardless of how realistic they are, and damned if anything

....

4   To learn more about the fascinating history of the symbol for Aquarius, see the recommended reading list at the back of this book.

gets in their way—but unlike cardinal signs, fixed signs freeze as soon as they encounter an obstacle. Change is hard for a fixed sign, especially because change so rarely unfolds as we might expect. This fixed-sign stubbornness also manifests as a desire to go against the grain; Aquarius may dye their hair an unnatural color on a whim, for example.

AQUARIUS SUN

The Sun is in Aquarius from January 20 to February 18, give or take a few days depending on the year. Aquarius Suns are remarkable friends. They are passionate and find great fulfillment in chatting with folks who have similar interests. In today's day and age, it is a breath of fresh air to meet someone so authentic.

For those with an Aquarius Sun, every section in this chapter will apply to some degree. The Sun is the most powerful planetary force, so it has a huge impact on personality. While an Aquarius Sun may not have an Aquarius Venus, for example, they will undoubtedly find something in that section that they relate to.

Pure Aquarius Energy

There is nothing average about an Aquarius. Even if an Aquarius blends in with the crowd, they will stand out in a big way once you get to know them. They have creative brains that think up one-of-a-kind ideas, phrases, and inventions.

★ **Aquarius is the free spirit of the zodiac.** This sign couldn't care less about social norms—they follow their heart, and they do so proudly. Depending on Aquarius's home environment, it may take time for them to feel secure in their individuality; for some, this is a lifelong endeavor. At their core, Aquarians dream of a world where everyone is accepted and valued for their unique contributions. This humanitarianism is the foundation of their core beliefs.

★ **No matter what they do or where they go, Aquarius will feel disconnected from the people around them.** There is something lost in
translation between an Aquarius and every other zodiac sign; often,
relationships feel "off." This is especially heartbreaking because
Aquarius desires close friendships more than anything, but they have
a difficult time forming them. Rest assured, there are people who will
appreciate Aquarius's outside-the-box thinking.

★ **Many Aquarians are fascinated by the unusual and unexplained.** They
enjoy reading about conspiracy theories, cryptids, or unidentified fly-
ing objects. This is likely due to the fact that Aquarians often feel alien
in comparison to the people around them. They dream of a community where they feel "normal," even if it's not on this planet.

★ **At their core, Aquarius knows that "normal" is a fallacy.** Whereas
some signs want nothing more than to follow society's rules (*cough,
cough,* Capricorn), Aquarius actively rebels against them. They loathe
the monotony of a predetermined life: school, work, marriage, children . . . Aquarians may be the black sheep of their families because
they refuse to conform to generational expectations. Their rejection
of "normal" keeps the rest of us on our toes, and this attitude will be
lauded as society progresses.

★ **This is a friendly sign.** Aquarians are rarely quiet for long. If they're
not texting a buddy or chatting with a family member, they can be
found filling awkward silences with random conversation. Aquarius
knows that each of us is so much more than meets the eye, so they
relish chitchat.

★ **Aquarians have a liminal view on life.** They know that nothing lasts
forever, and this laissez-faire attitude leads to many spontaneous
decisions. If a stranger were to offer an Aquarius a free stick-and-poke
tattoo, for example, they would be tempted to say yes, if for no other
reason than because it would be a cool story.

Gifts for an Aquarius Sun

It's hard to buy a gift for an Aquarius because they enjoy being unpredictable. Unlike Taurus, who would be happy with a candle, Aquarius rebukes unimaginative gifts. When in doubt, shop small and support local businesses.

★ **Donate to a charitable cause in Aquarius's name.** Choose an organization that aligns with Aquarius's values—bonus points if it's one you've heard them talk about before. In an Aquarius's eyes, a donation in their honor is the ultimate gift because it will go on to serve others, which warms their humanitarian heart.

★ **Similarly, you could do a symbolic adoption on behalf of the Aquarius in your life.** There are all kinds of things you can "adopt" nowadays: You could adopt a sloth, a panda, a great white shark, or a whole host of other animals through the World Wildlife Foundation; you can adopt a star, with your donation going toward astronomy research; there is even Project Honey Bees, a jewelry company that lets you adopt and name one queen bee for each item purchased.

★ **Find the wacky, intriguing products on the market**—Aquarius is willing to give anything a try. Sure, you could buy your loved one a new pair of slippers, but you could also buy them a dozen strange miniatures or pickle cotton candy.

★ **Board games are always a hit with an Aquarius.** They love any excuse to gather with friends.

★ **Buy tickets to an event that gives back in some way.** Are any local organizations hosting fundraisers in the near future? Even if they've never heard of the organization before, Aquarius will happily attend a pancake breakfast if it benefits those in need.

So Your Boss Is an Aquarius Sun . . .

Aquarius bosses are a bit of a rarity, not because they lack the skillset to achieve a leadership position, but because they have no interest in it.

★ **It will be difficult to obtain clear, measured expectations from your boss.** Your boss's mind works in mysterious ways, which means they struggle to remain focused on one task. They'll ask you to do something, and that's as far as it gets—they likely haven't thought through how the task should be executed. Ask plenty of clarification questions, or just wing it!

★ **Work-life boundaries will be fuzzy.** Aquarians see everyone as a friend, and consequently, they have no hesitation sharing details about their personal life. They blur lines, inviting friends and colleagues alike to every party they host. Aquarians don't even give this a second thought, but more austere signs prefer to keep their personal and professional lives separate.

★ **Your boss feels more like a friend than a superior.** Professionalism is overrated as far as Aquarius is concerned—after all, we're all living on a floating rock. So if something is going on in your personal life that is impeding your ability to meet a deadline, your boss wants to know. No need to make life harder than it has to be! Your boss values you as a person, which may lead to a lovely friendship.

★ **Your boss wants what is best for you, so they will bend to support your needs.** For example, if extenuating circumstances require you to reduce your hours a few days a week, your boss will sign off on the change without a second thought. There are plenty of advantages to having an easygoing boss.

So Your Coworker Is an Aquarius Sun . . .

Even if you've never talked to your Aquarius coworker, you've probably heard of them. They're notorious for the unique ways they solve problems.

★ **Conversation with an Aquarius Sun may be pleasant and flowing one day and awkward and stilted the next.** Aquarians have a hard time reading people and situations, and they struggle to know just what to say. They may say the wrong thing, throwing their coworker for a loop, or they may get so hung up on saying the *right* thing that they say nothing at all.

★ **Your coworker has plenty of interests, and they love sharing their passions with others**; if they are not part of a club, group, or team at work, they may start their own. If you'd like to bond with your Aquarius coworker, discover what they enjoy, then express genuine interest in learning more. Just know that once you open that door, Aquarius will consider you their go-to person any time there's a new development in their special interest.

★ **No office space is complete without a work friend, and if you have not found one yet, have no fear! Aquarius is here!** Aquarians can get along with just about anyone. They aren't picky about who they spend their time with. As long as an individual is respectful and conscientious, Aquarius is open to developing a friendship.

★ **While some signs dread team-building exercises, holiday parties, and company happy hours, Aquarius actually looks forward to them.** In their mind, there's nothing better than bonding with the people they see almost every day. Aquarius sees work friends as real-life friends, and they cherish those relationships.

So Your Partner Is an Aquarius Sun . . .

What a delightful, unique partner you have! They are effortlessly interesting.

★ **Freedom of expression is crucial for your partner's well-being.** An Aquarius Sun's ideal partner is someone who loves them uncon-ditionally and encourages them to be whomever they want to be. Dismissive comments about their interests, appearance, or charac-teristics—which are always harmful in a relationship—are especially hurtful for an Aquarius.

★ **Your partner is down for just about everything.** They have an open mind and a never-ending list of things they find fascinating. Take them on atypical date nights, travel to uncommon destinations, and defy expectations of what you "should" be doing at your age. Closer to home, think of ways you can shake up your routine. Is there a new food you can cook or a new TV show you can binge?

★ **Your partner finds solace in a group of like-minded individuals.** If they are not part of a group, virtually or in person, they should find one to join. Perhaps they could join a book club, an online gaming chat, an adult sports league, a trivia team, a live-action role play (LARP) group, or even an active group on Facebook. Whichever they choose, it's crucial that you support your partner's social endeavors. It's best that they pursue this interest independently.

★ **There will be something atypical about your partner.** (Remember, your idea of "typical" depends on the kind of household you were raised in—what is normal for you may be totally abnormal for someone else.) This difference between you and your partner could be a source of discord, or you could enjoy the "opposites attract" component of your relationship. Remind yourself that life would be boring if we were all the same.

★ **Your partner likely has at least one friend who is an ex.** Maintaining friendships with their previous romantic partners is common for Aquarians. Do not assume they still have feelings for their ex; if anything, they maintain a friendship because they truly want the best for that person. When Aquarius cares for someone, it is hard for them to cut ties completely. This is a beautiful reflection of their compassionate nature.

☽
AQUARIUS MOON

The Moon is the planet of emotion, and Aquarius is the rule-breaker. Aquarius Moons feel like they are always on the outskirts of society. No matter how comfortable they are with the people around them, they are distinctly aware that they are a square peg trying to fit into a round hole. This is not a character flaw—Aquarians think and feel differently from other people, which can be a very isolating experience, but it can also lead to innovation.

Aquarius Moons are most compatible with other air Moons (Gemini, Libra, and Aquarius). Air Moons prefer to bounce back from a challenge instead of ruminating on it, and they are uncomfortable with heavy conversations and emotions. Aquarius Moons do all right with fire Moons (Aries, Leo, and Sagittarius) because they move on from things pretty quickly.

Aquarius Moons are least compatible with water Moons (Cancer, Scorpio, and Pisces). Aquarius will be unable to meet their partner emotionally, no matter how hard they try, and water Moons will be frustrated by Aquarius's cerebral responses.

Aquarius Moons may be compatible with earth Moons (Taurus, Virgo, and Capricorn). Specifically, they may click with Capricorn Moons, who, while being very different fundamentally, also process emotions in a detached way. Ultimately, compatibility will be determined by other placements.

Restorative Activities for an Aquarius Moon

Aquarius Moons seem to have a detached response to emotion, but beneath that perceived detachment is a lot of overthinking. Clear your head on a regular basis.

★ **Think of something you enjoy, then pursue that interest independently.** Solitary exploration can be healing. If you like to read, wander around a bookstore; if you like to go on long walks, visit a trail you haven't been to before. Sometimes, we are so hesitant to do things on our own that we stop ourselves from new experiences. You can have just as much fun on your own, I promise.

★ **You tend to spend a lot of time in your head.** To balance yourself, devote time to being in your body. Practice somatic work: Breathing exercises, mindfulness, and walking meditation are good options. Alternatively, you could work out, do some form of group exercise, or practice yoga. Focus on the cadence of your breath and nothing else.

★ **Shadow work can be immensely useful for working through your feelings of otherness.** When you are in a safe space, take out a sheet of paper. Start listing moments when you felt like you did not belong. Go into as much or as little detail as you'd like. This can be an incredibly painful exercise, so take your time, and be gentle with yourself. If you're feeling up to it, continue with the exercise. Otherwise, you can return to the paper at a later date. When the list feels finished, rip, cut, burn, or shred the paper, then toss the scraps in the trash.

★ **To activate your creativity, tap into your inner child by inventing something.** Think about an item, no matter how realistic, that would improve your life greatly. Sketch, draw, or create an image of this invention in a way that feels fun to you. Share your idea with a friend. If you are more of a tangible person, embrace the concept of innovation by doing something you've never done before.

Journal Prompts for an Aquarius Moon

Aquarius Moons naturally observe thoughts, emotions, and experiences from a distance. Journaling is a healthy way to work through everything you've observed.

★ When was the last time you felt truly accepted? Who were you with? Can you think of at least two other times you have felt accepted recently? How can you invite more of those experiences into your life?

★ What social causes are important to you? Why? How do you honor these causes in your everyday life? Are there manageable ways you could become more involved in supporting these causes? For example, are you part of a group of likeminded individuals, either in-person or virtually?

★ How do you go against the grain? What social norms do you rebel against? Are these differences something you are proud of, or something you are ashamed of? How can you cultivate more pride for your uniqueness?

★ You have high hopes for the world. What do you hope to see change in the next year? The next decade? How do you hope the world will change by the end of your lifetime? What small steps—or large steps—can you take in that direction?

So Your Partner Is an Aquarius Moon . . .

Aquarius Moons want to date someone who will join in on their zany behavior and support their wildest dreams. They believe relationships should be fun, not staid.

★ **Your partner may seem to shut down when emotions become heightened.** This is because Aquarius Moons respond to things mentally rather than emotionally. They are uncomfortable with strong emotions like rage and despair because they rarely allow themselves to reach those emotional depths. Arguments are unlikely to get heated with an Aquarius Moon unless they have fiery placements in their chart.

★ **Embrace your partner's eccentricities.** Your Aquarius Moon partner is odd in an endearing, lovable way, and they are sure to be unlike anyone you have dated in the past. Their behavior may feel unfamiliar, unpredictable, or challenging at first, but with time, you will come to love their quirks.

★ **You may become frustrated by your partner's apparent lack of emotion.** Aquarius Moons *do* feel, but from a distance. Thus, they rarely have strong reactions. Emotional responses are simply anathema to an Aquarius Moon. Your partner's ability to separate themselves from emotion can be a superpower depending on the scenario. Go to them when you need to problem-solve, not when you want to be consoled.

★ **Your partner will be atypical in some way.** Maybe they have an unusual career, or perhaps their romantic ideals deviate from the norm. Aquarius Moons believe rules are meant to be broken, and they have no problem defying systems that don't serve them. This trailblazing energy is an asset in a cookie-cutter world.

★ **Prioritize the friendship component of your relationship.** Aquarius Moons are emotionally fulfilled by their friendships, none more so than the one they have with their romantic partner. Lean on your friendship during disagreements. When you are upset with each other, take a walk together instead of rehashing an argument. You might be surprised how quickly the two of you "make up" when you simply enjoy each other's company.

↑

AQUARIUS RISING

The rising sign is how we come across when people are getting to know us. It indicates the kind of first impression we leave, and Aquarius risings certainly leave a memorable one!

Aquarius risings are naturally drawn to people with Leo placements. They are attracted to Leo's pride and confidence, two traits that they wish they embodied so naturally. Aquarius risings may feel especially close to colleagues, friends, or family members with Leo placements, and single Aquarius risings should seek partners who have Leo placements.

Ways to Spot an Aquarius Rising

Aquarius rising is one of the most awkward rising signs. There is something different about them. This is not necessarily a bad thing—awkwardness can be quite endearing, depending on who you ask!

★ **Aquarius risings typically deviate from the norm in some way.** This may be obvious, like a funky hairdo or a one-of-a-kind tattoo, or less overt: Perhaps something about their communication style is uncommon. However they show up, it will be apparent that they are not your average Joe.

★ **The way Aquarius risings interact with their environment may be unusual.** They become aloof and detached in unfamiliar settings. For example, if Aquarius rising attends an event where everyone is seated in a circle, they might stand near the back of the room on their own. Others could perceive them as standoffish or awkward.

★ **When meeting new people, Aquarius risings look to others for help blending in.** Whereas charismatic rising signs naturally assimilate to any group or setting, making friends in a matter of moments (*cough, cough,* Gemini), Aquarius rising's attempts to assimilate take effort. They mimic how others behave because, although they are genuinely friendly people, Aquarius risings often struggle when conversing with strangers.

Downsides of Being an Aquarius Rising

Like all rising signs, Aquarian characteristics may rub some people the wrong way.

★ **Others perceive you as unpredictable.** Because you do things your own way, social norms be damned, people have no idea what you will do next. You quite like this about yourself, but humans love predictability and sameness, which means your uniqueness disrupts the status quo. It may be difficult for you to find people who accept you as you are.

★ **Something about you is otherworldly.** People will not be able to put their finger on what exactly it is—there is just something different about you. Realistically, this difference is your one-of-a-kind communication style and outlook on life. However, you may go through life feeling disconnected or alienated from the people around you.

★ **You can be difficult to understand.** Aquarius risings are eccentric and innovative, and your mind may move faster than your mouth can keep up. It's not uncommon for you to stumble over your words or to have a hard time explaining things. In situations where clarity is crucial, slow down and try again.

Using Your Aquarius Rising to Your Advantage

I think having an Aquarius rising sign is a fantastic way to weed out the dull, uptight people of the world. Those who take the time to get to know you will be rewarded.

★ **You appear calm under pressure**—it's almost as though nothing can disturb your inner tranquility. This sense of calmness is misleading; you are actually detached from your surroundings, especially if they are unfamiliar. However, use this sense of calmness to your advantage. Assure potential employers (and lovers) that you are able to keep a level head in intense situations.

★ **Your energy is laidback and friendly.** While communication can be a struggle for you sometimes, others do pick up on your pure intentions. You come across as someone who would be a remarkable friend.

★ **You make people feel safe to express their individuality.** It is clear that you are not like everyone else. It takes courage to go against the grain, and your bravery inspires others. Whether you are aware of it or not, others look to you for inspiration as they navigate their identity.

☿

AQUARIUS MERCURY

When Mercury, the planet of communication, is in zany Aquarius, conversation will be fun yet random.

Communicating with an Aquarius Mercury

This is one of the most challenging Mercury signs to communicate with. Like its fellow fixed signs Taurus and Scorpio, Aquarius has a communication style that requires some effort on the other person's behalf.

★ **Aquarians don't abide by the status quo, so an Aquarius Mercury communicates in ways that are atypical.** They have a language of their own, written or verbal, with code words. Aquarius Mercury is quick to adapt slang and other modern manifestations of language.

★ **It can be hard to keep Aquarius Mercury focused on one topic.** Nothing about their communication style is linear; their focus may meander from one subject to the next. This can be particularly frustrating if you're crunched for time and trying to get specific information out of an Aquarius Mercury, but if you have all in the time in the world, relax and see where the conversation takes you.

★ **During a conversation, Aquarius Mercury chimes in with random additions.** They may share a seemingly unrelated personal anecdote, for example, or a phrase or two that doesn't make sense in the current context. These quips and tidbits occur when Aquarius Mercury makes connections between subject matter. With a bit of patience, you can work with an Aquarius Mercury to untangle the common thread.

Questions to Ask an Aquarius Mercury

These are great questions to ask an Aquarius Mercury because they could take the conversation in so many interesting directions. Be prepared for Aquarius Mercury to throw you for a loop.

★ Do you have a favorite conspiracy theory?

★ What social norms do you think we should do away with completely?

★ If you were in charge, how would things be different?

★ Who do you look up to?

♀
AQUARIUS VENUS

When Venus, the planet of love and pleasure, is in Aquarius, a friendly sign that pushes boundaries, individuals may prefer unconventional relationships.

Self-Love for an Aquarius Venus

The most important thing you can do for your well-being is surround yourself with like-minded individuals, whether the connection is romantic or platonic.

★ **Reflect on every relationship you have been in by answering this series of questions.** (If you have not been in a relationship, you can still do this exercise by reflecting on your relationships with close friends.) Grab a notebook or laptop. How have you molded yourself to accommodate your partner(s) in previous relationships? Did you ask your partner(s) to change anything about themselves? What positive qualities did your partner(s) bring out in you? What about negative qualities? Were there any aspects of your relationship that felt stifling? Were there any aspects that made you feel free? How can you honor your authenticity in your current or future relationship?

★ **You understand that love is not one-size-fits-all**—each of us needs different things to feel loved unconditionally. Name three things that make you feel cared for. Then, name one thing that you do for yourself that makes you feel cared for. Set aside time in the next week to do that one thing. If you can integrate the other three things you listed, all the better!

★ **Visit a museum and focus on everything *except* the art.** What interesting takeaways do you find on the artist placards? How has the museum laid out its materials? Are there intricate details on the ceilings, walls, or trim? What kinds of people are wandering about? What paintings, rooms, and exhibits are visitors drawn to? Repelled by? How do people behave when they do not think they are being observed? Before you leave, wander through the museum and look at the art itself if you'd like.

★ **Spend time with friends.** This is important for all signs, but especially so for an Aquarius Venus. Your friends are your family, and they understand you in ways that your relatives can only aspire to. If you are feeling socially unsupported, challenge yourself to attend an event where you can meet people who share your interests.

★ **Take a walk and intentionally wander off the beaten path.** What do you find? What is waiting to be discovered?

Seducing an Aquarius Venus

Like all air signs, Aquarius Venus is attracted to intelligence. They are also drawn to individuals with strong personalities. However, unless they have strong earth sign placements, being in a committed relationship has never been *that* important to them.

★ **Aquarius Venus is attracted to someone who marches to the beat of their own drum.** They will be unfazed by your choice of career, your fashion sense, or your financial status—in fact, they couldn't care less about those things. Aquarius Venus's ultimate goal in life is to find a partner who fearlessly pursues whatever makes them happy. There is nothing sexier to an Aquarius Venus than confidence.

★ **Talk about your interests and hobbies proudly**—Aquarius Venus isn't here to judge. On the contrary, they will be inspired by your passion. Whereas some signs may feel threatened by a potential partner's successes and aspirations, Aquarius Venus is excited by them. They, too, have plenty of interests and goals for themselves. To an Aquarius Venus, a perfect relationship is one where all passions are welcome.

★ **All happy relationships start as a friendship.** This does not mean you are destined to stay in the friend zone; it means you must make cultivating your friendship a priority. Take the time to build your connection mentally and emotionally before adding in the physical. Seduction for an Aquarius Venus is cerebral, not bodily.

★ **Be patient when it comes to establishing a commitment.** Aquarius Venus will be happiest if they are the one to start that conversation. If you do decide to broach the subject, try to remain open-minded. Traditional terms like *boyfriend*, *girlfriend*, and *partner* make them feel suffocated, especially if the conversation happens too early on. Know that they will form an emotional bond with you long before they are able to verbalize it.

So Your Partner Has an Aquarius Venus . . .

Entering a long-term relationship with an Aquarius Venus is not for the faint of heart! This placement loathes the idea of relationship "rules," such as the assumption that dating must lead to marriage. Perhaps you, too, are open-minded about what love looks like. All the better!

★ **When it comes to a relationship structure, anything is possible.** Monogamy or polyamory? Your partner is intrigued by both. Perhaps they are monogamous now but explored polyamory in the past, or vice versa. They may be open to the idea of adding another person to the relationship, or they may be perfectly content with a one-on-one connection at this moment in time. Aquarius Venus will follow your lead here.

★ **A long-lasting relationship must be one where spontaneity is present.** Your partner will become bored by the same old, same old; they don't care much for routines or traditions. For a relationship to truly stand the test of time, they will want to be kept on their toes. No matter how long you have known each other, there is always something new to learn or somewhere new to explore.

★ **Your partner loves you exactly as you are, and they hope for that same love in return.** Asking your Aquarius Venus partner to change something about themselves will not go over well. Your intention may be innocent enough, but to an Aquarius Venus, it feels like a betrayal. Their individuality is sacred, and they believe true love is unconditional.

★ **Your partner likely has a very interesting relationship history.** If asked, they will tell you they do not have a "type"; they have dated many different kinds of people and had several different types of relationships. They've likely had a few very serious connections and plenty of unserious ones. Do not be threatened by their history. All their adventures (and misadventures) have helped them recognize what sort of person they want to settle down with, and that's what really matters, right?

♂
AQUARIUS MARS

Mars, the planet of passion, aggression, sex, and chaos, charges forward. The sign of Aquarius rebels against expectations, fueling that chaos, but air signs are flighty and unpredictable. An Aquarius Mars will not stay the course for long.

Aquarius Mars Behind Closed Doors

When individuals have an Aquarius Mars, they are incredibly open-minded and chase new experiences.

* **Sexually, Aquarius Mars is incredibly versatile.** They are willing to try just about anything at least once, though they tend to follow their partner's lead. Don't be shy about telling Aquarius Mars your innermost desires—they'll be happy to explore with you.

* **Aquarius Mars does not play mind games, though those on the outside looking in may make that assumption.** Aquarius Mars has a limited attention span because the focus of their passion changes on a dime. If they don't respond to your text, it isn't a personal slight. They genuinely forgot. No matter how close the two of you are, you will always have to pursue an Aquarius Mars.

* **The way that Aquarius Mars chooses to live their life is unconventional.** Perhaps they live a nomadic lifestyle, visiting new cities and countries regularly, or are saving up to buy a van that they can travel around in. Perhaps they remain perpetually single by choice or practice relationship anarchy. Or maybe they work a night shift, making their way through the world while most of us are asleep. In one way or another, they choose a life that goes against the grain. If an

Aquarius Mars has strong earth sign placements, however, those may motivate them to live a more "stable" life.

★ **Aquarius Mars is not prone to rage; they are more likely to become frustrated or irritated.** If they do become angry, it will fizzle out quickly when they become distracted by something else.

Things *Not* to Do to an Aquarius Mars

Crossing an Aquarius Mars is not as ruinous as crossing other signs—they move on quickly. Plus, as a humanitarian sign, Aquarius Mars generally does give people the benefit of the doubt.

★ **Don't boss around an Aquarius Mars.** If you demand an Aquarius Mars do something, they will intentionally do the opposite. They are a fixed sign, which means they are stubborn, and they also enjoy challenging authority. Instead, ask nicely, or try reverse psychology.

★ **Don't expect Aquarius Mars to follow through 100 percent of the time.** Air signs are notorious for changing their mind, and Aquarius is no exception. They don't flake on purpose—schedules, deadlines, and timeframes simply don't mean as much to Aquarius Mars as they do to other signs.

★ **Don't try to place limitations on their humanitarian heart.** Aquarius Mars cares about making the world a better place, and they want to positively impact as many people as possible. While they have the purest intentions, Aquarius Mars struggles with time management, so they are not nearly as charitable as they would like to be. Remind Aquarius Mars that something as innocuous as paying for someone else's drink in a drive-thru still has a ripple effect.

★ **Don't assume Aquarius Mars will behave in a run-of-the-mill way.** There is nothing predictable about this placement. Expect the unexpected!

Things an Aquarius Mars Probably Needs to Hear (But Definitely Doesn't Want To)

Aquarius Mars is a trailblazer on a solitary path. Not everyone will understand the choices you make, but that's okay—it's *your* journey. However, be intentional about how you respond to people's comments. There are nice ways to go about this.

★ **While some rules were made to be broken, it would benefit you to go along with things once in a while.** To you, challenging expectations is a hobby, and a fun one at that. To the people around you, it becomes tedious, especially when you're killing the mood for everyone. Pick and choose your battles.

★ **Is your behavior genuine, or are you hoping to get a reaction?** You like the shock factor, but it loses its impact if you're surprising people constantly. Be more selective about when you will stir the pot or throw a curveball. Most people lose patience with this sort of behavior pretty quickly. If you're lucky, you'll find friends and family who think it's funny.

★ **Stay true to your word.** You do not like to abide by a firm schedule or strict rules, but if you tell someone that you are going to do something, you should do it. You don't have to pinky promise or solemnly vow, but any form of commitment is better than none. Really, constantly changing your mind gets exhausting, doesn't it?

QUICK GUIDE TO

AQUARIUS

PLACEMENTS

If someone in your life has Aquarius placements . . .

DO

★ Embrace their individuality.

★ Support their hopes and dreams, no matter how realistic.

★ Seek their unique perspective.

DON'T

★ Pressure them to conform to what you perceive to be "normal."

★ Ask them to shrink any aspects of themselves.

★ Rely on them as your sole source of emotional support.

★ 12 ★

PISCES

Pisces, sweet Pisces. The twelfth and final sign of the zodiac is gentle and dreamy. Pisces live in their own little world, a world that is peaceful, kind, and equitable. They are also the most intuitive sign, and they possess a quiet wisdom. Every Pisces I have ever met has immediately put me at ease.

At their best, Pisces are benevolent, optimistic, idyllic, serene, and all-knowing. Because Pisces easily tap into their intuition, this is considered the most psychic zodiac sign. Pisces may behave in uncanny ways, like knowing exactly what is on someone's mind, for example. The other thing Pisces are known for is having their head in the clouds; this contributes to that sense of serenity that they carry with them. They have big dreams for themselves and for all of humanity, and they naturally see the good in the world.

At their worst, Pisces are unrealistic, easily overwhelmed, muddled, and reclusive. When the world becomes too much, Pisces chooses to get lost, either in their head or in an unhealthy coping mechanism. Most likely, they will withdraw so that they can wallow in their emotions in peace.

Pisces rules the twelfth house, the house of isolation, spirituality, and the subconscious, among other things. If Aries is the child of the zodiac, Taurus is the preteen learning the value of money, Gemini is the teenager preparing to leave home, Cancer is the young adult building a home of their own, Leo is the new parent, Virgo is the adult who has established a routine, Libra is rediscovering the importance of relationships, Scorpio is the adult coming to terms with mortality, Sagittarius is the expert with a flair for adventure, Capricorn is the adult at the pinnacle of their career, and Aquarius is the retiree seeing the world through fresh eyes, then Pisces is the elder who has amassed a lifetime of wisdom. They share this wisdom freely with anyone who asks, seeing no point in keeping it to themselves.

Pisces's symbol is the fish. More specifically, two fish swimming in opposite directions. Like the fish, Pisces goes with the flow. They adapt to the currents, whether they need to swim upstream or downstream. These characteristics perfectly represent Pisces's element, water, as well as their mutable quality. Additionally, the two fish swimming in opposite directions can represent Pisces's indecision, confusion, and uncertainty about which way is the way forward.

Pisces is the third and final water sign, in addition to Cancer and Scorpio. Like Cancer and Scorpio, Pisces is emotional and tender. Water signs experience all-encompassing highs and extreme lows. They are prone to bouts of sadness when their innate capacity for empathy overwhelms them. Water signs make others feel safe, which oftentimes results in them becoming an unpaid therapist. They need plenty of alone time to replenish their social battery and must learn to protect their energy.

Pisces is a mutable sign. Like the other mutable signs (Gemini, Virgo, and Sagittarius), Pisces adapts to whatever circumstances life throws at them. They understand that sometimes things go awry, just as they understand that they will be in the wrong now and then. Mutable signs want everyone to be happy and will gladly sacrifice their own needs and wants if it benefits the collective. They don't look forward to change, nor do they dread it.

⊙

PISCES SUN

The Sun is in Pisces from February 19 to March 20, though these dates may differ slightly depending on the year. Individuals with the Sun in Pisces are dreamy and wise. They have high hopes for themselves and for everyone around them, and they wholeheartedly believe that anything is possible. Pisces trust that everything happens for a reason. Religion and Pisces go hand-in-hand; they find comfort in a relationship with a higher power. Even nonreligious Pisces tend to be spiritual in some regard.

For those with a Pisces Sun, every section in this chapter will apply to some degree. The Sun is the most powerful planetary force, so it has a huge impact on personality. While a Pisces Sun may not have a Pisces Mercury, for example, they will undoubtedly find something in that section that they relate to.

Pure Pisces Energy

Pisces energy is wholesome yet goofy. They find wonder in everything.

★ **Pisces is more sensitive than other signs.** They are closely connected to their emotions and can be brought to tears when experiencing all sorts of things: sadness, anger, happiness, even confusion. This is the sign most likely to cry watching those ASPCA commercials.

★ **Pisces Suns enjoy spending time with children and the elderly**; it's fellow adults that they have the hardest time with. Adults are too serious and too focused on all the wrong things: money, status, power. Children and the elderly are concerned with life's simple pleasures, which suits Pisces perfectly.

★ **It's not uncommon for strangers to walk up to a Pisces and start baring their soul.** Their welcoming and open demeanor is like a beacon of light for those who are struggling. If Pisces has time to listen, they certainly will. They may not understand the trials and tribulations the person is going through, but they do their best to help in some way.

★ **Similarly, Pisces Suns are taken advantage of.** They see the best in people and are very trusting. This makes them easy targets for manipulators and narcissists. Because Pisces is honest to a fault, they are oblivious to the fact that some people make a habit out of lying and cheating. If Pisces is beginning to doubt the authenticity of a person or situation, they should ask a trusted friend for their input.

★ **Pisces are often called old souls.** They keep the peace in chaotic situations and notice things that others overlook. When they offer their unique perspective, it is valuable. If they can withstand the emotional turmoil, they make skilled mediators, therapists, practitioners, and healers. They may be drawn to working with children or the elderly.

★ **This is a very imaginative sign.** Pisces's favorite coping mechanism is getting lost in their own little world. Reality is harsh, but their fantasies are sweet. Pisces need some form of creative outlet; perhaps they write, sing, or paint. Creativity is how they experience catharsis, and without regular artistic expression, Pisces will begin to feel stir crazy.

★ **As mentioned before, Pisces is the most psychic sign of the zodiac.** They have an uncanny ability to predict what is going to happen. If your Pisces friend crosses your mind, don't be surprised if you receive a text from them a few minutes later. This connection to the otherworldly makes them excellent astrologers and tarot readers.

★ **Pisces benefit from isolation.** Whether this isolation comes from locking themselves in the bathroom and soaking in the tub, attending a week-long retreat, or taking a solo vacation, they will learn much about themselves and the world in solitary reflection. Because they benefit from a rich inner world, Pisces are often drawn to spiritual paths such as organized religion.

Gifts for a Pisces Sun

This is one of the easiest Sun signs to purchase gifts for because they genuinely appreciate everything they receive.

★ **Any gift that inspires nostalgia is welcome, as is anything connected to an inside joke.** Pisces Suns are sentimental people. If all else fails, give Pisces a framed photo of the two of you. They will display it proudly.

★ **Take the time to complete one of those fill-in-the-blank books for Pisces, answering the prompts thoughtfully.** This will become one of Pisces's most cherished possessions. The idea that someone devoted that much time in their honor could move Pisces to tears.

★ **Purchase a journal for Pisces, something high quality.** Alternatively, if they are more of an artist than an author, buy them a nice sketch pad or drawing materials. Pisces Suns are creative people who may neglect this much-needed outlet.

★ **Water is incredibly healing for a Pisces.** If they like to take baths, purchase gifts such as a bath tray, a bathtub pillow, bath bombs, bath salts, or other items. If they prefer to shower, buy shower steamer tablets or luscious body washes and lotions. Perhaps Pisces likes to swim or sail, or maybe they like their home to be filled with beachy decor or images of mermaids. Whatever their connection to water, this is a wonderful starting point for a gift.

★ **If Pisces is spiritual, gift them a tarot deck, an oracle deck, crystals, herbs, or essential oils.** If they have not yet tapped into their spiritual side, a new age or self-help book is an excellent place to start.

★ **When all else fails, buy Pisces something that embodies the energy of a cozy rainy day**: a scarf, blanket, or shawl; a good novel; a candle; an assortment of teas; or a new mug.

So Your Boss Is a Pisces Sun . . .

It's uncommon to have a Pisces boss. Unless they have strong Capricorn placements, a Pisces Sun rarely has the drive to climb the corporate ladder.

★ **Your boss may struggle with tasks that you find incredibly simple.** They may need your help creating a graph in an Excel document, for example, or moving an email into a different folder. This surprises you—how can a person in power be so disconnected from modern technology? You see, technology and Pisces don't mix. Pisces are old school, and they have a hard time wrapping their head around all that technology can do nowadays.

★ **Instructions will be unclear.** Your boss does their best to explain things in a concise way, but they don't think like everyone else. They may overlook circumstances entirely, jumping straight from point A to point C, totally neglecting point B in the process. If the parameters of a task feel foggy, work with your boss to clarify their expectations.

★ **Your boss may cross work-life boundaries at times.** This isn't intentional; they see you as a person first and a colleague second, so they may ask questions about your personal life that cause you to bristle. They mean well, and they won't be offended if you change the subject. Likewise, your boss may share more than you deem appropriate.

★ **If you are going through a hard time, you should be honest with your boss.** They will do their best to help you through it in every way possible, from granting extended time off to bringing you a casserole.

So Your Coworker Is a Pisces Sun . . .

Pisces Suns are wonderful coworkers. They willingly offer a friendly face and a helping hand.

★ **This is the coworker to run to if you are having a bad day.** Pisces will listen with open ears and an open heart. They don't hesitate to set aside their work for a person in need. Do not take advantage of this kindness, though. If you are unloading on your Pisces coworker multiple times a week, you should reevaluate your systems of support.

★ **Pisces really does do their job to the best of their ability, but they miss the mark from time to time.** They take every failure personally. Pisces is their own worst critic. If you sense something is getting your Pisces coworker down, try to cheer them up. Remind them how valued they are.

★ **A true mutable sign, Pisces is not terribly ambitious.** They would be content to work the same role for most of their career. In the process, they come to see their coworkers as family. If a coworker leaves to pursue a job elsewhere, Pisces will be sad to see them go. They will hope to stay in touch, but it will rarely pan out that way—too often, people are out of sight, out of mind. At the very least, Pisces will remain friends with their former coworker on Facebook and wish them well from afar.

So Your Partner Is a Pisces Sun . . .

Pisces Suns are phenomenal partners. They wear their heart on their sleeve and love unconditionally and easily.

★ **Your partner celebrates your successes and mourns your sorrows.** They are empathetic and in tune with your emotions, unconsciously taking them on themselves. Unsurprisingly, they are deeply affected by arguments and disagreements. It is best for both of you to repair after conflict as quickly as possible.

★ **A Pisces possesses unending trust and loyalty.** The downfall of their idealism is that they stay in situations that do not serve them for far too long. Perhaps they work somewhere they are not valued, for example, but they don't want to quit because they know it would disadvantage the people they work with. Encourage your partner to make choices that benefit their own well-being first and foremost.

★ **Pisces views connections as lifelong.** They remain friends with their exes; they maintain relationships with people who have crossed them one too many times; they keep in contact with difficult family members. This might boggle your mind or frustrate you. Respect the fact that soul ties are near impossible for Pisces to break.

★ **Pisces's mind doesn't work like everyone else's; they can't be bothered with manmade problems like finances or taxes or insurance.** Managing money will be a challenge, as will paying bills on time. You will likely have to bear the brunt of these responsibilities.

★ **Your partner is forgetful, and remembering anniversaries, birthdays, and appointments is not their strong suit.** If you ask your partner to do something, be prepared to remind them. Likewise, they shouldn't go to the grocery store without bringing a list. To make both of your lives easier, get in the habit of writing things down on a shared calendar.

☽
PISCES MOON

The Moon rules emotion. Pisces, a water sign, is one of the most emotional signs of the zodiac. When their Moon is in Pisces, individuals are deep thinkers and visceral feelers. They are compassionate and hopeful. They are also incredibly intuitive and may be drawn to new age pursuits like meditation, divination, or reiki.

Pisces Moons are most compatible with other water Moons (Cancer, Scorpio, and Pisces). A fellow water sign is the only element that stands a chance of matching their emotional capacity. Water Moons love with their entire being, and when two water Moons choose to partner, they connect on a spiritual level.

Pisces Moons are least compatible with air Moons (Gemini, Libra, and Aquarius). Picture the sea, which reaches unfathomable depths. Now picture the distance between the sea and the sky. No matter how hard they try, Pisces Moons and air Moons simply cannot reach each other. At best, they will meet on a surface level. An emotional connection will be unfulfilling for both parties.

Pisces Moons may get along with earth Moons (Taurus, Virgo, and Capricorn) or fire Moons (Aries, Leo, and Sagittarius). Of these options, Pisces Moons have much in common with the mutable signs Virgo and Sagittarius. However, true compatibility will depend on other placements.

Restorative Activities for a Pisces Moon

While some signs have endless energy reserves, Pisces Moon's depletes quickly. It is crucial for you to practice self-care on a regular basis, or you will burn out.

★ **When you feel overwhelmed, disconnect from the outside world.** Turn your phone on do not disturb or, better yet, turn it off completely. Spend time in contemplation, meditate, or create—write, draw, play an instrument, listen to music, or read a book. To prevent feelings of overwhelm, maintain strict boundaries. Do not have your work email on your phone, and don't check your emails outside of working hours. Don't use your phone for at least an hour before bed. Learn to say no to situations or people that make you feel depleted.

★ **Create something.** It doesn't matter if you like the end result—the process of creation is what is valuable here. Notice how your body feels while you work. Are there parts of your body that are holding tension? Parts that feel as though they are vibrating with energy? Parts that are numb or heavy? Aim to relax your entire body by the time you finish your creation. Practice this skill until you are able to relax your body at will.

★ **Sleep for long periods of time unapologetically.** Nap often. You need more rest than the average person. If you struggle to fall asleep or stay asleep, create a sleep routine and stick to it. If you are still struggling to get adequate sleep, schedule a check-up with your primary care provider.

★ **Find activities that feel cathartic.** Perhaps this is putting together a puzzle, cross-stitching, washing dishes, or watching YouTube videos that you know will make you cry. (Personally, *Got Talent* videos always do it for me.) Whatever you choose, commit to healthy forms of catharsis. Too often, Pisces Moons are drawn to unhealthy methods of coping with the outside world.

Journal Prompts for a Pisces Moon

If you have a Pisces Moon, you should journal often. A regular journaling practice will help you unpack your emotions, reactions, and experiences. Your head will feel clearer as a result.

★ When was the last time you cried? Why?

★ How do you nurture your psychic abilities? Do you believe you are psychic? Why or why not? What role does spirituality play in your life?

★ What is something you wish more people knew about you? Is this something you feel inclined to share? Why or why not?

★ Which relationships or experiences in your life have taught you what love is? What is your definition of love? Can you name three people or actions that feel like love?

So Your Partner Is a Pisces Moon . . .

Pisces Moons are incredibly caring, but they are also very emotional people, and their emotions can overwhelm those closest to them.

★ **Your partner offers you a rare kind of love.** Pisces Moons are nurturers, so being selfless in a relationship comes naturally: If you are happy, they are happy. You partner is constantly showing you that they care, but they tend to do so in small ways that are often overlooked. Try not to take these simple gestures for granted.

★ **You may perceive your partner as a bleeding heart.** Seemingly inconsequential things upset or disturb them. They may have a hard time watching the news and looking at violent or graphic scenes on television. Don't make light of your partner's sensitivity—their ability to remain soft in our hard world is admirable.

★ **Pisces Moons don't have one love language—they have all five!** Your partner glows when you offer them words of affirmation; they are happiest when they have gotten plenty of quality time and physical touch; small gestures and gifts make their day. This may sound daunting, but don't fret! Yes, Pisces Moons need an attentive partner, but because all love languages make them feel special, they are easily placated.

★ **Your partner absorbs your emotions.** Your victories are their victories, and your pain is their pain. Because of their vast capacity for empathy, pause before venting carelessly. Even if a matter is frivolous to you, your partner does not take what you say lightly—they will have a physical and emotional response. Think before you speak.

↑
PISCES RISING

The rising sign is the way we present ourselves in the world, and it provides clues to how we come across to people we've just met. When the rising sign is in Pisces, individuals immediately appear shy yet kind. Of course, depending on their other placements, looks can be deceiving.

Pisces risings are drawn to people with Virgo placements or Virgo characteristics. They appreciate that Virgo is put together and resolute. Virgos seem to have everything figured out, and Pisces risings wish they were more like that. Pisces risings would benefit from surrounding themselves with Virgo friends, colleagues, and lovers.

Ways to Spot a Pisces Rising
Pisces is one of the most unassuming rising signs.

★ **Unless they have prominent air sign placements, Pisces risings are very quiet.** Pisces is not a talkative sign—they spend most of their time in their own head. When Pisces do speak up, they may second-guess themselves or downplay their contributions to the conversation.

★ **Pisces risings are shy.** In group settings, they will follow someone else's lead. They are amenable and friendly when spoken to, but they rarely if ever initiate conversation on their own.

★ **Pisces risings like to wrap themselves in soft, comfortable fabrics.**
They own plenty of sweaters, shawls, and scarves. They may even
wear items that they have made themselves!

Downsides of Being a Pisces Rising

This is a placid rising sign placement, which is a blessing and a curse.

★ **You seem soft and impressionable.** Judgmental strangers will (falsely)
assume you are weak or a pushover. Be careful, as the cruel people of
the world will try to take advantage of you and the dominant people
will try to control you.

★ **It is not uncommon for people to speak on your behalf,** especially
when you are among outgoing folks. For example: At work, a
coworker elevated your concern to the higher-ups because they
assumed you wouldn't do so yourself; on a first date, your date took
it upon themselves to order for the table; at family gatherings, loved
ones talked about you as if you weren't present. When you do try to
speak up, you are frequently talked over. This is deeply frustrating and
demoralizing.

★ **Acquaintances presume you won't have much to add to conversation.**
Your demure demeanor is not a permanent part of your personality—
you're just reserved at first! However, others become so accustomed
to assuming you have nothing to say that you may have to fight to
make your voice heard.

Using Your Pisces Rising to Your Advantage

Don't be dismayed—there are plenty of benefits to being a Pisces rising.

★ **You appear contemplative.** Complete strangers assume you are a deep
thinker, as you seem to radiate wisdom. Because of this, you may be
trusted with confidential or high-stakes tasks. This is professionally
advantageous. However, you are prone to burnout, so be careful not
to take on too much!

★ **Because you are gentle and quiet, people will mistake you for being weak, but that couldn't be further from the truth.** It is always good to be underestimated. When you struggle, it will fly under the radar. When you succeed, others will certainly notice—and the humble will apologize for misjudging you so.

★ **Without you having to say a word, people feel safe in your presence.** They know you will hold space for whatever they need to get off their chest. Your peaceable demeanor makes you well-suited for a career in social services, hospitality, counseling, or healthcare.

$$\text{☿}$$

PISCES MERCURY

Mercury is the planet of communication. It is quick and straightforward. When Mercury is in Pisces, the sign of rest and introspection, the planet's energy becomes quite muddled.

Communicating with a Pisces Mercury

At first, you may leave conversations with a Pisces Mercury feeling flummoxed. The more you get to know them, the more fulfilling your conversations will become.

★ **Pisces is the most psychic sign of the zodiac**, so don't be surprised when Pisces Mercury says something that makes you think, *Wait, how did they know?* They have a sixth sense about certain things. More specifically, they have a built-in lie detector that can sense dishonesty from a mile away, though they probably won't call you on your BS. Similarly, they may uncover your secrets effortlessly.

★ **Pisces Mercury often stumbles over their words.** This is because their mind works faster than their mouth, and in their effort to keep up, they may trip over their own words. Speech becomes tangled or confused. As Pisces Mercury becomes more comfortable, this will happen less and less.

★ **Do not be surprised if Pisces Mercury shares a compliment or another warm sentiment.** Their communication style is naturally affectionate, and they will make their love known, whether they do so in writing or aloud. Pisces Mercury shares this affection with friends and strangers alike. They believe small acts of kindness have a significant impact, so even though this people with this placement prefer to bite their tongue, they will speak up in hopes of making someone's day.

Questions to Ask a Pisces Mercury

Pisces Mercuries may lose their train of thought easily. They enjoy discussing topics that require introspection, such as their innermost hopes and dreams.

★ When you think about your golden years, what do you look forward to?

★ What have you been dreaming about recently? Do you often remember your dreams?

★ How do you hope society will progress in the next decade?

★ Do you believe our destinies are predetermined, fully in our control, or somewhere in between? Why?

♀
PISCES VENUS

Venus is the planet of love, beauty, and pleasure. Pisces is a whimsical, ethereal sign. Thus, Venus in Pisces is an incredibly romantic placement. Some may describe Pisces Venus as an idealist.

Self-Love for a Pisces Venus

You freely offer your love to others, so much so that you may fall to the bottom of your priority list. Setting aside time to "fill your own cup," so to speak, will make you even more attentive to your loved ones.

★ **Write a song, a poem, or another burst of artistic expression.** The goal here is to pour your feelings into another medium. If you prefer to use your hands, that's an option too: Sculpt, paint, stitch, or sketch. Even those who don't think they have an artistic bone in their body have one form of expression just waiting to be explored: Dance!

★ **Look at an old photo of yourself and make a list of at least five ways you have grown as a person since the photo was taken.** Then, take a moment to think about who you want to become. What are five qualities you would like to adopt or grow into? Write them down and place your list in an envelope. Write a date on the envelope at least one year in the future, then seal it and set it aside. When that time comes, read your list and reflect on whether or not you are growing in alignment with your goals.

★ **Make time to read.** Ideally, read lighthearted and feel-good books. Think beach reads or novels that have been selected for celebrity book clubs. This is a healthy way for you to escape the real world now and then. If you struggle to prioritize reading, or if you have a limited attention span, audiobooks are a fantastic alternative.

★ **Every once in a while, do something selfless.** Generosity restores your spirit. You can volunteer for a local organization, donate to charity, or even deliver a small gift to a loved one. Whatever you choose to do, keep it as private as possible. Notice how it feels to keep this sacred moment to yourself.

Seducing a Pisces Venus

Romancing a Pisces Venus is relatively easy. These individuals want nothing more than to find their happily ever after, so they swoon when someone offers them undivided attention. Be gentle with their heart, because this placement falls in love easily!

★ **Nothing is more attractive to a Pisces Venus than emotional availability.** When you see they've texted, respond sincerely. Keep in mind that as far as Pisces Venus is concerned, there's nothing embarrassing about a double text. If you're enjoying spending time with them, let them know! Ask them to go on another date. Above all else, be straightforward with your intentions.

★ **Acts of service are the way to Pisces Venus's heart.** They are naturally selfless when it comes to the people they love, so when someone cares for them, it is totally unexpected and very appreciated. Acts of service can be minor—Hold the door for them! Help them put on their coat!—or more overt: Pick up the tab, fill the tank up with gas, and rub their shoulders after a long day. If your relationship stands the test of time, continue to integrate acts of service.

★ **Pisces Venus is emotionally intelligent.** Depending on their Moon and Mercury placements, they will have varying degrees of comfort *verbalizing* their emotions, but they will always be astutely aware of how they feel and why. Do your best to match their level of emotional intelligence by recognizing how you feel and naming it. Take accountability for the ways your emotions may influence your connection. For example: "I'm feeling a little cranky today because I spilled coffee all over myself this morning, so I'm sorry if I'm not as upbeat as normal."

So Your Partner Has a Pisces Venus . . .

Pisces Venus is a dreamer, so they may have unrealistic expectations for their long-term relationships.

★ **Never stop dating your partner.** This is good advice for any long-term relationship, but especially so for a romantic like Pisces. Pisces Venus doesn't believe that the honeymoon phase needs to end—they fantasize about fairy-tale love, and they want to be wooed for their entire life. Whenever you notice yourself neglecting romance, plan a date, and don't overthink it: A date can be any time set aside for the two of you.

★ **If you are both spiritual people, practice your spirituality together** (e.g., praying together, attending services together, etc.) to create an unbreakable bond. If spirituality is not something you have in common, find something else the two of you can do together. Choose something that occurs on a set date and time at least once a month. For example, you could join a bowling league, a trivia team, or a book club.

★ **Pisces Venus wants their love life to resemble a storybook happily ever after.** This means the nitty-gritty, mundane moments of a committed relationship will make your partner feel disillusioned. Squabbles about laundry or what to have for dinner, cooling passions, and periods of disconnection are normal occurrences in a long-term relationship—but to Pisces Venus, they might as well be the kiss of death. Make sure to have regular conversations about your relationship satisfaction and expectations.

★ **Your partner deeply commits to people, sometimes to their detriment.** They rarely end a relationship (either platonic or romantic) no matter how toxic it has become. This is because Pisces Venus idealizes people. When relationships turn sour, Pisces Venus uses empathy and rationalization to forgive bad behavior, always hoping things will improve. Have honest, gentle conversations with Pisces Venus about when it may be time to let someone go.

♂

PISCES MARS

Mars—the planet of passion, aggression, drive, and sex—is a fiery planet. When combined with watery Pisces, its spark fizzles quickly. Thus, Pisces Mars often feels as though they lack direction in life.

Pisces Mars Behind Closed Doors

Pisces Mars is more sensitive than they may appear. They are incredibly hard on themselves.

★ **Sexually, Pisces Mars tends to be submissive, though because Pisces is a mutable, changeable sign, they are open to exploring their preferences.**

Pisces Mars sees sex as a sacred act and rarely sleeps with people they are not in a committed relationship with.

★ **The Pisces Mars tendency toward change may manifest as breaking off relationships in search of the elusive "perfect" partner.** Pisces Mars has surges of emotion in which they act impulsively. They often feel guilty about their actions once they have returned to a more even-tempered state of mind and begin to second-guess the decisions they made. This placement is prone to on-again, off-again relationships because they struggle to cut people off completely.

★ **A Pisces Mars may use sex, alcohol, or drugs to escape the harsh realities of everyday life.** Pisces rules the twelfth house (the house of isolation and all things unseen), and Pisces placements tend to cope with unpleasant emotions in unhealthy, even dangerous, ways. It is imperative for Pisces Mars to set boundaries, practice self-care, and establish a support system.

★ **People with a Pisces Mars don't really get angry.** Instead, they become frustrated and overwhelmed, often bringing themselves to tears. Sadness is more familiar to them than rage, and when situations get heated, Pisces Mars withdraws. They may sulk or become sullen after a disagreement. They also tend to feel sorry for themselves.

Things *Not* to Do to a Pisces Mars

When crossed, a Pisces Mars may burst into tears. Alternatively, if they have fire sign placements, they become all bark and no bite.

★ **Don't assign them a bunch of responsibilities.** Pisces Mars is easily overwhelmed and can only handle having a few things on their plate at a time. If Pisces Mars is not careful, they will become burdened by others' expectations, and their relationships may become strained. It's best to keep your asks low.

★ **Don't express disappointment when they change their mind.** This will make Pisces Mars feel terrible about themselves. Pisces is a mutable sign, so they are supposed to change! Criticism eats away at them; no matter how unaffected they seem, they will experience tormenting self-doubt. Instead, go with Pisces Mars's flow.

★ **Don't criticize their goals, even if they don't seem realistic to you.** Pisces is a dreamy sign, and their sense of hope is admirable. Life is hard enough, and feeling like their loved ones don't believe in them destroys a Pisces Mars.

★ **Don't try to make decisions for them.** Confident, bold placements may want to swoop in and "save" Pisces Mars, but Pisces Mars doesn't need to be saved! It may take Pisces Mars a while to make up their mind, but they're entitled to take as much time as they need. Whether or not their decisions lead to success or failure is largely irrelevant—it's all part of the journey.

Things a Pisces Mars Probably Needs to Hear (But Definitely Doesn't Want To)

This placement doesn't mind being a little delusional; sometimes, it's more pleasant than facing the truth.

★ **Live life for yourself and no one else.** If you don't think this advice applies to you, ask yourself: If no one was watching, would you make the same choices? You are easily swayed by others' opinions, so much so that you may end up adopting different personality traits around certain people or pursuing a career path that doesn't feel authentic. This is *your* one wild and precious life—own it.

★ **You are prone to unhealthy coping mechanisms.** All of us cope with things in less-than-favorable ways once in a while, but for a Pisces Mars, there is danger of unhealthy methods becoming the norm. Assess your relationship with addictive behaviors: substance use, financial compulsions such as online shopping, overindulging in food and drink. If you need help choosing healthier patterns, consult a mental health professional.

★ **Systems of support are crucial for you.** They keep you from spiraling. Support can come from trusted family and friends, licensed professionals, or even an online community. Don't be afraid to reach out to someone in times of need—there are more compassionate hearts than you realize.

★ **If someone is treating you poorly, consider ending the relationship.** You tend to give people second, third, and even fourth chances, but they are not always warranted. Giving people the benefit of the doubt is a superpower, but be careful of people who take advantage of this kindness. Remember, not everybody you lose is a loss.

QUICK GUIDE TO

PISCES

PLACEMENTS

If someone in your life has Pisces placements . . .

DO

★ Respect their sensitive nature.

★ Serve as a constant source of support.

★ Initiate deep conversations.

DON'T

★ Contribute to their overwhelm.

★ Pressure them to make up their mind.

★ Minimize moments that they deem significant.

CONCLUSION

Now that you have a good understanding of how certain placements present, you can further develop your astrological skills by zooming out and putting the pieces together. Remember that a birth chart is the sum of all its parts. Our placements influence each other, which adds complexity to astrological interpretation. For example, you cannot assume that all Libra Suns want to find their other half. If a Libra Sun has a Leo Moon, Aquarius Venus, and Sagittarius Mars, they are unlikely to be married with kids. In fact, they probably really enjoy being single and pursuing what makes *them* happy. Similarly, Aquarius Suns are notorious for being detached, but if an individual has an Aquarius Sun and a Cancer Moon, for example, they will be a deep feeler. And, to further complicate matters, the house a planet is in impacts our placements too! All of this is to say, a person's birth chart is as unique as a fingerprint. Having access to a person's entire chart is the best way to fully assess their quirks, preferences, and desires.

WHAT NEXT?

If you have enjoyed this book, there is so much more you can learn about astrology. First and foremost, study the houses. Understand what the houses represent and how planets manifest in each house. Research the outer planets (Jupiter, Saturn, Uranus, Neptune, and Pluto), especially Saturn. Learn about the North and South Nodes. Memorize aspect patterns and their meanings. Familiarize yourself with Chiron. All these things will usher you toward the intermediate level of astrological know-how. In my eyes, intermediate knowledge makes you qualified to offer birth chart interpretations to family and friends or even clients.

FINAL THOUGHTS

When I started writing this book, I never dreamed it would be read by anyone but myself. I wrote the first few chapters just for me, for no other reason than I thought it would be fun to think about all the ways astrology impacts our modern lives. As I continued to work on the book, it became so much more.

Astrology was a hobby that has turned into a passion. It has revolutionized the way I see the world, and it fills me with a profound sense of hope. To believe in astrology is to believe in a cosmic order, a divine purpose.

Unfortunately, the topic of astrology will probably always be met with skepticism and derision. It is hard for people to wrap their heads around the idea of planets and stars influencing us—but we do not question that the moon impacts our tides or that the sun's solar flares disturb radio communication on Earth. Even Jupiter and Saturn, which are over half a billion miles away, have such a strong gravitational pull that they warp Earth's orbit into a more elliptical shape![5] And yet, to some, the idea of the planets being able to impact our personalities is unbelievable.

....

5   NASA Science Editorial Team, "Milankovitch (Orbital) Cycles and Their Role in Earth's Climate," NASA, February 27, 2020, https://science.nasa.gov/science-research/earth-science/milankovitch-orbital-cycles-and-their-role-in-earths-climate.

★　★　★

My hope for you is that this book has helped you learn more about yourself and the people in your life. I hope it has inspired you to remain curious and to meet people with empathy and curiosity. More than anything, I hope this book fueled your interest in astrology. There will always be something new to learn, and that is a remarkable gift, for knowledge is power.

All the best,

Nicole

ACKNOWLEDGMENTS

To GUS (God, Universe, Spirit), for this miraculous life. I am constantly in awe of the magic all around me. Your divine guidance is recognized and appreciated. Thank you.

Thank you to my parents, who shaped me into the woman I am today. You have shown me what unconditional love is. My interests and hobbies were nurtured my entire childhood, and you both selflessly set me up for success. I knew from a young age that no matter what I chose to do or who I became, you would be right alongside me, cheering me on. I wish everyone had parents as wonderful as you, and I'm so glad you're mine.

To Mom, my number one fan. You have always loved me in a way that seems effortless. You are a natural caretaker and an above-and-beyond mom. Thank you for rubbing my tummy when I had a stomachache; for taking me to every appointment and finding me the best care, no matter the cost; for coming to every piano recital, dance show, and volleyball game; and for the patience you have shown me and my anxiety. Thank you for texting me good night and for picking up the phone no matter what time it is. Thank you for Bella, for supporting me through the hello and the goodbye. I love that we laugh together and cry together. If everyone had a mother as selfless, kind, and gentle as you, the world would be a much better place. I cannot wait to see you embody the role of Grandma someday. My future children will be so lucky to have you. *I* am so lucky to have you.

To Dad, my favorite man on Earth. Thank you for helping me see the humor in life. Thank you for always making me smile and for the sage advice, in those rare moments when you are serious. Thank you for helping me pick up the pieces when He-Who-Shall-Not-Be-Named left; you gave me hope when I couldn't find it myself. I look up to you. When I was a child and I wrote my first story, you offered to be my agent. While you said it in a joking way—because let's be honest, almost everything is said in a joking way—that exchange showed me that you believed in me and my writing. I know I can do anything and be anything because you have always told me so. More than anything, I want to be like you. You've shown me that a person can work hard *and* play hard. I love our shared passion for horror movies, beer, and the Vegas Lounge, and I cherish every moment we spend together.

To Rev, my match and the loveliest surprise. The Universe brought us together at the perfect time. Thank you for being curious when I brought up astrology on our first date. Thank you for supporting my interests whole-heartedly, even if you don't understand them. I will never forget when I told you I was writing a book on astrology and you said, "I call dibs on the first copy," even though you don't remember my Sun sign half the time. Sweetheart, you bring so much joy to my life. Thank you for encouraging me to use my voice. Thank you for reminding me that life begins outside of my comfort zone. Thank you for all the phone calls and the endless advice and support you offer. And of course, thank you for being my personal Mr. Fix-It. You are my best friend and my safe place. Together, we can do anything. I love you.

To Bella, my sweet Cancer Sun, the love of my life and the greatest gift I have ever received. I miss you every day. I hope you hear me talking to you. I hope you feel me loving you, wherever you are. I'll see you at the gate when the time comes—I know you'll be waiting.

To Brynn. Thank you for decades of friendship, love, and support. You are my lifelong best friend. The nights spent playing *The Sims*, eating Goldfish, and drinking Coke are some of my fondest memories of being a kid. Many of my favorite adult memories include you too—car wash raves, trips to the bingo hall, falling asleep on the couch while watching *Shrek*. When we hang out, I wish I could freeze time because I never want to say goodbye. It takes a special relationship to grow together instead of apart. No matter what changes, our friendship stays the same. I love you forever.

To Maddie. Thank you for literally saving my life, and thanks for all of the times you figuratively saved my life too. I would not have survived Oxford without you. I also would not be nearly as worried about getting scurvy. You make me laugh out loud more than anyone I've ever met. Even though you're waaaaay younger than me, I look up to you. You are smart and strong and sharp, and I learn something from every conversation we have. Your messages have gotten me through some of the lowest points of my life, and I'll never be able to repay you. But I have been the president of your fan club for years, and I don't plan on ever stepping down.

To Lauryn, Amy, Nanette, Shira, and Markus, the best team a girl could ask for. Lauryn, this would not have been possible without you. Thank you for believing in me and cheering me on. I am so lucky to have a friend in you. Amy, thank you for always being a kind, safe space to land. You truly care about the people in your life and the work you do, and it shows. You have a heart of gold. Nanette, thank you for the endless support. You've guided me through some challenging times and helped me believe in myself. And you have recommended some really, really good books too! Shira, you are a powerhouse of a woman. I am blessed to know you. You and your family have welcomed me with open arms, and I am honored to be a part of your lives. (Hi, Lilah and Theo!) And, finally, Markus, thank you for the years of friendship and laughter. I love goofing around with you, and I'm so excited for all the beautiful things in store for you and Daniel.

To all the friends I did not mention by name. You know who you are! Thank you for making me laugh, letting me cry, and supporting me through everything in between. I am beyond fortunate to have so many amazing people in my life.

To Makayla, Melannie, Natalie, Savannah, and Dawn. Thank you for volunteering to be my advance readers and generously sharing your feedback with me. This book is better because of you. I appreciate you all!

To the wonderful people I have met on TikTok, who always hold space for whatever is on my mind. The kindness you have shown me restores my belief that there is far more good in the world than we realize.

And, finally, to everyone who has ever listened to me talk about astrology: Thank you.

RECOMMENDED READING

Astrology is a vast subject, but anyone can learn more about its nuances with enough time, patience, and dedication. There are countless resources available in our modern age, but not all resources are written by experienced astrologers. My goal for this section is to share some of the resources that I have used in my own development.

ASTROLOGICAL RESOURCES

These four accessible books are beginner-friendly and can take your practice to an intermediate level:

★ *Birth Chart Interpretation Plain & Simple* by Andrea Taylor

★ *Discover the Aspect Pattern in Your Birth Chart: A Comprehensive Guide* by Glenn Mitchell

★ *Astrology for Beginners: Learn to Read Your Birth Chart* by David Pond

★ *Llewellyn's Complete Book of Astrology: The Easy Way to Learn Astrology* by Kris Brandt Riske

ASTROLOGICAL TIPS AND TRICKS

The more you learn about astrology, the more fun facts you uncover. After all, astrology has been around for a *long* time. With enough study, you will pick up on relevant anecdotes you can share when interpreting someone's chart. Here are some resources I found interesting:

★ To learn about Scorpio's ruling planet, which has changed over the years:
https://www.bustle.com/life/what-planet-rules-scorpio-pluto
-astrologer

★ To learn about what roles Venus and Mars play when it comes to sex:
https://getinthegroove.com/astrologist-explains-your-sex-life
https://berrylemon.com/blogs/berrylemon/guide-to-sex-astrology

★ To learn more about Aquarius's symbol, the water bearer:
https://youtu.be/XA1KckgYuOw?si=O7fe7symCZ_rQEvs

I've also picked up plenty of tips and tricks for guessing people's placements over the years. (I *love* guessing people's placements—it's one of my favorite ways to win over a skeptic.) For example, the planet Venus is always within two signs of the Sun, meaning that it is actually impossible for a Virgo Sun to have a Pisces Venus.[6] Therefore, an individual with a Virgo Sun must have a Cancer Venus, Leo Venus, Virgo Venus, Libra Venus, or Scorpio Venus. I love utilizing this "trick" when guessing someone's Venus sign because it narrows down the possibilities, making my birth chart guesses even more accurate. Share your favorite astrological tips and tricks with me on Instagram or TikTok at @nicolewellwell.

....

6   Jake Register, "Your Sun and Venus Signs Have a Special (Sexy) Relationship That Tells You Alllll About Your 'Type,'" *Cosmopolitan*, August 12, 2020, https://www.cosmopolitan.com/sex-love/a33587153/sun-sign-venus-sign-meaning.

ASTROLOGY ON SOCIAL MEDIA

One of my favorite ways to learn is via social media. There are tons of astrologers out there who are constantly sharing their knowledge *for free*! These are my go-to Instagram accounts for planetary transits and astrology updates (and/or memes).[7]

@gottesss

@solelunastro

@itskemimarie

@notallgeminis

@risingwoman

@kayxstars

@alizakelly

@tarotreaderpeter

@jakesastrology

@spiritdaughter

@thepulpgirls

@astrologys_space

@thegoddessgem

@thethreadsoffate

@sanctuarywrld

@starchild.app

@mymoongirlreadings

....

7   These Instagram handles were current at the time of publication.

TO WRITE TO THE AUTHOR

If you wish to contact the author or would like more information about this book, please write to the author in care of Llewellyn Worldwide Ltd. and we will forward your request. Both the author and the publisher appreciate hearing from you and learning of your enjoyment of this book and how it has helped you. Llewellyn Worldwide Ltd. cannot guarantee that every letter written to the author can be answered, but all will be forwarded. Please write to:

Nicole Wells
℅ Llewellyn Worldwide
2143 Wooddale Drive
Woodbury, MN 55125-2989
Please enclose a self-addressed stamped envelope for reply,
or $1.00 to cover costs. If outside the U.S.A., enclose
an international postal reply coupon.

Many of Llewellyn's authors have websites with additional information and resources. For more information, please visit our website at http://www.llewellyn.com.